# Essentials
# of
# Management

# Essentials
# of
# Management

## Anita Satterlee
## Liberty University

SYNERGISTICS Roanoke, Virginia 24024

ESSENTIALS OF MANAGEMENT: CORE PRINCIPLES, CONCEPTS, AND STRATEGIES

Published by Synergistics Inc. Copyright ©2007, 2006

11 10 09 07/ 1 2 3 4 5

ISBN - 10:  0-9788748-4-6
ISBN - 13:  978-0-9788748-4-1

Editorial director: *Kerry Hogan*
Cover photograph: *Paul Yates*
Cover design: *Kelly Pittman*
Interior design: *Gene Miller and Kelly Pittman*

Printed in the United States of America

# Table of Contents

Preface     XIV

Introduction     XVII

**Chapter One**

**Introduction To Management     2**

What is Management?     3

   Managerial Decision Styles     4

   Leadership     4

   Followership     6

   Types of Power 8

   Why Managers are Important  8

      Roles     9

   Types of Managers and Their Typical Duties     10

      General     10

      Operations  11

      Finance     11

      Human Resources     12

      Executive     12

   Managerial Skills     12

      Technical skills     13

      Human skills     13

      Conceptual skills     13

   Characteristics of Successful Managers 13

   Organizational Levels  15

      Simple structure     15

      Machine bureaucracy     15

      Professional bureaucracy     15

      Adhocracy bureaucracy     16

      Functional structure 16

      Divisional structure  16

      Matrix organization  16

      Span of control     16

      Strategic  management     17

      Tactical management     18

      Operational management     18

   Organization Environments in which the Manager must Operate     19

   Systems Approach     21

Resource Inputs      22
Transformation Process        22
Product Outputs     22
Feedback     22
Total Responsibility Management        22
Career Development    23
Conclusion        24
Brief Summary of Major Points 24
Impact on the Organization, the Manager, and Employees       25

**Chapter Two**
**History Of  Management  30**

Introduction       31
Industrial Revolution     32
Scientific Management    32
Frederick W. Taylor      33
Frank and Lillian Gilbreth        34
Administrative Management      35
Henri Fayol     36
Max Weber     37
Behavioral Management 38
Robert Owen   38
Hugo Munsterberg      39
Mary Parker Follett      39
Chester Barnard        40
Elton Mayo     41
Abraham Maslow       42
Douglas McGregor      43
Chris Argyris   43
Quantitative Management       44
Operations Research   44
Inventory Modeling    45
Linear Programming   45
Queuing Theory       45
Simulations    46
Modern Management Theories 46
Systems Approach     47
Contingency Thinking 48

Fiedler's Contingency Model    48
Quality Management Gurus    49
    W. Edwards Deming               49
    Joseph M. Juran       51
    Peter Senge  52
Conclusion        53
    Impact on the Organization, the Manager, and Employees      57

**Chapter Three**
**The Functions Of Management    62**
Introduction       63
    The Basic Planning Process      64
        Conduct a Situational Analysis            64
        SWOT        65
        Select Specific Goals and Plans            67
        Implement the Selected Goals and Plans          68
        **Monitor Results and Use Information to Control the Process              68**
Effectiveness/Efficiency  69
    Strategic planning         69
        Establish Mission/Vision/Goals            69
        Benchmarking        70
        Strategy Formulation—Corporate Level (Concentration, Vertical, Concentric, Conglomerate)  71
        Implementation        72
    Operational Planning  72
        Policies      72
        Procedures and Rules          73
        Budgets      73
        Project Management          74
        Scenario Planning   75
Controlling        76
    Types of Control        77
        Internal Controls    78
        External Controls    79
    Control Systems and Tools       79
        Management by Objectives 79
        Information and Financial Controls (Ratio and Breakeven Analysis)        81
        Operations Management and Control             81
    Steps in the Control Process    82
        Establish Objectives and Standards       82
        Measure Actual Performance 83

            Compare Results with Objectives and Standards          83
            Take Corrective Action          83
    Organizing          83
        Structures          84
            Traditional Structures          84
            Contemporary Approaches to Structure          87
        Corporate Governance 90
            Chain of Command 90
            Span of Control          91
            Delegation and Empowerment          91
            Centralization/Decentralization          92
            Downsizing—Doing More with Less Staff, etc.          92
    Conclusion          93
        Brief Summary of Major Points for Planning, Controlling, and Organizing     93
        Impact on the Organization, Manager, and Employees          94

**Chapter Four**
**Function Of Leadership    98**

    Leading    99
        The Nature of Leadership          100
            Vision          100
            Power and Influence 101
            Ethics          102
        Leadership Styles          103
            Autocratic   103
            Democratic  104
            Laissez-Faire 104
        Trait Theories  104
        Behavior Theories          105
        Contingency Models of Leadership          105
            Fiedler Contingency Model   106
            Hersey-Blanchard Situational Leadership Model          107
            House Path-Goal          109
            Vroom-Jago Decision-Making Model 110
        Transformational vs. Transactional          112
        Collins' Good to Great Concept on Leading    113
        Servant Leadership          115
        Principle-Centered Leadership 115
        Change Leadership          116

Conclusion        118
    Brief Summary of Major Points        118
    Impact on the Organization, the Manager, and Employees     119

**Chapter Five**
**Effective Communication  122**

Interpersonal Communication   123
    Communication Process—Sender, Receiver, Meaning, Encoding, Message Transmittal, Channel, Decoding, Interpreting, Feedback     124
    Barriers to Communication     125
        Noise        125
        One-Way vs. Two-Way         125
        Perception   126
        Filtering       126
        Non-Verbal  127
        Mixed Messages        128
    Professional Presentations        128
        Strategy      129
        Substance   129
        Structure     129
        Style            129
        Support       130
        Supplement 130
        Presentation Taboos  130
        The Perfect Presentation        131
    Meetings        132
  Business Etiquette        134
    Email Etiquette        134
    Phone Etiquette        135
    Dining Etiquette        135
    Office Etiquette        136
    Introductions  136
    Rumor Mill     137
    Office Politics  137
        Norms        138
        Groupthink 139
        Dress Codes 140
        Office Layout        141
    Proxemics        142

Conclusion        143
**Chapter Six**
**Organizational Behavior    148**
Motivation Theories        149
Behavioral Based        149
Thorndike's Law of Effect        149
Skinner's Behavior Modification (Reinforcement, Punishment, Extinction)        150
Vroom's Expectancy Theory  152
Need Based        153
Maslow        153
ERG Theory                154
McClelland's Trichotomy of Needs        155
Job Based        156
Herzberg's 2-Factor Theory  157
Hackman and Oldham Job Design Model        157
Equity Theory                158
Managing Conflict        159
Functional vs. Dysfunctional Conflict  159
Causes of Conflict        160
Task Conflict                160
Relationship Conflict                160
Process Conflict        160
Conflict Management Styles        161
Avoidance   161
Accommodation        161
Competition        161
Compromise        161
Collaboration        162
Teams        162
Pros and Cons of Using Teams 163
Informal and Formal Teams        163
Primary Types of Teams        164
Workgroups 164
Committee/Taskforce        164
Cross-Functional Teams        164
Quality Circles        164
Self-Managed Teams 165
Benefits of Teams        165
To an Organization  165

        To an Individual     165
    Stages of Team Development   166
        Forming    166
        Storming   166
        Norming    166
        Performing 166
        Adjourning 166
    Task vs. Maintenance   167
    Characteristics of High Performance and Low Performance Teams     167
        Shared Vision and Goals      167
        Shared Leadership   167
        Continuous Learning and Development        168
        Customer Focus      168
        Feedback and Data   168
Conclusion          169
Impact on the Organization, the Manager, and Employees    169

**Chapter Seven**
**Human Resource Management    174**
    Importance of Human Resource Management 175
        Recruitment    176
        Selection          178
            Application Forms & Résumés          178
            Ability Tests 178
            Performance Tests     178
            Personality Tests     179
            The Interview Process          179
        Orientation    181
        Training       182
        Employee Development       182
        Performance Management      183
        Compensation and Benefits    183
    Legal issues       185
        Major United States Federal Laws and Regulations Related to HRM (1963–2005)  185
        Best Practices   188
    Strategic Human Resource Planning Process    188
        Five Aspects of Implementing Strategy 189
            Strategic Alignment  189

      Leadership and Knowledge Management        189
      Results-Oriented Performance Culture        189
      Talent Management 189
      Accountability        190
   Job Analysis    190
   Job Description        190
   Job Specification        191
Current issues    191
Managing Workforce Diversity 191
   Sexual Harassment        192
   Hostile Work Environment        193
Career Management        194
   Career Paths    195
      Linear        195
      Spiral        195
      Steady-State        195
   Job Hunting    195
Conclusion        197
Impact on the Organization, the Manager, and Employees    197

**Chapter Eight**
**Working and Traveling Abroad    200**
Introduction        201
Working Overseas        201
   Motivations to Accept an Expatriate Assignment        201
   Selection Procedures and Success Indicators    202
   Adjusting to Cultural Change  204
   Communication Barriers and Training 204
      Cultural Norms        205
      Non-verbal Communication 205
   Expatriate Compensation        207
   Tax Considerations        207
   Personal Security and Terrorism        207
Business Travel Abroad   209
   Planning an Itinerary   209
   Proper Documentation 210
      Passports    210
      Visas        210
      ATA Carnets        211

Extra Copies of Documents   211
Current Documentation        212
Assistance from U.S. Embassies and Consulates        212
Medical Concerns        212
Vaccinations213
Food Allergies        213
Water Contamination        213
Disease and Disaster 214
Safety Procedures        214
Safety on the Street   215
Safety in the Hotel   215
Safety on Public Transportation        215
Travel and Medical Insurance  216
Currency Guidelines   216
Check List for Business Meetings and Travel Abroad   217
Cross-Cultural Communications        218
Language Barriers   218
Foreign Holidays        219
Time-Zone Changes 219
Acceptable Forms of Business Communications        220
Acceptable Forms of Body Gestures   220
Other Cultural Factors 221
Religious Factors        221
History        221
Local Laws   221
Customs and Foreign Goods 222
Transportation Modalities        222
Index        226

# PREFACE

For the first half of the 20th century, collegiate business education courses were considered primarily skill-intensive—deficient in the application of scientific research methodology. Such practical courses were taught by faculty who had business experience and demonstrated expertise in the specific skill being taught. During the 1960s, the emphasis on a specific-skills business curriculum was abandoned in favor of the management science approach, taught by faculty who were trained in the scientific method of research. These faculty members possessed little or no business experience. Critics of the management-science-only method believed that the specific skills were abandoned in favor of teaching critical thinking, though many believed students had nothing to think about that they could use beyond the ivory tower of academia. Business students, though well versed in theoretical constructs, were not being equipped to confront the realities of the business world.

This shift in the approach to teaching business courses was reflected in the type of textbooks published for use in the class. The new business textbooks, typically written by career academics, were essentially being published more for the benefit of the professors than students—as more institutions of higher learning instituted faculty polices, such as "publish or perish." This policy stimulated textbook publishers to flood the market with book packages that had added features and ancillary teaching materials to make the teaching process easier—as the ancillary materials provided lecture outlines, test banks, videos, and CDs—all of which greatly added to student textbook costs. These "extra materials" were used as incentives for faculty to adopt the textbooks. In addition, the instructor could now devote the time normally spent on class preparation to other activities that contributed to earning tenure and career promotion. Tenure and career promotion was based on publication—an end result of "publish or perish" policies. It is interesting to note that many institutions of higher learning view books written by non-academics or practitioners as not fitting the "publish or perish" paradigm. The erroneous presupposition is that these books are perceived by some in the academy as deficient in academic rigor, due to the so called "lack of scientific research" methodology. Thus, the typical business textbook of the late 20th century was written by those motivated more by research than teaching—for the primary benefit of the author who possessed little or no business experience. The student was a secondary consideration and "paid the price" as textbook prices escalated at very high levels each year.

The 20th century collegiate teaching model was based on the proposition that the teacher was the purveyor of knowledge and was the one responsible for student learning; transmitting course knowledge via passive learning methods required little or no interaction on the part of the student. The development of the Internet during the last decade of 20th century ushered the 21st century model of collegiate learning: online education. In contrast to the 20th century emphasis on the role of the teacher, the 21st century model places at least equal emphasis on the role of the learner. Students have become more involved (active) in the new learning model, as the role of the faculty has shifted from an emphasis on "teaching the student what is to be learned" to "being a mentor and facilitator of the learning process." Mentoring and facilitating is a more empowering approach to teaching, as the student essentially learns how to learn, thus moving away from being dependent on the need for a teacher to explain everything to becoming a more independent learner.

Synergistics Publishing was established in response to the growing concern that the typical textbook used in college classes today, based on the old 20th century model, is obsolete in light of the realities of the 21st century. Textbooks should be written and published, first and foremost, with the student needs in mind. Obviously, there is nothing inherently wrong with the author enjoying the fruits of the labor of publishing, yet the primary purpose of publishing textbooks for student use must uphold the needs of the student—high-quality academic content that is usable in a timely manner and low cost.

The 21st century student rarely has the leisure time that was available to the 20th century student. Today's typical college student balances a full time schedule of classes, demands of a job, socialization with family and friends, and church/community volunteer activities. The student is always connected to someone or some organization via email, instant messaging, cellular telephone, personal digital assistant, corporate intranets and extranets, and so forth. Time is a precious commodity to the 21st century student. Hence, a textbook needs to provide the essentials of high-quality academic content in an easy-to-read format—one that does not require exhaustive hours of reading for comprehension. Synergistics Publishing authors are scholar/practitioners, who combine academic knowledge with real-world experience in developing a textbook that delivers the essential high-quality subject matter in a reader-friendly format.

The second student need is low cost. The typical business textbook is sold by college bookstores well in excess of $100, and many exceed $200. Synergistics Publishing textbooks are sold by college bookstores for less than half the price of traditional publishing houses. This is the result of an innovative business model using the latest in management processes and information technologies. Our scholar/practitioners develop high-quality textbooks that are relevant to Internet-Age learners and contemporary in coverage of essential core concepts. Our publishing processes engender the development of a personalized approach to instruction, allowing professors who adopt our textbooks to add value to their courses, whether online or in the physical classroom.

This textbook—part of a series being developed to provide essential core concept knowledge to business students that meet the dual objectives of high quality and low cost—is suitable for use in both undergraduate and graduate classes. While the core concepts at both academic levels remain the same, the level of learning and application is higher at the graduate level than at the undergraduate level. This concept is supported in the literature concerning Learning Theory. In 1956, Benjamin Bloom led a team of educational psychologists who developed a classification of levels of intellectual behavior important in learning. Bloom's team found that over 95 percent of the test questions students encountered required them to think only at the lowest possible level—the recall of information. Bloom identified six levels within the cognitive domain— from the simple recall or recognition of facts, as the lowest level, through increasingly more complex and abstract mental levels—to the highest order which is classified as evaluation. Thus, in the undergraduate course, the concepts of this book would be dealt with at the Bloom lower-domain levels of knowledge, comprehension, and application. In the graduate course, the higher learning domain levels of analysis, synthesis, and evaluation would be emphasized.[1]

The Publisher is committed to helping professor's who teach business courses by providing both a Student Guide and an Instructor's Resource Manual to accompany this textbook. The Student Guide is appropriate for use at the undergraduate level. The Instructor's Resource Manual contains power-point presentation slides, a test bank, answers to Student Guide questions, and suggested resources, including current IB-events video clips, for use in teaching the course in both online and residential format. Faculty who adopt this textbook for use in their courses may contact the Publisher by email to request the Instructor's Resource Manual.

Synergistics Inc.
P.O. Box 12274
Roanoke, VA 24024
info@synpub.com

---

1    Bloom's Taxonomy. Retrieved January 1, 2007 from http://www.officeport.com/edu/blooms.htm

# INTRODUCTION

This textbook provides students from diverse academic backgrounds an overview of the essential knowledge needed to be literate and competent in the field of business management. While the book assumes that students will have limited knowledge in the area of business and management prior to enrolling in the course, the content provides exit learning and competencies comparable to those experienced in courses that require prerequisite knowledge or prior coursework in the field. Thus, this textbook is suitable for undergraduate and graduate courses in Business and Management for which no prerequisite knowledge or prior coursework is required for enrollment.

**Chapter One** provides an introduction to the field of management. The introduction is based on five essential concepts:

1. Management vs. leadership,
2. The roles, work, and importance of management,
3. The effective vs. ineffective manager,
4. The manager's relationship with organizational constituents, and
5. Managerial career development.

First, the similarities and differences between management and leadership are discussed, as well as the related concept of followership. Second, the reader is introduced to the work of management, specifically why managers are important to the organization, the differing organizational roles managers play, and the general types of managers. The first essential concept focuses on the work and relevance of management to the organization. The second and third essential concept focuses on the relationships of managers within the organization. The fourth essential concept focuses on the skills and characteristics of the effective and ineffective manager and how they differentiate. The fifth essential concept concerns managerial relationships—in terms of the overall organizational levels, environments, and stakeholders. The chapter concludes with a discussion of managerial career development.

**Chapter Two** provides the historical development of the field of management, covered in four essential categories:

1. Scientific management theory,
2. Administrative management theory,
3. Quantitative management theory, and
4. Modern management "gurus."

The chapter begins with a summary of the historical development of modern management thinking, from Adam Smith (1776) through the Industrial Revolution (late 1800s). Next, the three historical eras of modern theory are discussed, specifically scientific management (early twentieth century), administrative management (mid twentieth century), and quantitative management (later twentieth century). Finally, the chapter concludes with historical development of management gurus, including their impact on contemporary management thought.

**Chapter Three** provides coverage of three of the four major functions of management, categorized as follows:

1. Planning,
2. Controlling,
3. Organizing, and
4. Leading.

Leading is a function of management, when considered as the process of influencing others in an organization to act in a certain manner. However, in the broader sense, if leadership is considered a transformative act, it is considered as its own discipline, separate from the functions of management. Thus, Chapter Four will deal with the important issue of leadership.

Planning, the first function considered, includes the basic planning process, the issue of effectiveness and efficiency, goal setting, the role of strategic planning, and operational planning. The second function, Controlling, includes types of controls, control systems and tools, managerial control processes (employee, financial, operations), and measurement tools and metrics. Finally, the function of organizing is discussed. Essential topics in this function include organizational structuring and approaches, systems thinking, corporate governance, and current issues impacting managers.

**Chapter Four** provides an introduction to leadership as a discipline separate from management, which is categorized as follows:

1. The nature of leadership,
2. Leadership styles, and
3. The theoretical basis.

Topical coverage for the nature of leadership includes vision, power, and ethics. Styles include the classical concepts of autocratic, democratic, and laissez-faire. The theoretical basis includes trait and behavioral theories, models, transformational leadership, and concludes with a description of Collins' *Good to Great* concepts.

**Chapter Five** discusses the importance of professional communication for managers. The essential concepts of communications center on the following:

1. Interpersonal communications,
2. Professional presentations and meetings, and
3. Business protocol for professionals.

Coverage of interpersonal communications includes the communication process and ancillary issues. Developing and making effective presentations, as well as conducting professional meetings, are delineated. Finally, the importance of business protocol is considered, including office etiquette, rumor mill, office politics, norms (formal vs. informal), dress codes, office layout, proxemics, and etiquette.

**Chapter Six** provides the essentials of behavior in organizations and is categorized as follows:

1. Theoretical basis,
2. Conflict management, and
3. Teamwork.

The major motivational theories include behavioral based, need based, and job based. Managing conflict includes concepts such as functional vs. dysfunctional conflict, causes of conflict, and conflict management styles—avoidance, accommodation, competition, compromise, and collaboration. Teamwork includes the pros and cons of using teams, types of teams (formal/informal, committee, task force, cross-functional, quality circles), stages of team development (form, storm, norm, perform, adjourn), task vs. maintenance, groupthink, characteristics of high performance and low performance teams.

**Chapter Seven** covers human resource management (HRM), which is categorized as follows:

1. Importance of HRM,
2. Legal issues concerning employment,
3. The HRM planning process,
4. The employment process, and
5. Current HRM issues impacting managers.

HRM is an important organizational aspect impacting managers in both large and small firms. Legal issues coverage includes major US federal laws and regulations related to HRM (1963-2005). The strategic human resource planning process includes phases such as job analysis, job description, and job specification. The employment process includes the recruitment, selection, orientation, training, performance management, and compensation and benefits. Current issues include managing workforce diversity and sexual harassment.

**Chapter Eight** concludes the textbook with an overview of working overseas and business travel. While many traditional business texts provide a chapter which gives an overview of global business, the author of this text believes the topic of working and traveling overseas will be of more benefit to students of management. This chapter is divided into two inter-related sections. The first section deals with working overseas as an expatriate, including motivations to accept an expatriate assignment, expatriate selection procedures and success indicators, the expatriation process as a bridge, managing the expatriation process, adjusting to cultural change, compensation and taxation issues for expatriates, and personal security in the Age of Terrorism.

# Essentials
# of
# Management

# CHAPTER 1 — Introduction To Management

## MEASURABLE LEARNING OBJECTIVES

1. Define management and the value which managers add to an organization.

2. Differentiate between management and leadership.

3. Define the different roles which managers have within an organization. Identify tasks executed by managers in each role.

4. Explain the different types of skills that managers should possess.

5. Describe an ineffective manager.

6. Define the different levels of management within an organization. Identify tasks performed by managers in each level.

7. Identify the different environments in which a manager must operate.

8. Explain the role of stakeholders.

9. Describe how an organization is an open system.

10. Determine personal career development.

# What is Management?

Management includes planning, organizing, leading, and controlling human and other resources to achieve organizational goals efficiently and effectively. Resources are organizational inputs that include people, technology, raw materials, financial capital, and skills. Therefore, the act of management requires knowledge and skills necessary for the functions of management and how those functions are completed internally and externally to the organization. Planning is the development of organizational goals, which leads to the development of an overall strategy for achieving those goals. Top executives defining the mission statement of the company and determining how the organization can maintain its competitive advantage serve as examples of planning.

Organizing determines what needs to be done, who is to do those tasks, how tasks are to be grouped, and who reports to whom.

Leading deals with motivating employees, directing the activities of subordinates, and selecting the most effective forms of communicating with subordinates. Leading also entails resolving conflict that occurs within an organization. This function requires an expertise in human behavior in order to understand what motivates others in the organization.

Controlling is monitoring activities to ensure that they are being accomplished as planned and correcting any significant differences between a planned result and the actual result.

In addition to having expertise in all four of the functions of management, managers who operate within the different levels of an organization will also need to understand their individual roles and duties, which are dependent upon the organizational level in which the manger operates. An organization is comprised of three different levels, each of which has a corresponding level of management. The three levels of management are first line managers, middle managers, and top managers.

Top managers, referred to as strategic managers, are responsible for making decisions that will help the organization meet its overall mission and vision. These decisions affect the organization in the long-term: one to five years. A strategic decision may determine whether the organization will enter a particular market or discontinue the production of a particular product. Examples of top managers are Chief Executive Officer (CEO), Chief Operating Officer (COO) and President. Top managers are considered critical to an organization's success or failure.[1]

Middle managers, often referred to as tactical managers, supervise first line managers and find the best way to utilize both human and non-human resources in order to achieve the organizational goals received from top managers. Tactical managers are given the goals set by strategic managers and determine how to translate those broad goals into specific goals for the units that the tactical manager oversees. The decisions that tactical managers make will affect the organization in the next six to twenty-four months. Examples of middle managers are project managers and district managers.

First line managers, also known as operational managers, supervise non-managerial workers. Operational managers take the goals of tactical managers and make specific goals and action plans. The decisions made by operational managers are short term and will take place in one to twelve months.

## *Managerial Decision Styles*

Many disagree over the extent to which managers should include their subordinates in the decision-making process. While an autocratic manager is one who makes a decision and then informs the group about the decision, a democratic manager asks for input from others prior to making a decision. A study found that subordinates whose managers used democratic decision styles had more positive attitudes; however, the autocratic decision style resulted in subordinates having a somewhat higher performance level.[2] A laissez-faire manager, one who essentially did not make any decisions, resulted in negative attitudes and lower performance.

Neither the democratic nor autocratic decision style is inherently bad, because the decision style utilized will depend on the follower, the situation, and the leader. Decision-making will be discussed more thoroughly in a later chapter.

## *Leadership*

Management and leadership are not synonymous. While a manager must deal with planning, controlling, and organizing, the act of leadership is about coping with change.[3] In *A Force for Change*, author John Kotter, a Harvard Business School professor, separates the role of a leader from that of a manager:

> . . . good leaders produce important, positive change by providing vision, aligning people's efforts with the organization's direction, and keeping people focused on the mission and vision by motivating and inspiring them. Good leadership, like good management, helps an organization to succeed.[4]

Leadership, as the ability to influence others, is also dependant upon whether the leader possesses that which his or her followers seek. Leadership can be classified as transactional leadership or transformational leadership.

J.M. Burns' research showed that transactional leaders lead by understanding the underlying principles of management and then applying those principles in the workplace; a transactional leader will guide followers to achieve organizational goals.[5] Transactional leaders guide and motivate their followers in the direction of established goals by clarifying roles and task requirements. In other words, transactional leaders define the purpose of the organization's existence to followers and then provide them with the plans and means to attain goals.

Bennis and Nanus studied 90 top leaders and determined that transactional leaders differed from transformational leaders.[6] Transformational leaders channel the efforts of those in the organization by ensuring followers are aware of the issues, paying attention to the concerns of followers, and inspiring followers to achieve organizational goals. Tichy and Devanna identified many characteristics of the transformational leader: perceived visionary, risk taker, confidence in the organization's personnel, communicator of organizational goals, high learning curve, able to handle complex and uncertain issues.[7]

Charisma, a characteristic of transformational leaders, is the ability to affect followers and inspire extraordinary accomplishment. Charismatic leaders have a vision, take risks to make their visions a reality, and are sensitive to the needs of followers. Followers of a charismatic leader are stimulated to exceptional performance and satisfaction.[8]

Effective transformational leaders rely on the expression of feelings to help convey a message; therefore, they should possess a high level of emotional intelligence. Emotional intelligence is the ability of an individual to detect emotional cues and adapt their feelings and behaviors accordingly. Emotional intelligence consists of five dimensions:
1. Self awareness—being aware of what one is feeling.
2. Self management—the ability to manage one's emotions and impulses accordingly.
3. Self motivation—the ability to persist in the face of adversity.
4. Empathy—being able to feel another's pain or suffering.
5. Social skills—the ability to communicate effectively with others.[9]

The terms manager and leader refer to different skills and abilities. Although managers are often considered leaders, they may only direct an organization's day to day activities and not act as a change agent within the organization. Similarly, even without having a position of authority, one can be a leader within a group, based on a special skill or knowledge. Management is about coping with complexity, while leadership is about coping with change. Managers overcome complexity by designing formal plans and organizational structures; leaders overcome change by developing future visions, and encouraging followers to overcome the hurdles of change.

## *Followership*

A leader cannot lead without followers. Although there is an abundance of research on leadership, the importance of followership is often overlooked. One should remember that organizational success depends on both followers and leaders:

> Leaders matter greatly. But in searching so zealously for better leaders we tend to lose sight of the people these leaders will lead . . . Organizations will stand or fall partly on the basis of how well their leaders lead, but partly also on the basis of how well their followers follow.[10]

Just because one is a manager does not mean that he or she knows how to lead, and just because one is a subordinate does not mean that he or she knows how to follow. Effective followers do not require constant praise and share a number of essential qualities, including intelligence and self-reliance. Findings have shown that effective followers "managed themselves well . . . [were] committed to the organization  and to a purpose principle, or person outside themselves . . . built their competence and focus[ed] their efforts for maximum impact . . . [and ] are courageous, honest and credible."[11]

Another aspect of followership is the responsibility to leadership. In *Ten Rules of Good Followership*, Colonel P. Meilinger of the U.S. Air Force states that within an organization the role of followership is as important as the role the leadership.[12] A subordinate, by mastering the role of followership, prepares himself or herself for the role of leadership. Meilinger's rules of followership are based upon his experiences as both a follower and a leader:

1. Don't blame your boss for an unpopular decision or policy; your job is to support, not undermine.
2. Fight with your boss if necessary, but do it in private—avoid embarrassing situations, and never reveal to others what was discussed.
3. Make the decision, then run it past the boss; use your initiative.
4. Accept responsibility whenever it is offered.
5. Tell the truth and don't quibble; your boss will be giving advice up the chain of command based on what you said.
6. Do your homework; give your boss all the information needed to make a decision; anticipate possible questions.
7. When making a recommendation, remember who will probably have to implement it, which means you must know your own limitations and weaknesses, as well as your strengths.
8. Keep your boss informed of what's going on in the unit; people will be reluctant to tell him or her of any problems and successes. You should do it for them and assume someone else will tell the boss about yours.

9. If you see a problem, fix it; don't worry about who would have gotten the blame or who now gets the praise.
10. Put in more than an honest day's work, but don't ever forget the needs of your family—if they are unhappy, you will be too, and your job performance will suffer accordingly.[13]

Noted author Warren Bennis adds that an effective follower must be willing to tell the truth: "In a world of growing complexity, leaders are increasingly dependent on their subordinates for good information, whether the leaders want to or not. Followers who tell the truth and leaders who listen are an unbeatable combination."[14]

Leaders may agree with the concept of followership wholeheartedly, but for a subordinate to fully embrace followership, he or she must trust in the leader/follower relationship:

[Trust is] [t]he willingness of a party to be vulnerable to the actions of another party based on the expectation that the other will perform a particular action important to the trustor, irrespective of the ability to monitor or control that other part as a positive expectation that another will not act opportunistically.[15]

According to Kouzes and Posner, in *The Leadership Challenge* there are five dimensions of trust:

- *Integrity* requires honesty and trustworthiness. Of the five concepts, this is the most critical, because employees assess a leader's trustworthiness.
- *Competence* is interpersonal and technical skill. While leaders do not have to know everything, they must exhibit a proficiency level so that people will respect them.
- *Consistency* is the correlation between what a leader says and what a leader does and the uniformity of those actions. Managers who are inconsistent in their discipline or praise lose the respect of his/her workers. Authority is also undermined.
- *Loyalty* is the willingness to remain faithful to the interests of others and a concern for followers.
- *Openness* is about managers communicating effectively with their employees, without hidden agendas.[16]

At some time each day, even those in an organization's leadership take on the role of follower and must remember that being an effective follower is as important as being an effective leader.

## Types of Power

One factor managers use to persuade workers to meet organizational goals is the exercise of power. Power is the ability of A to influence the behavior of B—so that B complies with A's wishes. French and Raven first discussed the five types of power a manager could have, based on the manager's position to make workers behave a certain way. [17] The five types of power are as follows:

1. *Legitimate power* is the power of a position, such as an organization's president. Managers have legitimate power based upon their position within an organization. Employees follow the position, not the person.

2. *Reward power* is having the ability to give something that an employee values as a reward (or to withhold a reward) to manage employee behaviors. Rewards are giving employees what they want in exchange for doing something the manager wants. Rewards do not have to be tangible but could be intangible, such as verbal praise.

3. *Coercive power* is having the ability to force compliance. Again, this type of power does not have to have tangible results, such as threatening an employee with dismissal, but can be intangible, such as not including the employee in future staff meetings.

4. *Expert power* is power an individual has when they possess a special knowledge, skill, or ability that others lack. People seek advice and guidance from those with expert power.

5. *Referent power* is the display of admirable characteristics that others seek to possess. An individual will choose to follow someone with referent power because the person who holds such power has traits and characteristics that the individual admires. Charismatic persons and celebrities have this type of power.

## Why Managers are Important

Managers are very important to an organization because they are responsible for using resources, both financial and human, to increase performance and profits. Without the proper managerial leadership, individual employees would be left to attempt to meet organizational goals through their individual efforts. Employees may lack the passion, motivation, direction, and purpose required to run an organization.[18] Managers are the people who give the organization a vision—by establishing an organizational mission statement that will define how the vision will be realized.

The mission statement tells why the organization exists; it gives the organization a sense of direction. Without the mission statement, an organization may operate in a state of confusion, where workers would not know the reasons behind decisions made at any level of the organization.

*Roles*

Managerial roles are tasks a manager is expected to perform based on the position he or she holds in the organization. In 1960, Henry Mintzberg undertook a study of executives to determine what they did on their jobs. Mintzberg concluded that managers perform different roles that are grouped into three categories: interpersonal roles, informational roles, and decisional roles. [19]

*Interpersonal.* Managers engage in interpersonal roles to provide direction and supervision for both the organization as a whole and the employees within the organization. When managers perform the interpersonal role, they are referred to as a figurehead, leader, or liaison. The role of manager as a figurehead is inspirational in nature; the leader acts as a symbolic head of the organization and represents the organization in all formal matters. When managers take on the role of leader, they are responsible for motivating and directing employees; this role defines the relationship between leaders and employees. In the liaison role, the manager maintains a network with contacts outside of the organization.

*Informational.* A manager holds an informational role by receiving information regarding the external or internal environment and communicating that information to an organization's members or contacts. As the manager receives information about what the company needs to do in order to remain competitive, that individual communicates it with other members of the organization. The manager fills the spokesperson role when conveying information to the public or speaking on behalf of the organization. An example would be when a manager goes public to inform investors about the company's profitability and future plans for growth. A manager fulfills the disseminator role by communicating information received from the environment to members of the organization.

*Decisional.* The manager's decisional role is determining the direction an organization should take. Growth requires action, and the responsibility to move rests with the manager. When a manager searches the organization and the industry market for opportunities and anticipates choosing an opportunity to become a reality, he is acting as an entrepreneurial manager. A manager becomes a disturbance handler by taking corrective actions when the organization experiences unexpected disturbances. Disturbances could include conflict between subordinates, but in general a manager fills this role when fixing problems. A manager becomes negotiator when making organizational decisions or representing the organization at major negotiations. In this role, the manager is working with others, both inside and outside of the organization, to accomplish the organization's goals.

## *Types of Managers and Their Typical Duties*

Due to the number of different tasks that are performed within an organization, many different types of managers exist. Some tasks will be common to all managers, while other tasks will only be required in a manager's specific area of expertise. Generally, two types of managers run an organization: functional and general.

### *Functional*

The functional manager is responsible for just one function/activity in the organization, which includes functions such as operations, finance, and human resources. When hiring either a general or functional manager, the hiring committee should look for the qualities common to all managers and those required for a specific function.

### *General*

An essential quality for any manager is the desire to lead. Without that desire, a manager will not be able to lead and motivate others to achieve the company's objectives. Effective managers should also have the proper training and experience. A manager must understand how the business runs and possess a vision of where it is going so that he or she is competent in guiding others to success. Effective managers must also be able to handle the pressures and responsibilities for the success or failure of the business.
Yukl summarized the general duties of a manager in six points:
1. The manager should be able to agree with corporate objectives and priorities.
2. The manager must be committed to a task when difficulties are encountered.
3. Managers must be able to rally people within their organization toward a common goal.
4. Managers must be able to multi-task, utilizing the available resources and personnel.
5. This individual must be able to rally support from company stakeholders.
6. Finally, the successful manager will have clear, definable, and knowable boundaries for his or her job.[20]

Jack Welch, former Chief Executive Officer (CEO) of General Electric, states that the most fundamental quality a manager must have is self-confidence. Self-confidence gives birth to the courage required to face the many trials that will be experienced by a manager. In addition, Welch believes that if a person has courage, that individual will be more apt to take risks, which he believes is a requirement for success. A manager who is willing to take calculated risks will stretch themselves to become more talented and achieve more. However, it all starts with developing self-confidence and believing that one can achieve great things—things that seem impossible to most individuals.[21]

## Operations

Operations management is concerned with how a company's products are produced—from the CEO in the boardroom to the individual on the manufacturing floor and everything in-between. Managing the operations of an organization requires the skills of a general manager and the ability to communicate and identify with the average worker. Individuals who make good operations managers communicate the desires of top management to the employees in a manner that motivates and inspires. The operations of an organization includes organizational design, product development, production planning, supplier management, quality assurance, distribution, and risk management.

The operations manager should have an expert knowledge of how things work in the areas for which he or she is responsible; however, being an expert in every task is not as important as realizing the potential for every piece of equipment and for each employee. An operations manager must be knowledgeable of the basics of the organization itself and the business environment in which the organization operates. Care must be taken in selecting the individual to occupy this managerial position, because the manager's philosophy must mirror that of the organization.

## Finance

Individuals managing the financial component of a business must have very specific skills to ensure that this critical facet of an organization is accurately and efficiently performed. Financial managers must have knowledge of the following concepts:
- Local, national, and international laws regarding investments, taxes, and import/export procedures, and business monopolies.
- International labor and banking practices dealing with fixed vs. variable loans, debt financing, bonds, revenue sharing, tax waivers, interest rates.
- Knowledge of depreciation of materials, employee wages, labor bonuses, accounting, budgeting, surpluses, and the economy are all critical for success as a financial manager.

*Human Resources*

Human resource managers address employee-related issues such as development and management of the organization's human resources and organizational development. Human resource development focuses on the improvement of individual performance, while organizational development focuses on the improvement of group performance. Human resources managers oversee the staffing process within an organization, including employee assistance programs, workplace violence, recruiting, staffing, and payroll issues. Because human resource managers deal with people and their livelihood, the stress associated with this job is significant. Individuals who elect to manage in this area must have attributes of compassion, decisiveness, discernment, organization, administration, and commitment to the company.

*Executive*

Top managers establish organizational goals, determine how departments will interact, and monitor the performance of middle managers. Top managers employ the skills of strategists to help the organization gather, analyze, and organize information through the strategic management process. The strategic management process consists of three activities: (a) strategy formulation, (b) strategy implementation, and (c) strategy evaluation.

Strategy formulation is the planning stage. During this phase, strategic managers determine (a) what business to enter, (b) how to allocate resources, (c) the development of a vision statement, (d) a mission statement, and (e) the formulation of a SWOT analysis, in order to give the organization a sense of direction. The final step in strategy formulation is to set measurable objectives. This phase ensures the formulation of the organization's identity and provides long-term direction for the organization's members. Strategy implementation occurs when employees, with the guidance of top managers, begin work to accomplish the organization's strategies. Strategy evaluation compares the organization's actual performance with the organization's planned performance to determine any necessary corrective actions.

## Managerial Skills

In his studies in the 1970s, researcher Robert Katz determined that managers, through education and experience, acquire three different types of skills: technical, human, and conceptual.[22]

*Technical skills*

A technical skill is the job specific knowledge and expertise required to perform a particular role within an organization. This requires that managers have a thorough understanding of the job specific tasks which can be gained through both formal education and/or training programs. Because such managers provide guidance and direction to the organization's front line, operational managers should possess technical skills, which emphasize a manager's performance expertise.

*Human skills*

Human skills are a manager's ability to interact and work well with others. Since managers get things done through people, they must have good communication and motivational skills. A manager provides instructions to subordinates through communication; therefore, managers must communicate clearly in both written and oral formats so that subordinates understand what is required. Human skills also include understanding what motivates subordinates within the organization. These skills are important for the top, middle, and lower levels of management.

*Conceptual skills*

Conceptual skill is a manager's ability to see the big picture and how all parts of the organization work together as a whole. Managers use conceptual skills to identify problems, develop alternative solutions, evaluate the alternatives, and select the best alternatives. Conceptual skills are important for top managers who must deal with complex problems that involve the organization and its macroenvironment.

## Characteristics of Successful Managers

In a twelve-year study, conducted by the Hagberg Consulting group, 25 percent of executives in high technology companies were deemed to be ineffective managers.[23] Effective managers must be able to build trust, motivate workers, adapt to change, build relationships with internal and/or external customers, and communicate effectively.

Successful managers are those that build a relationship of trust with their subordinates. Since human effort is an organization's most important resource, mutual trust must exist between an employee and his or her manager. If an employee trusts his manager, he is more likely to perform his best while striving to achieve organizational goals.

Another characteristic of an effective manager is the ability to motivate workers. In order to motivate workers, managers must understand how to motivate employees according to individual preferences.  In a diversified workforce, successful managers must learn to cope with individual differences, based on culture and gender, and develop a way to motivate each individual accordingly.

A successful manager must be able to adapt to change.  Today's organizational environments constantly change because of technological breakthroughs, global competition and consumer demands.  The development of new technology is making the prior obsolete, and as a result, managers must upgrade their personal technical skills and the technology utilized within their organization in order to remain competitive.

Because of changing customer demands, a manager must maintain a relationship with his or her customers in order to understand the changes in consumer preferences. The more information a manager can get from consumers concerning improvements to products and/or services, the more successful the manager will be in working towards those improvements and keeping the organization competitive.

Lastly, successful managers must be able to communicate effectively. As the one that employees look to for direction, managers must be able to communicate in such a way that subordinates comprehend what is required. In addition to being able to communicate what is required of employees, managers must also establish open communication to get the proper feedback, so that if any changes are needed to ensure effective and efficient performance, the proper actions can be taken immediately.

High self-esteem and self-efficacy are factors that determine the success of a manager. While self-efficacy and self-esteem are often used interchangeably, the two concepts differ. Managers with high self-esteem believe that they have the ability to succeed, regardless of the circumstance.  Self-efficacy is a person's self-evaluation of their ability to perform a task successfully.[24] Experience performing a task and the level of difficulty has an impact on whether a person's self-efficacy is high or low.  The concept is related to one's ability to perform something.  Contrast that with self-esteem, which is a global feeling about self. The perceptions are rather fixed, but can be altered. In practice, a person can have a low self-efficacy regarding their ability to complete a task, yet maintain a high self-esteem. Similarly, the reverse could also be true.

Mintzberg offered that successful management was a blend of craft (experience), art (insight), and science (analysis).  Balanced, dedicated individuals, who practice an "engaging" style, are needed for management success.[25] An engaging manager is one who is personally engaged with others in the organization and believes that his purpose in the organization is to leave it stronger than when he arrived.  Mintzberg believed that by defining successful management as a craft implied that it could not be learned in school;

that one has to experience the complex phenomena found in organizations first-hand to be able to understand the nuances and tacit processes of practical management.

## *Organizational Levels*

Organizations are not structured by any standardized blueprint; however, an organizational structure states the authoritative hierarchy and is the framework by which job tasks are divided, grouped, and coordinated. The traditional organizational chart is the visual representation of an organization's structure.

The type of structure utilized within an organization depends on both the organization's environment and its technical work process. The types of organizational structures include (a) the simple structure, (b) machine bureaucracy, (c) adhocracy and professional bureaucracy,[26] (d) functional structures, (e) divisional structures, and (f) matrix structures.

### *Simple structure*

The simple structure has no formal managerial hierarchy; authority is principally the responsibility of one person. Labor does not follow strict, identified guidelines; therefore, planning and training are limited, and few rules exist. An entrepreneurial start-up would be an example of this organizational structure.

### *Machine bureaucracy*

The machine bureaucracy is an inflexible structure found in mature organizations that are stable and simple. Characteristics of the machine bureaucracy include work procedures, communication procedures, task assignments, and operating procedures— that are standardized. Management, staff, and clear authority figures are distinctly separated in a machine bureaucracy.

### *Professional bureaucracy*

A professional bureaucracy has a standardization of skills. An organization that operates as a professional bureaucracy will have a series of autonomous organizations that answer to a central authority—usually a corporate headquarters—in a stable, complex environment. The professional bureaucracy merges the standardization of the machine bureaucracy and needed autonomy of professionals. The faculty of a university serves as an example, where strict departmental rules are in place; however, the instructors have some autonomy regarding research, teaching methodology, etc.

### Adhocracy bureaucracy

An organization that operates as an adhocracy does not have formalized or standard levels of management but is characterized by flexibility in task and group assignment. Very few standardized procedures and very little centralized control exist. The organization is split up into groups who converge to accomplish company goals. Managers of each department work together in problem solving and goal attainment.

### Functional structure

A functional structure groups together employees that perform similar duties. In an accounting firm, the functions may be divided by the accountants whose specialty is tax preparation, auditing, forensic accounting, or financial advising. In a manufacturing plant functions may be human resources, production, marketing, accounting, and sales.

### Divisional structure

A divisional structure groups employees based upon product, geographical regions, or customers. While each corporate office has a centralized authority, each division is focused on a different product, region, or customer. An auto manufacturer that has different divisions for different models of cars—Daimler Chrysler has both the PT Cruiser and Mercedes 350z—has different target markets and different manufacturing processes.

### Matrix organization

A matrix organization is one that combines divisional and functional structures so that a subordinate working on a project reports to two supervisors—the functional supervisor where the subordinate works and the project supervisor. However, as the number of individuals or teams reported to increases, so does the chance for error, loss of information, time, and money.

### Span of control

The span of control which managers possess depends upon the type of organization in which they operate. A span of control is the number of subordinates who report directly to a manager. The optimal span of control depends upon the type of work being done and the skill level of subordinates, but Napoleon Bonaparte considered five subordinates to be the optimal number that should report to a single manager. Many managers today still believe this to be a good number.[27]

Historically, the mindset of management was that as a company grew in size, the layers of management required to oversee the additional personnel or production would also grow by necessity. Peters and Townsend believe that most of the Fortune 500 companies are over-managed—a narrow span of control—which produces wasted resources, time, and profits.[28] Therefore, as organizations grow, management layers should not. Excessive layers of management are costly and contribute to confusion and operational inefficiency.[29] Thus, the purpose for inserting additional managerial levels often does not produce the desired effect.

What is the optimal number of levels of corporate management? Peters and Townsend suggest that any company that has over $50 million in annual sales should have no more than three levels for optimal performance. They believe that additional managerial levels creates layers of personnel that are not needed; and even worse, they divert the energies and resources of the business away from their goal of making a profit.[30] More is not better when deciding upon the number of layers of management an organization should adopt. A critical factor in making this decision is performing an evaluation of personnel, departmental, and organizational needs.

A critical factor to the success of any business is assessing the organization's structure to ensure the personnel, departments, and management are working together toward the same goals. Without the cooperation between departments and without upper-management providing critical information to middle- and lower-level managers, the ability to successfully complete a project or reach a goal can be hindered or impeded. The different components of an organization must work together to perform efficiently.[31] Brockman and Morgan found that the level of organizational cohesiveness was critical in the development and use of a new product.[32] Thus, an organization must coordinate its various levels and function as a unit in order to enhance production and profits.

*Strategic management*

Strategic management, business strategy, and organizational strategy are terms that are used synonymously; they focus on an organization's external environment and mission statement. A strategic manager assesses what the organization is doing currently and then determines what changes need to take place for the organization's goals to be accomplished. Strategic management is "[t]he set of decisions and actions that result in the formulation and implementation of plans designed to achieve an organization's objectives."[33] Strategic management includes action plans that evolve from the mission statement, the inclusion of both internal and external environmental factors, and the reward system that will be utilized for goal attainment. Development of a good strategy is often neglected when trying to improve a company's performance.[34]

A mission statement answers the question, "What is our reason for being?" An organization's board of directors and top leaders have the responsibility of determining a clear and concise mission statement, because "[o]nly a clear definition of the mission and purpose of the organization makes possible clear and realistic [goals]."[35]

A SWOT analysis looks at an organization's strengths, weaknesses, opportunities, and threats. When reviewing strengths and weaknesses, one is looking at matters internal to the organization, which includes work processes, culture, staff, etc. Opportunities and threats are matters external to the organization and may include competitive analysis, governmental regulations, new technology, etc.

Developed by Kaplan and Norton, the balanced scorecard (BSC) gives managers a comprehensive look at an organization.[36] While traditional management systems focused on profits, the BSC recognizes that if strategic managerial objectives are going to be achieved, additional factors need to be considered. Specifically, BSC acknowledges the importance of both financial and non-financial issues in the realization of organizational goals. The key to the BSC's effectiveness is its ability to encompass financial and non-financial matters and link them to the organization's strategy. The BSC is a tool that can effectively facilitate the identification of strategic goals and the clarification of necessary procedural methods to achieve desired results.[37] To employ the BSC, an organization should first develop a clear vision of where the company is going by writing a mission and vision statement. Next, clear goals should be established. Finally, the strategies to achieve those goals should be determined. The BSC considers customers, marketing, operations, finances, growth, and personnel training.

Critical for the strategic manager's duties is the ability to determine organizational goals, how those goals will be accomplished, and the skill to make strategic decisions. The effective manager utilizes tools, such as the balanced score card, and determines the proper time to act, what actions to take, and utilizes feedback to take any necessary corrective action.

### Tactical management

Tactical planning is performed by the middle level of management and is performed after an institution has established broad strategic goals and objectives.

### Operational management

Operational managers take the goals devised by tactical mangers and devise specific goals and action plans to ensure a positive outcome. Operational management is a complex phenomenon involving corporate governance and project management—both of which must be synchronized with technology. Although the components of a business are complex, operational management attempts to simplify potential problems in the details of business.[38]

When attempting to improve a company's operational efficiency managers should avoid tunnel vision—simply looking at the numbers to determine the viability of making any change. Rather, managers must determine if changing business operations would help a company achieve its goals by having the appropriate information technology (IT), by aligning departments in a manner that will streamline production or service, and by avoiding radical, sweeping changes that overhaul the entire organization.[39]

The flaw in many operational management strategies is that a manager cannot simply list the activities each department is required to perform. Those who oversee the company's operations must ensure that departmental activities are consistent with the organization's strategic goals and that the strategic goals cascade from the top of the organization to the lowest level within the organization.

## Organization Environments in which the Manager must Operate

The organizational environments in which management must operate differ vastly from those of even ten years ago, mainly due to globalization. The amount of information managers have to process has increased exponentially. Due to the increasingly competitive nature of business today, management faces significant pressure to make wise decisions, using the most up-to-the-minute information.

Managers must be aware of the internal and external factors of the organization. Internal factors are those which reside within the business, such as the internal stakeholders (employees, owners, and the board of directors), organizational goals, corporate structures, and policies. External factors are those which are external to the organization but affect and are affected by the organization: external stakeholders, including customers, suppliers, local, state, federal, and international governmental agencies, and other competitors. The external environment is constantly changing and requires regular review. External factors constantly affect the decisions that organizations make. A competitor's marketing/advertising campaign or world events easily influence customers' attitudes. Different variables can prevent a supplier's ability to provide the needed materials. Governmental agencies make laws to pacify their constituents, often to the detriment of local and national businesses. Other companies are constantly seeking to discover new and creative ways to identify and connect with the consumers.

According to Jack Welch, the successful manager of the future will be able to multi-task, handle inside politics and adversity, make tough decisions courageously, and be a team player with a staff that regularly changes.[40]  Because the manager's chief duty is decision-making, he or she must be able to discern how to handle different situations.

Managers must be aware of environmental and organizational entities to succeed in business.  The emerging global economy demands that managers be aware of the corporation's totality—see the "big picture."  As the world shrinks because of technology, the business environment continues to be increasingly competitive and unstable. Therefore, a business that wishes to be successful will need to possess the ability and plan for change within the organization.[41] Due to the fluidity of markets, nations, consumer demand, and public opinion, companies must prepare for change internally and externally. Internal factors that need to be considered include corporate management structure, rules, required job skills, employee abilities, motivation, facilities, available finances, present clients, and different personnel roles. Intangible concepts, such as tradition, corporate history, bias, local culture, and personal habits must also be processed in one's managerial duties.[42]  Because the individual's job performance depends on the ability to work through many of these issues, managers who fail to consider this information will have a short managerial life.

While managers greatly influence many of the internal factors, their ability to control external factors is almost nil.  However, managers must be aware of external factors and use environmental scanning when making decisions.  External factors include information technology, the political atmosphere, economic conditions, competitors, the public's perception, local and international laws, media habits and practices, and cultural trends.

A daunting task for any manager is to remain current with the latest corporate–business technology.  While managers do not have to be aware of how technology works, they must know how it can help or harm their organization.

Managers must maintain an environment where the needs and desires of the stakeholder and the company's vision are considered in every decision.[43]  A manager must lead a workplace that encourages teamwork, collaboration, and information sharing.  Finally, many business environments demand that the leader be an effective communicator to both individuals and management teams.

Effective managers must be aware of the social and political climate of the country in which the organization is located and where its products are sold or services provided. Failure to attend to these variables can mean disaster. Many corporations experienced huge losses when Fidel Castro became the head of the Cuban government in 1959 and confiscated U.S. owned sugar mills in Cuba.[44]

## Systems Approach

A systems approach to management has been defined as "the ability of the organization in either absolute or relative terms to exploit its environment in the acquisition of scarce and valued resources."[45] This particular approach recognizes that corporations do not operate in a vacuum; rather, they interface with their external environments—suppliers, customers, cultures, etc.—and form mutually beneficial relationships to produce better products or services. An organization operating in an open system has four stages: inputs, transformation, outputs, and feedback. Individuals outside the organization provide supplies, service, and/or personnel to enable business operations to function. Tangible output of an organization generally includes products or services, but output also includes intangibles such as the organization's reputation, influence of others, and knowledge of people or organizations.[46]

Organizational stakeholders are "persons or groups that have or claim ownership, rights, or interests in a corporation and its activities, past present, or future."[47] A stakeholder is an individual or group who has an effect or is effected by the success of a business enterprise.[48] The number of individuals and groups classified as stakeholders is essentially endless. Commonly labeled stakeholders are the consumers, employees, suppliers, special interest groups, political groups, other competing businesses, etc. Thus, in a systems approach, anyone with whom the organization interacts is a stakeholder.

One of the more complicated problems facing managers today is the fact that in an open system, the needs, wants, and demands of every stakeholder are in a constant state of change due to their interaction with new information.[49] As stakeholder's expectations change, so do the goals of the organization. Managers must monitor the satisfaction levels of stakeholders to enable the best product or service to those who are invested in a company.

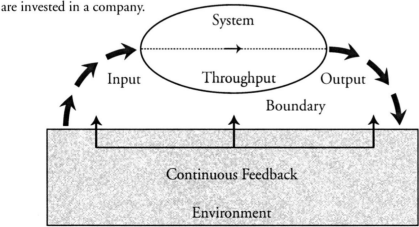

*Resource Inputs*

The resource inputs with which each organization must interface are suppliers and the communities in which the organization operates. Researchers have identified the need for small and large businesses to make a profit and be socially responsible. Corporate social responsibility is, "a company's commitment to operating in an economically sustainable manner while recognizing the interests of its stakeholders."[50] Corporations that are perceived to care about their social and physical environment are often thought to have a greater identification with consumers. While countries differ in the amount of governmental regulation of corporate social responsibility, many corporations have found it to be good business to be labeled environmentally or socially sensitive.[51] Companies should include corporate social responsibility in its strategy, because businesses should be accountable for their actions in society and the environment.

*Transformation Process*

With the inputs received from the environment, an organization utilizes its management expertise and technology to add value to the product or service, converting the inputs into outputs.

*Product Outputs*

An organization's output includes not only the product or service produced but also the financial gains, losses, or reputation that is generated through the organization's actions in both the local and global communities.

*Feedback*

Customers sustain a business and provide the capital for growth and expansion.[52] However, they are only one group that provides feedback to an organization that is operating as an open system. Anything that is a reaction to the organization's outputs, such as financial statements, employee feedback, or community response to an issue is utilized as feedback.

## Total Responsibility Management

The pressure exerted on international corporations is so great that total responsibility management (TRM) teams have become commonplace. TRM teams have been given a daunting task: to balance the demand for greater profits while remaining environmentally sensitive.[53] TRM adds another layer of management to the already cluttered corporate structure. In an attempt to clarify and appease the needs of stakeholders, companies may have caused greater confusion and loss of profits through the establishment of TRM. It is a fine line to satisfy both economic and environmental concerns among chief stakeholders, but pressure from public, private, and governmental sources demand that the effort be made.

An examination of the focus of the banking industry found that the concerns of the stakeholders in the community had become the primary core of business operations.[54] The problem with this mindset was that it caused the basics of the banking business to be neglected—namely the owners and customers. Profits were negatively affected and customers were not satisfied. In order to correct the situation, the banking industry changed its mindset from profit-making to customer-assistance. When banks satisfy customers, profits will naturally result.[55]

## *Career Development*

If one were to ask a hundred people how to build a management career, he or she would receive one hundred different answers. While people each have their own opinion regarding the issue, everyone can agree that certain aptitudes and skills will benefit a future manager.

Those who aspire to management positions should carefully consider the following:
- Take initiative with and responsibility for the development of your career.
- Be introspective, know yourself.
- Commit to learn new skills and obtain new knowledge throughout your career. This could include communication and presentation skills or learning about another specialization in the organization. For example, if you work in the marketing department, learn about the financial component of your organization. This will make you valuable to the organization.
- Build and maintain a network of business acquaintances and contacts.
- Carefully document your achievements in the workplace. This allows you to accurately promote your accomplishments and manage your reputation.

A survey of individuals who wanted to go into business and become entrepreneurs showed that the factors associated with the desire to be proprietors were both intrinsic, such as prestige, and extrinsic, such as earning power and greater independence. Results also found that the reasons for failing to start a business were lack of capital, skills, confidence, and compliant costs.[56] Therefore, if one desires to work as an entrepreneur, he or she should consider locating resources to fund business ventures, develop the skills required of a CEO, attend every workshop available, and begin each day envisioning success.

# Conclusion

## *Brief Summary of Major Points*

It is incredible to think that in the 21$^{st}$ century man is still asking the question, "What is management?" Hundreds of journals and thousands of books have been dedicated to explaining the latest trends and theories that will enable man to out-perform the competition. As the business world becomes more global, greater attention must be given to studying international management. Managers who operate in the manner that is most comfortable for them, regardless of the penchants of their stakeholders, will quickly find themselves looking for a new line of work. Today's business world is not fixed but fluid and always changing. The manager of the future must learn to adapt and learn how to lead amid an ever-changing environment. One of the characteristics of management is that no theory, strategy, or mechanism works in every type of business or situation. Therefore, each industry and business must decide for itself which method to use to operate its organization. The consumers will determine if the correct decision was made.

Despite the ever-evolving appearance of business, the functions of a manager have remained the same—planning, leading, organizing and controlling. However, the methods used to perform these functions vary between individuals and tasks. To lead some individuals, such as novices, requires a high degree of supervision, while professionals can often be led by giving a request. A good manager must determine the best methods to motivate so that company goals can be achieved; they must constantly be analyzing and learning how to spur those under them onto fulfilling the company goals. The question naturally arises, "How can a manager motivate his/her workers?" A more complete answer will be addressed in a future chapter; but suffice it to say, due to the complexity of mankind, managers will be pondering this question for many years to come. Motivational theories and techniques abound, each seemingly having a piece of the puzzle. Researchers must focus their attention upon discerning the motivational tendencies of people from different ethnic backgrounds, cultures, socio-economic levels, and gender. As differences emerge between groups, managers will be better equipped to lead others.

Another question that has yet to be answered is how many managers are needed for an organization to operate effectively? The recent managerial trend has been to downsize the levels of management within the organization, but this practice is not beneficial for all businesses. The fluid nature of business has been discussed, citing the need for flexibility in management styles and size. Because no two people are alike, one could accurately conclude that no two businesses are alike. One of the objectives of this chapter was to identify some commonalties that can be found in many organizations and allow the reader to select those which would work best for him/her. Researchers need to target the tendencies of people from various backgrounds and come to an understanding of how different people prefer to operate in business. Organizations will be birthed when they recognize and identify these tendencies as more efficient and cost effective.

Managers need to be diligent in examining the expectations of owners, workers, suppliers, customers, and communities to anticipate change. The great challenge for every company and researcher will be to predict cultural, community, and business tendencies, followed by a plan or map to help organizations achieve their goals amidst our ever changing world.

Some recommendations have been offered for the individual who wants to be successful in the business world. These suggestions would help any manager improve his or her performance, but this list is not exhaustive. Senior management would be wise to offer workshops for other senior and junior level managers where these principles and their application within the organization were taught. Management will never completely understand human behavior, but they can do their best to acquire the best information available and apply it to their personnel. This will be a constant challenge and frustration due to the inconsistency of human behavior.

## *Impact on the Organization, the Manager, and Employees*

The impact management has on the organization is immeasurable. Theories of management have continued to evolve; and with this, a level of managerial uncertainty has permeated the elite ranks. Ever-changing technology has altered the way managers practice. Real-time communication is available worldwide, and managers need to take advantage of this opportunity. However, management must never forget that business is about people. The public and personnel within the organization must be treated well if organizational goals are to be achieved.

Employees have been and always will be the bedrock of a successful organization. Without concerned, motivated, passionate, and well-trained workers a business may fail. However, employees must be willing to change as the structure of business changes. With the emergence of IT, the methods and application of business have changed and will continue to do so. Employees must look for opportunities for training and experience in unfamiliar areas to strengthen their value to business. This was true one hundred years ago and is more true today.

# Endnotes

1   Hambrick, D.C. & Mason, P.A. (1984).  Upper Echelons: The Organization as a Reflection of Its Top Managers." Academy of Management Review 9, No. 2 :193-206.

2   White, R. & Lippitt, R. (1960).  Autocracy and democracy: an experimental inquiry.  New York: Harper & Brothers.

3   Kotter, J.P. (1996).  Leading Change, Boston: Harvard Business School Press.

4   DeGrosky, M. (2006, May 1).  Management not leadership.  *Wildfire.*  p. 12.

5   Burns, J. M. (1978).  *Leadership.*  New York: Harper & Row.

6   Bennis, W. & Nanus, B. (1985).  *Leaders: The strategies for taking charge.*  New York: Harper & Row.

7   Tichy, N. M., & Devanna, M. A. (1986).  *The transformational leader.*  New York: Wiley.

8   House, R.J. Woycke, J., & Fodor, E.M.  *Charismatic and noncharasmatic leaders: Differences in Behavior and Effectiveness.*  In Conger and Kanungo *Charismatic leadership.*  pp. 103-104.

9   Goleman, D. (1995).  Emotional intelligence.  New York: Bantam.

10  Kelley, R. (1988)  "In Praise of Followers" (*Harvard Business Review:* 66.6 [Nov.-Dec. 1988]: 142-48).

11  Ibid.

12  Meilinger, P.S. (n.d.)  *Ten Rules of Good Followership*,  AU-24 Concepts for Air Force Leadership. Retrieved from the World Wide Web September 23, 2006:  http://www.au.af.mil/au/awc/ awcgate/au-24/meilinger.pdf

13  Ibid.

14  Bennis, W. (1993) An Invented Life; Reflections on Leadership and Change.  Cambridge, MA; Addison-Wesley Publishing.

15  An Integrative Model of Organizational Trust   Roger C. Mayer, James H. Davis, F. David Schoorman *Academy of Management Review*, Vol. 20, No. 3 (Jul., 1995), pp. 709-734.

16  Kouzes, J. & Posner, B. (2002)  The leadership challenge. 3$^{rd}$ ed.  Jossey-Bass.

17  French, J. R. P., and B. Raven. 1959. The bases of social power. In D. Cartwright, ed., *Studies in social power*, 150–67. Ann Arbor: University of Michigan.

18  Stanley, A. (1999).  *Visioneering.* Sisters, OR: Multnomah Publishers.

19  Mintzberg, H, (1973).  *The Nature of Managerial Work*, Harper & Row.

20  Yukl, G. (1989)  Leaderhip in Organizations. 2$^{nd}$ ed. Albany,  Prentiss Hall.

21  Welch, Jr., J. F. (2001).  *Jack: Straight from the gut* (pp. 3-20). New York: Warner Books.

22  Katz, R. (1974).  Skills of an effective administrator.  Harvard Business Review, Vol 52, Issue 5, p 94 (pp90 – 102).

23  Silicon Valley/San Jose Business Journal - January 2, 1997.

24  Bandura, A. (1986).  *Social foundations of thought and action: A social cognitive theory.* Englewood Cliffs, NJ: Prentice Hall.

25  Mintzberg, H. (2004).  Managers not MBAs: A hard look at the soft practice of managing and management development. San Francisco: Berrett-Koehler.

26  Mintzberg, H. (1989).  *Mintzburg on Management*,  New York: Simon & Schuester.

27    VanFleet, D. & Bedeian, A. (1977). A history of the span of management. *Academy of Management Review, 2* pp. 356-72.

28    Peters, T. & Townsend, R. (Speakers). (1986). *Excellence in the organization* (Cassette Recording No. 199-2). Chicago, IL: Nightingale-Conant Corporation.

29    Glander, P. (2006, June 19) It's not easy being lean. *Wall Street Journal,* 247(142), B1-B3; 2p; 1c.

30    Peters & Townsend (1986).

31    Sinickas, A. (2006, June/July). Evaluating your cascade process. *Strategic Communication,* 10(4), 12-13.

32    Brockman, B. B. & Morgan, R. M. (2006). The moderating effect of organizational cohesiveness in knowledge use and new product development. *Journal of the Academy of Marketing Science,* 34(3), 295-307.

33    Pearce, J. & Robinson, R. (2005). *Strategic management* (9th ed.). Boston: McGraw-Hill Irwin.

34    Levitt, T. (1991). *Thinking about management,* p. 112-115. New York: The Free Press.

35    Drucker, P.E. (1954). The Practice of Management. New York: Harper and Row, p. 122.

36    Kaplan, E.S. & Norton, D.P. (2004). Strategy maps: Converting intangible assets into tangible outcomes. Boston: Harvard Business School Press.

37    Balanced scorecards help to measure what matters, (2006). *Law Office Management & Administration Report,* 6(9), 1-12.

38    Bielski, L. (2006). The new efficiency alignment. *ABA Banking Journal,* 98(5), 43-47.

39    Ibid.

40    Welch, (2001).

41    McLean, J. (2006). We're going through changes …, *British Journal of Administrative Management,* 54, 31-32.

42    Hernandez, R. A. (2002). *Managing sport organizations* (p. 158). Champaign, IL: Human Kinetics.

43    Ward, J. L. (2005). Project management: Techniques for adaptive action. *Chief Learning Officer,* 4(12), 20-23.

44    Grun, B. (1963). *The timetables of history* (p. 544). New York: Simon & Schuster.

45    Yuchtman, E. & Seshore, S. E. (1967). A systems resource approach to organizational effectiveness (p. 898). *American Sociological Review,* 32, 891-903.

46    Gamson, W. A. (1966). Reputation and resources in community politics. *American Journal of Sociology,* 72, 121-131.

47    Clarkson, M. B. E. (1995). A stakeholder framework for analyzing and evaluating corporate social performance (p. 106). *Academy of Management Review,* 20, 92-117.

48    Freeman, E. R. (1984). *Strategic management: A stakeholder approach* (p. 46). Marshfield, MA: Pitman.

49    Davis, C, & Stevens, E. (2006). Tired of reading? Listen to the webinar. 22-24.

50    Durand, A. (2006). CSR continues to define itself globally (p. 48). *Caribbean Business,* 34(18), 48.

51    May, J. (2006). Triple-S offers tips for effective corporate social responsibility (p. 48). *Caribbean Business,* 34(18), p. 48.

52    Richard, W. C. (2002). The responsible shareholder: a case study. *Business Ethics,* 11(1), 14-24.

53   Waddock, S. A., Bodwell, C. B., & Graves, S. (2002). Responsibility: The new business imperative. *Academy of Management Executive*, 16(2), 132-148.

54   Kaplan, N. I. (2000). Needed: New face in executive suite to act as surrogate for the customer. *American Banker*, 165(217), 13.

55   Ibid.

56   Choo, S. & Wong, M. (2006). Entrepreneurial intention: Triggers and barriers to new venture creations in Singapore. *Singapore Management Review*, 28(2), 47-64.

# CHAPTER 2

## History Of Management

## MEASURABLE LEARNING OBJECTIVES

1. Summarize the historical background of the study of management.

2. Discuss Scientific Management theories and theorists and identify their impact on modern management. Identify the contributions of Taylor and the Gilbreths.

3. Discuss Administrative Management theories and theorists and identify their impact on modern management. Identify the contributions of Fayol and Weber.

4. Discuss Quantitative Management theories and theorists and identify their impact on modern management. Identify the contributions of Owen, Musterberg, Parker Follett, Barnard, Mayo, Maslow, McGregor, and Argyris.

5. Describe trends and theories that are affecting modern management practices.

6. Identify management gurus that are affecting modern management practices.

7. Discuss the impact of management theories on an organization, the manager and employees. Identify the contributions of Deming, Juran and Senge.

# Introduction

The roots of current management practices are found in the historic events of the past few centuries. This chapter follows the evolution of management from its embryonic stage in the eighteenth century to modern theories of today, with changes driven by economic, environmental, political, and cultural factors. Theorists and innovators met the forces of change by challenging the status quo and seeking new methods to be more efficient and productive. Management emphasis shifted from one of rules and authority to industrial psychology; from production to employee; from a pyramidal management structure to one that is flat; and from a static organization to one that is flexible.

In 1776, Adam Smith (1723-1790) of Scotland, published The Wealth of Nations, in which he shifted the economic focus to efficient production through specialized tasks and the division of labor. At the time of publication, the focus of industry was on small farms and home-based factories where owners were trying to earn an income to support their families. Smith believed that there were two requirements necessary for work to be productive: the work must create both a tangible end product and a surplus, which would be reinvested into production.

The annual labor of every nation is the fund which originally supplies it with all the necessaries and conveniences of life which it annually consumes, and which consists always either in the immediate produce of that labor, or in what is purchased with that produce from other nations. Therefore, as this produce, or what is purchased with it, bears a greater or smaller proportion to the number of those who are to consume it, the nation will be better or worse supplied with all the necessaries and conveniences for which it has occasion.

Smith was the first to recognize the relationship of job specialization with efficiency. To explain the relationship, he used as illustration the manufacturing of pins. Smith concluded that ten workers could produce approximately forty-eight thousand pins daily if each performed only a specialized task in the manufacturing process. He asserted that if those same ten individuals had to construct a pin completely from start to finish, it would be unlikely that they could make even ten pins a day. This illustration emphasized that division of labor increased an employee's manual dexterity and speed, resulting in increased production.

# Industrial Revolution

With the onset of the industrial revolution in Great Britain in the eighteenth century, the economy moved away from an agricultural focus to one of commerce; it was a time of transfer from human and animal power to machine power—of technological and economic growth. With new sources of energy, raw materials, and a migration of the population to urban areas, labor shifted from the farms located in rural areas to factories located in metropolitan areas. Consequently, it was much cheaper to produce goods in factories than in homes. That shift of workers from small farms to large factories encouraged economic growth and challenges that arose from managing large numbers of employees. Managers were needed to assign jobs, direct employees, order raw materials, and coordinate activities across the factory. In other words, managers had to plan, lead, organize, and control. During this time period, management focused on machine-like control, as much of the labor involved repetitive tasks.[3]

Prior to the onset of the industrial revolution, most factories produced guns, ammunition, or pottery; however, during the early years of the industrial revolution, factory production of textiles became prevalent. Technological advances during that time lead to the invention of a myriad of equipment and machinery to support mass production. Invention was not only occurring within the factory, however. The invention of the steam engine and the steam engine's use in steamboats and railroads allowed quick transport of manufactured goods to consumers.[4]

# Scientific Management

Scientific management emerged in the latter part of the nineteenth century on the heels of the industrial revolution. Primarily an American trend, scientific management focused on increased efficiency for the individual employee. The era of the craftsman diminished as more items were mass produced in factories. The replacement of small home-based businesses with large organizations brought about opportunities, but not without problems. When the small work shop was replaced with factories, which employed large numbers of people, those factories were run by managers who may have possessed technical skills but had no idea how to address the personnel issues that arose. Scientific management utilized scientific methods to determine the "one best way" for a job to be accomplished.

## *Frederick W. Taylor*

Frederick Winslow Taylor (1856-1915), is considered the father of scientific management.  As an engineer, Taylor established the guidelines associated with scientific management in his book *Principles of Scientific Management* (1911).  Unlike later management theorists, such as Henri Fayol or Max Weber, Taylor's interest was in efficiency, not authority.  Taylor studied the different physical motions involved in jobs performed at Philadelphia's Midvale and Bethlehem Steel Companies and was shocked at the inefficiencies of workers performing their jobs.  Taylor determined what he believed to be the most efficient way to complete each job.  Like a cog in a machine, each employee had a specific function.  The more precise the cog, or in Taylor's case the employee, the better the factory ran.

According to Taylor, successful management entailed sustained profitability for the employer and substantial wages for the worker.  The goal was for both to work together to increase the profitability of the organization. Taylor felt that a manager had two responsibilities: coordinating employee functions by assigning tasks and monitoring employees' work.  He believed that employees needed clearly defined guidelines to be successful.  In fact, Taylor believed that workers deliberately dawdled on the job—worked at less than full capacity—a term he called soldiering.  To eliminate soldiering, Taylor's theory espoused four guidelines that he believed would promote efficiency:

> The principles at the heart of scientific management were clear: break jobs down into their simplest parts; select the most suitable workers to fit the available jobs; turn those workers into specialists, each an expert in his own appointed task; arrange these specialized jobs along an assembly line; and design the right package of incentives (including bonuses and prizes) to ensure that the workers did indeed work.[5]

Rules and clarity of function or role delineation were of the utmost importance to Taylor, so the new processes were documented as written rules and standard operating procedures.  The responsibility of the manager was to assure that the worker was appropriately trained to function within the parameters that had been created. Finally, an established acceptable level of performance, which was associated with a specific level of pay, had to be set.  Taylor believed that any performance that exceeded the expectations should be rewarded.

Taylor's Four Principles of Management

| Principle 1 | Study each aspect of the worker's task and develop a plan to improve performance. |
|---|---|
| Principle 2 | Secure new processes with written rules and standard operating procedures. |
| Principle 3 | Select workers according to their skill sets that coordinate with the task. Train to function within the rules and standard operating procedures. |
| Principle 4 | Establish an acceptable level of performance and associate it with a specific level of pay. Reward performance that exceeds the accepted level. |

Things were not always implemented as planned. By the early 1900s, Taylor's four guidelines were being utilized throughout the United States to increase efficiency. Organizations raised their performance expectations; but in some cases, management neglected to reward employees when they exceeded predisposed expectations. Instead of receiving monetary bonuses, the workers were simply rewarded with more work and higher expectations. The backlash against such abuse towards Taylor's principles led to his methods falling out of favor.

## Frank and Lillian Gilbreth

Frank (1868-1924) and Lillian Gilbreth (1878-1972) pioneered motion studies and the psychology of management. They first met in Boston where he had risen from a bricklayer's apprentice to one of the most prominent industrial contractors in the United States. She was about to embark on a trip to Europe with friends prior to entering a doctoral program. Frank was decades ahead of his time; he wanted his wife to have a career and encouraged her to work with him and to pursue a degree in psychology.

Frank and Lillian had a large family. As parents of twelve children, the Gilbreth philosophy of efficiency carried over to their personal lives. They separated the home into designated work centers. The family recorded and displayed tasks and methods on charts. Unquestionably unique, two of the Gilbreth children commemorated the household organizational structure in the acclaimed book, *Cheaper by the Dozen*.[7]

The Gilbreths worked to eliminate useless effort by studying hand and body motions that a worker used to complete a task. They took the job study ideas of Taylor to the next level. The tools used in this process were called Therbligs, an anagram of the name, Gilbreth. Therbligs were developed as a system of categorizing basic tasks within a process and were symbols for a specific movement or action that a worker would make to perform his or her job. Workers were observed, and every task performed was dissected into individual movements. The movements were timed, filmed, and examined—frame by frame—to study every stroke. Each motion was assigned a Therblig. Each of the eighteen Therbligs was color coded and associated with a specific icon. The Therbligs were hand recorded on a Simultaneous Motion (Simo) chart, which was the precursor to a flow chart. The chart was then reviewed to discover easier ways to perform tasks. The intent of using Therbligs was not to save time but to promote efficiency and avoid wasted movements.[6] Through chart evaluation, the Gilbreths could eliminate the Therbligs that were unnecessary, decreased efficiency, or caused worker fatigue. Areas of delay also became obvious. Deletion of Therbligs in a process eliminated unnecessary movements. By streamlining the processes in this manner, the Gilbreths assumed that the process would naturally take less time and decrease worker fatigue.

An example of a Therblig is "Search." "Search" was represented by the color black and associated with an icon looking to the side, which signified the time spent searching for items to perform a specific task, such as a paper, tool, or switch. The Gilbreths discovered that colors, shapes, and embossed symbols made finding the items easier.

# Administrative Management

Administrative management theory is the study of organizational composition based on efficiency and effectiveness. Efficiency is measured by how well resources are utilized to achieve set productivity goals. Effectiveness measures the appropriateness of the goals set by the organization and how well the goals are achieved. An organization utilizes efficiency and effectiveness by measuring performance according to these combined standards. Businesses continually seek ways to achieve efficient and effective processes as a matter of competitive survival.

Henri Fayol and Max Weber played important roles in the development of the support of the theoretical structure of Administrative Management. They simply prescribed the basic properties of management function. Administrative management contrasts the viewpoint of scientific theory by concentrating on the efficiency of large numbers of individuals in an organization, whereas the scientific approach concentrates on the efficiency of the individual. Another contrast is that scientific management is associated with American culture but administrative theory is a more universal management structure.[8]

## *Henri Fayol*

Henri Fayol (1841-1925) was a French engineer, the CEO of a mining company, and is known as the "father of modern management." After his retirement in 1916, Fayol published a book in which he utilized his management experiences to identify four functions and fourteen principles of management. The functions of management included the processes of planning, organizing, leading, and controlling, while the principles of management were intended to be used as guidelines in managerial decision making and in the development and improvement of management skills. The fourteen principles included the following:

1.  *Division of work* increases efficiency by promoting job specialization. In order for this to be effective, the employee must not be allowed to become bored with the task and should be stimulated to assume different responsibilities.

2.  *Authority and responsibility* are components not only directed to the manager but also to those employees with informal authority associated with increased expertise or natural leadership skills.

3.  *Unity of command* means that employees should answer to only one person in authority. Having more than one authority figure could lead to disarray and confusion.

4.  *Line of authority* or chain of command should align from top to bottom and with limited layers.

5.  *Centralization* of authority assures that decision making occurs at the top of the chain of command.

6.  *Unity of direction* gives the workers and managers a single path to follow; a single vision.

7.  *Equity* represents the entitlement of all employees to be treated fairly.

8.  *Order* is the alignment of positions to provide the employees opportunity.

9. *Initiative* and creativity should be encouraged and supported by management for the benefit of the organization.

10. *Discipline* of employees is an entitlement of leadership and authority.

11. *Remuneration of personnel* is accomplished through the practice of provision of fair wages, bonuses and incentives.

12. *Tenure of personnel* offers job security by encouraging skill development to promote retention and decrease turnover.

13. *Subordination of individual interests to the common interest* indicates that the success of the organization is the primary goal and all others secondary. It is the responsibility of the manager to lead the initiative towards the organizational vision.

14. *Esprit de corps* is the driving force to camaraderie and enthusiasm that unifies and energizes the organization.[9]

Fayol adamantly believed that a manager's authority was based on his position in the organization, as well as intelligence, performance, and moral fortitude. His organizational model was depicted "as a pyramid of people with both personal power *and* formal rules as principles of organization."[10] Fayol's theory is considered controversial because it is not based upon scientific study but on anecdotes of his own experiences. Many have challenged his principles because they claim that Fayol thought the principles were sweeping truths for management; however, Fayol wanted the principles to be flexible in their application.[11]

## *Max Weber*

Max Weber (1864-1920) was a German scholar, professor of economics, and sociologist, who in his book, *The Theory of Social and Economic Organizations,* developed a concept of bureaucracy considered to be ideal for large organizations.[12] The power behind Weber's theory was found in the rules of the organization, which provided structure and efficiency and defined the power of the manager.[13] Over time, Weber's strict view of authority and command met with controversy, but components of the basic structure of bureaucracy have held firm over time.

Weber's works became the basis for current theories behind charismatic leadership. The charismatic leader has a magnetic pull on followers.

According to Weber, charisma occurs when there is a social crisis, a leader attracts followers who believe in the vision, they experience some successes that make the vision appear attainable, and the followers come to perceive the leader as extraordinary.[14]

Weber believed in well-defined rules and a strong hierarchy and supported his viewpoint with the theory of an ideal bureaucracy. Weber's bureaucracy was a set of guidelines intended for large groups rather than individuals and was divided into division of labor, authority, formal rules, impersonality, and career orientation.

1. *Division of labor* assured that the job was done by an expert so that the end result would be consistent and completed more quickly and efficiently.

2. *Authority* assured a clearly set out chain of command.

3. *Formal rules* assured that employees followed the same pattern of tasks so that the same level of performance was maintained. The expectation of compliance to rules was applied to managers as well as workers.

4. *Impersonality* removed emotion and camaraderie from the equation. Rules were equitably enforced, regardless of the employee's rank or status so that favoritism held no credence in the organization.

5. *Career orientation* designated that the company owners should not manage the departments. Instead, that task should be done by professional managers, hired by the organization.

# Behavioral Management

Behavioral management theory concentrates on the behaviors utilized by managers to motivate employees to work effectively and demonstrate commitment to the organization's goals. Behavioral management emerged in the 1930s following the introduction of industrial psychology. Theorists Robert Owen, Hugo Munsterberg, Mary Parker Follett, Chester Barnard, Elton Mayo, Abraham Maslow, Douglas McGregor and Chris Argyris are all considered behaviorists.

## *Robert Owen*

Robert Owen (1771-1858) was a Welsh businessman and factory owner, noted as a reformer, idealist, and entrepreneur. He married the daughter of the owner of New Lanark Mills and managed the mill's operations. He worked passionately to improve working hours and overall conditions for laborers. Owen sought to improve public education (at a time when many were illiterate), company provided meals for workers, and organizational support for community programs. One of Owen's most exhausting battles was his fight to abolish the use of child labor; he believed that children should not work in the mills before they were ten-years-old. He chastised businesses for treating their machines better than the laborers themselves.

> Owen's opinion that labor is a source of wealth and that workers have certain rights greatly contributed to the labor movement and the development of a new working class. Owen did not, however understand or promote class struggle, feeling that a transformation to a cooperative, egalitarian society would be peaceful and natural.[15]

## Hugo Munsterberg

German-born psychologist Hugo Munsterberg (1863-1916) is considered the "father of industrial psychology" and a champion for behaviorism. As a Harvard professor, he identified methods to improve employee selection through the utilization of psychological testing and the development of the best training techniques and methodologies for individual motivation. In 1913, he pioneered job analysis based on his study of streetcar operators.[16]

Munsterberg was able to establish a connection between scientific management and industrial psychology. He believed that both scientific management and industrial psychology increased organizational efficiency through alignment of a worker's skills with the requirements of a job.

## Mary Parker Follett

Mary Parker Follett (1868-1933), a social philosopher and social worker, based her theories around groups and community. A graduate of Radcliffe College, her ideas and opinions were well ahead of others of her time. Follett may be best known for her pursuit of the human relations side of management. She appreciated the advantages offered through diverse groups and transferred this to her theory, which attributed the success of organizations to group interaction, ethics, and teams—as opposed to hierarchal structures or rules. Follett believed in self-governance in the workplace. In her 1924 book *Creative Experience,* she presented her circular theory of power in which power flows from one individual to another, not from a hierarchal position but from intelligence and expertise. Power is developed and cultivated, not used to control. Follett believed that individuals control with power because they are too impatient to wait for the educational process to bring about expertise and intelligence.

As a lecturer and writer, she shared her views on developing a social conscience in the workplace. Follett compared the workings of an organization to that of a democratic community that thrived with cooperative socialization—managers and employees should work together instead of one giving orders and the other receiving orders. Many did not accept her viewpoints readily in her lifetime; however, other theorists elaborated upon them later in the twentieth century. One such person was Peter Drucker, who discovered Mary Parker Follett's writings in the 1950s and found them to be highly influential in his subsequent work. Her ideas were visionary and contributed to the promotion of the concepts of searching for win-win solutions and appreciation for diverse cultures.[17]

## Chester Barnard

Chester Barnard (1886-1961) worked at American Telephone and Telegraph and later became the president of New Jersey Bell. The writings of Max Weber influenced him in his early years. After Barnard became familiar with the Hawthorne studies, he took Weber's theories one step further by adding human relationship aspects of management to the mix. In 1938, Barnard published *The Functions of the Executive,* where he defined an organization as "a system of consciously coordinated activities or forces of two or more people."[18] Barnard believed that cooperation is the glue that holds organizations together and that cooperation was an inherent function that should be adopted to support an organization's survival. In doing so, the leader became responsible to provide training, support and, employee incentives. Barnard stated the following in *The Functions of the Executive*:

> I believe that the expansion of coöperation and the development of the individual are mutually dependent realities, and that a due proportion or balance between them is a necessary condition of human welfare. Because it is subjective with respect to both a society as a whole and to the individual, what this proportion is I believe science cannot say. It is a question for philosophy and religion.[19]

To achieve equilibrium, Barnard believed that if the pay was sufficient, organizations could recruit and retain employees. People would accept low paying jobs only if the alternative was no job at all.[20] "His underlying theme is that organizations are by nature co-operative systems but require sensitive management to maintain them in states of equilibrium."[21] In addition to his theory of equilibrium, Barnard promoted principles for effective communication. He suggested that communication is essential to every organization and is the key for sound decision-making.

Barnard also recognized that the structure of an organization is a community of people. Individuals convene to become groups, and the groups make up the organization. Managers carry the responsibility of motivating the individuals and groups to follow a single set of goals for the benefit of the organization.

## *Elton Mayo*

Elton Mayo (1880-1949), a Harvard professor and researcher, studied the affects of groups on individual behavior. Mayo's studies revealed the impact of the informal organization—the social group that exists inside all organizations. Mayo has been recognized for his research associated with the Hawthorne Studies of Western Electric in Chicago. The original experiment was conducted by Western Electric industrial engineers who studied the affects of the physical environment of the work area on productivity. The initial experiment was to determine whether the level of workplace illumination had an affect on worker productivity.

The control group worked in an area where the lighting levels remained constant. As lighting increased, so did productivity in both the experimental and control group. The result was the same when the illumination was decreased. Only when the illumination was adjusted to the level of moonlight was there a decrease in productivity. The results of the illumination studies baffled researchers and led researchers to the conclusion that multiple factors influence productivity in the workplace.

Mayo participated in a subsequent five-year experiment—the Relay Assembly Test-Room studies. In this experiment, a research assistant observed six employees in an area removed from the mainstream employee population. The experimental group of six workers was segregated from the rest of the factory, and various changes were introduced: monetary incentives, refreshments, changes in work hours and rest periods. In almost every case, productivity improved. Even after the employees returned to their original work areas, the trend of increased productivity continued. However, the experimental group differed from the rest of the factory in that communication was fluid and the group had created a cohesive bond. Experimenters concluded that the recognition of the employees as a select group and the interpersonal dynamics, combined with a perceived elite status, led to the increased productivity.[22]

> This groundbreaking study, which established a pattern for the examination of group behavior, led to a series of studies about the feelings and attitudes of workers and supervisors in relation to their output. Mayo's insights and interpretations guided the development of these studies. He published the first extensive report of them in *The Human Problems of an Industrial Society* (1933).[23]

## *Abraham Maslow*

Abraham Maslow (1908-1970) is noted for his motivational theory—depicted as a hierarchy of needs—developed in 1943. The needs are frequently depicted in the form of a pyramid with the lowest achievement on the bottom and the highest at the top. Maslow's hierarchy of needs is further separated into two levels: lower-order and higher-order. Physiological and safety needs are categorized as lower-order needs, which are satisfied through external conditions. Social, esteem, and self-actualization represent higher-order needs that are satisfied internally.[24]

Maslow's pyramid consists of five levels: physiological, safety, social, esteem, and self-actualization. The physiological needs are those very basic needs—such as food, water, and shelter. Safety needs are security-oriented in the form of protection from physical or mental harm. Social needs include emotional stability in the form of affection and belonging and can be met through family and friends. Esteem needs include self respect, autonomy, and recognition and arise from status and titles. Self-actualization involves meeting one's potential through the achievement of a victory or taking on a challenge. The theory essentially states that man will be motivated to embrace the next level of achievement only after meeting the needs of the current level.[25]  Although used as the basis for many management decisions, the hierarchy of needs was not established through any scientific research but based on anecdotal evidence gathered by Maslow.

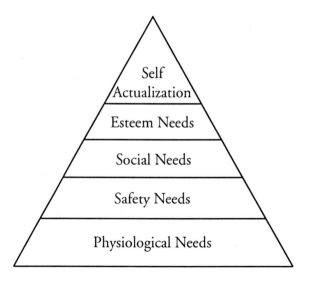

Maslow's Hierarchy of Needs

## *Douglas McGregor*

Douglas McGregor (1906-1964), a social psychologist and professor at Massachusetts Institute of Technology, was known for his human relations approach to management. In 1960, McGregor described his theories for which he is most famous in his book *The Human Side of Enterprise*. His Theory X and Theory Y are two methodologies for managing people. Theory X managers assume that employees are basically lazy, dislike work and responsibility, and will avoid work whenever possible. According to a Theory X manager, an employee will function only if threatened or coerced.[26] Theory Y managers assume a positive approach and assume that employees enjoy their work, can be self-directed, are creative, and will accept and seek responsibility. McGregor further stated that the only true management option to follow was Theory Y. Theory X managers rule with an iron hand and allow the employees no room for individualized thought process or innovation—management is all about control. Conversely, Theory Y managers foster motivation by giving staff the opportunity to assist in decision making. Employees experience greater autonomy and the manager acts as a facilitator and advisor, resulting in greater job satisfaction for both.

## *Chris Argyris*

Chris Argyris (1923- ) is an organizational psychologist, former professor at Yale, Professor Emeritus at Harvard, and author of the book, *Personality and Organization*. He proposed that the management approaches supported by Classical Management theories were not consistent with the personality of mature adults.[27] Argyris argued that employees who realize their full potential benefit not only themselves but the organization as a whole. This lead Argyris to conclude that the lack of focus on the employee, the use of autocratic management, and pyramidal corporate organizational structures hindered the intellectual growth and creativity potential in employees Argyris suggests that encouragement, reinforcement, and training opportunities foster growth. Furthermore, Argyris believed that allowing employees and managers the opportunity to offer input into decision-making, increases job performance and satisfaction.

As a major influence of the human relations movement, Argyris found that although many managers stated that they communicated openly, they did not actually practice an open communication style, thus their actual response was different than their espoused response. Argyris studied what people stated they would or should do in a situation and how those same people actually responded in the same situation. Argyris believed that people will often act in a way that is expected of them just because of the environment in which they are in at the time. For example, many places of business do not allow personal telephone calls during work time. A worker will follow all protocols while in the presence of the manager but might make personal calls when the manager is not around. The worker knows what he or she is supposed to do but does something else. Argyris found that in large organizations, employees were expected to behave in a compliant and subordinate way. Since such behavior goes against the human desire to control one's environment, it leads to employee dissatisfaction. The dissatisfaction leads the worker to seek employment elsewhere.

Argyris partnered with Donald Schon and proposed the concepts of single and double-loop learning.[28] Single loop learning involves modifying the actions of individuals or groups as a response to their errors or expected outcomes. Single-loop learning involves an action and a reaction. In double-loop learning, the individuals or groups solve complex problems by modifying the values and norms of the organization.[29] Double-loop learning involves the analysis of why the reaction occurred and uncovers the root cause of the issue. To explain, Argyris uses the example of a thermostat set to sixty-eight degrees. When the room temperature drops below the setting, the heat turns on. This is a simple example of single-loop learning. In the case of double-loop learning, several questions would be prompted: Why was the thermostat set at sixty eight? Is the house insulated? Were the doors and windows closed?

# Quantitative Management

Quantitative theory, also known as management science theory, utilizes mathematical processes to assist a manager in planning and making decisions concerning an organization's resources. Appropriate utilization of resources is pivotal to successful business management. Management science provides organizations with the decision-making tools to project fiscal planning, such as production volumes, target markets, and direction for capital investment. The quantitative processes covered in this chapter are (a) operations research, (b) mathematical forecasting, (c) inventory modeling, (d) linear programming, (e) queuing theory, and (f) simulation.

## *Operations Research*

First utilized during World War II to plan military initiatives, operations research, also referred to as management science, is used to evaluate all phases of the operations of industry and the military. Established by the British in the 1930s and utilized soon thereafter by the United States, operations research began as a team approach within each branch of the military. By the 1950s, operations research was taught in universities across the United States. Technology has promoted wide-scale use of specialized computer programs to assist in the process and widen the field from military to medical and broad business usage.

Mathematical forecasting is used in strategic planning to project demand for goods or services based on historical data and a myriad of variables. Components of forecasting include fixed and variable costs, sales projections, seasonal variation, projected profit margins, and demand forecasting, bringing the attributes of science to the field of management. Not only must the organization function efficiently, but it must also project the manufacturing costs, including labor, storage, and sales. Some of the variables in forecasting are the current economic environment, target market, available resources, and whether the product or service is a luxury or staple. Managerial decisions regarding production and marketing are based on the results of mathematical forecasting.

## Inventory Modeling

Inventory modeling is the process by which the appropriate amount of inventory required for an organization is available at all times. This means that enough of a product has been stocked to supply the customers without the cost of storing more than necessary on the shelves. Inventory can be controlled by automatic delivery for customers, based on normal usage or such processes as just in time inventory management, which keeps minimum supplies available to promote optimum usage and decrease capital tied up in slow moving supplies.

## Linear Programming

Linear programming "is a mathematical technique for solving constrained maximization and minimization problems when there are many constraints and the objective function to be optimized as well as the constraints faced are linear."[30] It is a mathematical planning tool that helps the organization plan for the future by analyzing its practices and deciding what steps are needed to maximize profitability and minimize expenditures.

## Queuing Theory

Queuing theory involves the use of mathematical tools, such as models, theorems, and algorithms to analyze systems to decrease customer waiting time and costs associated with customer service. The systems are analyzed under conditions of randomly varying demand. Queuing theory is utilized where holding patterns or lines of customers may occur due to lack of control over the demand or the amount required or both. This theory requires acute observation of the process.[31]

One application of the queuing theory evaluates the average arrival rate of customers, the amount of time it takes to wait on the customer after arrival, and the estimated cost of the wait, which determines customer satisfaction or dissatisfaction. One of the early uses of the theory was to estimate the number of operators needed to handle manual telephone switchboards. The average number of calls that arrived during given timeframes was evaluated, as well as how long it took the operators to connect calls. Queuing theory is still used today to monitor customer service and estimate the number of attendants needed, especially in areas where customers form a line, such as drive through businesses and retail stores.

### *Simulations*

Simulations are management models that are used to test different solutions under various assumptions. Simulations are usually based on the systems approach and utilize groups who converge to practice analytical skills in making managerial decisions. The participants are challenged to utilize quantitative processes to make such decisions as future pricing, marketing, product development, or capital investment.

Simulations are also human resource oriented and involve role-play and group problem solving. Prior to the simulation, participants are given background information charts and business documents. They are assigned roles to enact and make decisions—just as they would in a real organization. After the simulation is completed, feedback is given to the participants regarding their performance. Enactments are valuable for management training.

# Modern Management Theories

Modern management theory extends beyond that of conventional top to bottom management and focuses on decreasing the number of hierarchical layers in an organization. Management's aim is to discover the creative talents in a worker and cultivate those gifts. Modern management turns to the employee for input in efficient work processes and utilizes the expertise of multifunctional and multicultural groups to develop ideas in the business focus. Corporate missions and visions focus on quality and efficiency.

## *Systems Approach*

The systems approach to management looks beyond the boundary of the organization to explain how it interacts with its environment. Systems theory recognizes that an organization is connected to its larger environment and is constantly interacting with that environment. Outputs from the organization and inputs to the organization ultimately affect both the organization and its environment. In his 1938 book, *Functions of the Executive*, Chester Barnard identified organizations as a sequence of systems that integrated the efforts of individuals to accomplish a common purpose.[32]

An open system draws resources from outside and converts them into a service or product for resale. The input stage includes resources, such as raw materials, information, manpower, or money. Anything that goes into the system is an input. The second phase of the open system is the conversion stage, which uses the capabilities of the organization, such as technology and human skill to transform the raw materials into a product or service.

The next stage of systems theory states that the outputs of an organization are not only the product or service, which are the result of the transformation stage, but also includes the organization's profits or losses and the satisfaction or dissatisfaction of employees.

The final stage of systems theory is the feedback stage. Organizations obtain feedback from the environment regarding their product or service, which subsequently effects the inputs. Sales and customers' opinions are gathered and evaluated to determine what changes, if any, must be made to the system.

Although the classical management viewpoint viewed organizations as closed systems, business organizations cannot operate as such, because closed systems are self contained and not affected by events that occur outside of the system. An organization having any interaction with the environment would be considered an open system.

## An Open System

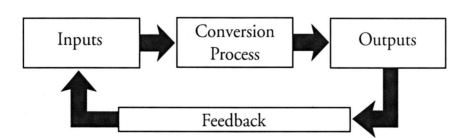

## Contingency Thinking

In the early years of management theory, many believed that there was a single best method for solving issues and motivating employees; however, new theories have shown that is not the case. In the 1960s, contingency thinking debuted. This theory proposes that different people approach issues with different values and varied levels of expertise. Similarly, organizations vary in size, mission, and overall culture. What motivates one individual may not motivate another, and what works in one organization may not work in all organizations. Therefore, contingency thinking does not have one best solution. The methods used by managers are contingent upon each situation and dependent upon the characteristics and culture of the organization. Several theories have been developed regarding this thought process.

## Fiedler's Contingency Model

The first model of situational leadership, in which the success of different leadership styles depends upon the situation, was the Fiedler Contingency Model, developed by Fred E. Fiedler (1922 - ).[33] Fiedler believed that leadership effectiveness was dependent upon two factors: the extent of influence and control held by the leader in the situation and the leader's personal style. Fiedler's Analysis of Situations looked at leader-member relations, the task structure of the organization, and the power held by the leader to determine whether a task-motivated leadership style or a relationship-motivated leadership style would be most effective in each situation.

Fiedler measured leadership style on the Least Preferred Coworker scale (LPC). Each manager considers all of the individuals with whom he or she had ever worked and completes a questionnaire that describes the person with whom the manager would least like to work with a series of 16 pairs of opposite characteristics—tense/relaxed, distant/close. The responses to those answers are summed and averaged. A low LPC score suggests the manager has a task orientation, while a high LPC score indicates the manager has a human relations orientation. The inference is that specific group types perform better when matched with specific leadership styles.

According to Fiedler, the effectiveness of a leader is determined by the degree of match between a dominant trait of the leader and the favorableness of the situation for the leader.... The dominant trait is a personality factor causing the leader to either relationship-oriented or task-orientated.[34]

Fiedler did not believe that a task-oriented leader could be easily transformed to a relationship focus; therefore, certain leaders were best suited for certain situations.

## *Quality Management Gurus*

### *W. Edwards Deming*

W. Edwards Deming (1900 – 1993) is known in part, as the statistical expert who brought quality to post-war Japan. He was responsible for placing emphasis on quality instead of quotas to increase production output.[35] According to Deming, organizations must have a defined mission or aim that is clear to all who work there. That mission acts as the foundation for the organization's purpose. Deming also stated that senior leadership was responsible for defining the aim and energizing the masses to obtain it.[36]

The essence of Deming's quality improvement model is to plan, do, check, and act (PDCA).[37] Many variations on the quality cycle have been proposed, but all are generally based on this model. The *plan* phase begins with identification of the issues. Once the problem is identified, the investigation begins with the gathering of data. The plan involves identifying underlying process issues and determining possible solutions to the problem. A test plan is developed. The next phase or *do* phase involves carrying out the proposed plan. During the *check* phase, the results of the pilot are checked for successes and failures. If the plan did not work, the areas of challenge are reviewed and evaluated. The end result is evaluated in the act phase, where success is determined or the plan is revised and the PDCA process is repeated.[38]

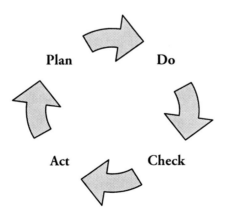

| Plan | Define the problem.<br>Gather data.<br>List possible solutions.<br>Devise a plan to test the proposed solution. |
|---|---|
| Do | Activate the plan. |
| Check | Analyze the results.<br>Identify barriers obstructing the plan's success. |
| Act | Based on the results, accept or revise the plan. |

Deming compiled fourteen points that he believed were the basis of industry transformation. The points stressed constant innovation and training in quality assurance. The fourteen points are as follows:

- Division of work
- Authority and responsibility
- Unity of command
- Order
- Discipline
- Initiative
- Equity
- Centralization
- Remuneration of personnel
- Unity of direction
- Scalar chain
- Stability of tenure of personnel
- Subordination of individual interest to the common interest
- Esprit de corps

Deming is also known for the "85-15 rule." He believed that when problems occur, an individual worker was at fault only 15 percent of the time. He felt that a majority of the time (85 percent) the problem was with the system, which could include not only machinery but management rules and systems. Deming believed managers often blamed employees when things went wrong, when it was actually the system that was causing the problem.

*Joseph M. Juran*

Joseph M. Juran (1904- ), known as the "father of quality," was born in Romania and came to the United States as a young child. Poor but hard working and extremely bright, he earned his engineering degree in 1924 from the University of Minnesota. After college, he worked at the Hawthorn Works in Chicago, where he participated in a training program and became one of two engineers chosen to work for the Inspection Statistical department. In 1937, Juran "conceptualized the Pareto principle, which millions of managers rely on to help separate the 'vital few' from the 'useful many' in their activities. [Many] commonly referred to [this concept] as the 80-20 principle."[39]

In 1951 Juran published his book, *Quality Control Handbook,* in which he summarized a quality trilogy that incorporated the concepts of quality planning, quality improvement, and quality control.[40] In quality planning the organization has to identify its customers, determine the needs of those customers, and develop a product that could meet those needs. Quality improvement included development of a process to produce the product. Quality control attempted to prove that the process developed during the quality improvement stage could actually produce the product with only minimal inspection.

The Quality Trilogy

| Quality Planning | Identify Customers<br>Identify Internal and External Needs<br>Create Quality Measures |
|---|---|
| Quality Improvement | Establish Quality Goals |
| Quality Control | Create Processes to Meet Goals |

Juran's focus was on training management to control quality. In quality management, the expectation is for upper management to control the strategic posture of the organization, while middle management is expected to handle the operational tasks and oversee the workforce. The workforce is then responsible for the actual labor and getting the job done. Consequently, quality management produces varied outcomes. One such end product can be workforce reduction. When asked if quality improvement led to downsizing, Juran replied that it does occur and that management needed to be prepared to address the issue.[41]

*Peter Senge*

Peter Senge (1947- ) is a graduate of Stanford and Massachusetts Institute of Technology and chairman and cofounder of the Society for Organizational Learning (SOL). SOL is a non-profit organization made up of researchers, consultants, and corporate participants that concentrates on decentralization of organizational leadership, corporate development, and enhancement of the contributions of individuals. Senge has had a major influence on modern business management, especially through his idealistic theories and promotion of flexibility in adapting to change. His book, *The Fifth Discipline* (1990), introduced the theory of learning organizations.

Senge names systems thinking as the fifth discipline. Systems-thinking integrates the first four disciplines-shared vision, personal mastery, mental models and team learning-to create synergy. Systems thinking then is "a conceptual framework for understanding patterns of events and behaviors to help see how to change them."[42] Systems-thinking is a concept that usually focuses on long-term issues and emphasizes how all of the disciplines are dependent upon the others and are needed to solve complex issues. In systems-thinking large patterns are dissected into small parts, which are analyzed to define their interdependence. Change occurs when the process' norms and assumptions are challenged. "The basic contribution of the fifth discipline of systems thinking is the art of seeing the forest *and* the trees."[43]

Senge proposes that the success of an organization depends on its ability to adapt to change; it must become a learning organization. In a 1991 interview, Senge described the innovative process of learning:

> In the innovation stage you are learning to do something that is reliable and replicable. I think that is where we are now with learning organizations. We are developing the key understandings, practices, and tools. There are four levels of this process as it unfolds: The highest is the level of values and vision. The second encompasses the skills and capabilities. Third are the methods we use to develop those skills and capabilities. The fourth is the infrastructure. By that I mean the design of an organization such that continual practice of the methods continually develops the skills and reinforces the values and vision.[44]

Senge admits that becoming a learning organization is not an easy process. Like people, organizations have learning disabilities. Individuals tend to focus on their own roles instead of the global results of their actions. The external environment is often blamed for organizational shortcomings because they neglect internal reflection. Instead of being proactive, they become engulfed in short term issues and often rely on consequences from experience, rather than engaging in strategic forecasting. To these organizations, challenge is viewed as a negative force instead of an opportunity for improvement.[45]

To overcome learning disabilities, the organization must focus on five areas:

1. *Systems thinking* can be briefly defined as the study of patterns of behavior and events to concentrate on developing processes for change.

2. *Personal mastery* requires probing within one's inner beliefs to be objective in accepting the reality of the environment and promote self-awareness and mental preparation for change. It is a state of continually learning.

3. *Mental models* are also internal reflections that determine individual comprehension and reaction to external forces. This is where the individual must shirk previous assumptions and start with a clear slate.

4. *Shared vision* entails the ability to cast aside simple compliance and redirect those energies to commitment. The individual has the enthusiasm to achieve.

5. *Team learning* breaks down barriers to communication and builds strength in group interaction and communal thinking. It is the culmination of the shared vision.[46]

Senge emphasizes the need for individual reflection and action to promote human values and learning for all roles within an organization. The roles include those of managers and employees. Internal reflection, growth, and collaboration foster the agility of an organization. The ability for organizations to thrive instead of survive is based on the forward thinking and ability to change direction quickly. The agile organization is one that will thrive.

# Conclusion

This chapter presented the accomplishments of engineers, economists, social psychologists, professors, sociologists, and entrepreneurs. All were visionaries whose work became the foundation for the management practices of today's world. Many did not achieve recognition until after their death, and others were recognized during their lives and then nearly forgotten, but all contributed ideas to improve functionality in the workplace. Management theories and practices were created through careful observation, intuitive thought processes, and determination. It was not enough to merely accomplish their goals, but they felt compelled to share the knowledge they acquired with the masses, allowing others to reap the benefits of their labors.

Management theory has evolved from its beginnings in the eighteenth century to the present day. Efficiency, effectiveness, and profitability are key points that have carried through the centuries, beginning with the industrial revolution, and are standards essential to organizational survival. Efficiency compares the amount of output created after a set amount of input, and effectiveness measures how well the goal was achieved. A process that is efficient and effective should increase profitability. Although the methodologies and processes have changed, the core components have remained the same.

Adam Smith and the concept of job specialization was the first step towards efficiency in the factory. He was also responsible for identifying the two requirements for productivity in the workplace: a tangible product and a surplus for the purpose of reinvestment. The industrial revolution emerged and changed rural life forever. People migrated into the cities; and because of the efficiencies of mass production, factory owners became prosperous. With the wave of change came the issues of managing large numbers of people, for which many were unprepared.

New techniques for management and production were needed; and thanks to men like Frederick Taylor, scientific management came into existence. Armed with a stopwatch, Taylor viewed the function of the organization as machine-like. The organization ran best with the right part in the right place and efficiency as the primary goal. Taylor is known for developing the four guidelines to promote efficiency of the workplace: appropriate worker selection, established rules, proper training (provided by management), and performance standards.

Frank and Lillian Gilbreth worked diligently with time-motion studies and employee satisfaction. Frank recognized that routine tasks created a potential for boredom, and Lillian sought employee input for job satisfaction. The most unique contribution of the Gilbreths was the introduction of Therbligs: eighteen color coded symbols used to represent individual timed movements within a task. Therbligs were displayed on a simultaneous motion chart and analyzed to see which, if any, could be eliminated. Elimination of a Therblig in a process decreases the steps, makes the process more efficient, and in some cases, decreases fatigue. The Gilbreths were among the first to study fatigue in the workplace and focus on improving ergonomics.

Administrative management theory followed and differed from scientific theory by concentrating on the efficiency of large numbers of individuals in an organization—versus individual efficiency. Henri Fayol and Max Weber brought administrative management into existence. Fayol developed the core criteria for management skills, which consisted of planning, organizing, leading, and controlling. He was also responsible for the development of fourteen principles of management, intended to be used as guidelines in decision making and improving management skills. The criteria are division of work, authority and responsibility, unity of command, order, discipline, initiative, equity, centralization, remuneration of personnel, unity of direction, scalar chain, stability of tenure of personnel, subordination of individual interest to the common interest, and esprit de corps.

Max Weber introduced the concept of ideal bureaucracy, based on rules and hierarchy, and intended for it to be a management model for large organizations. The guidelines for bureaucracy entailed division of labor, authority, formal rules, impersonality, and career orientation. Weber first introduced the concept of charismatic leadership. The charismatic leader is compelling, visionary, and sets an example that workers seek to follow. Weber's view of leadership was that of a hierarchy with strong authority.

Behavioral management theorists emphasized managerial influence on employee motivation. Pioneers in this realm were Robert Owen, Hugo Munsterberg, Mary Parker Follett, Chester Barnard, Elton Mayo, Abraham Maslow, Douglas McGregor, and Chris Argyris.

Robert Owen fought for the provision of educational opportunities and improved working conditions for employees. One of his first campaigns was to stop the use of child labor. Hugo Munsterberg promoted training and the alignment of scientific management with industrial psychology. He was a champion for behaviorism and developed methods for improvement of employee selection through the utilization of psychological testing and methodologies for individual motivation. Mary Parker Follett first discovered the importance of group interaction and the fluid movement of power.

Chester Barnard developed his theory of equilibrium, which suggested that employees could be recruited and retained based on the rate of pay received. Elton Mayo worked with the Hawthorne studies and developed theories based on the affect of groups on the individual and productivity. Abraham Maslow is noted for his motivational concept based on a hierarchy of needs. McGregor is noted for management based on Theory X and Theory Y, and Argyris developed single and double-loop learning. Single-loop learning involves an action and a result. Double-loop learning goes one step further to ask why the reaction occurred and uncovers the root cause of the issue. Chris Argyris is also responsible for the espoused theory, which is what people believe they would or should do in a situation but not necessarily what they actually do.

Quantitative or management science presents mathematical tools for utilization of resources and as a basis for rational decision making. The tools allow managers to strategically position themselves for the future. Some of the tools are operations research, mathematical forecasting, inventory modeling, linear programming, queuing theory, and simulation. Operations research optimizes productivity by applying scientific and mathematical approaches to analyze organizational performance. Mathematical forecasting is used in strategic planning to project demand for goods or services based on historical data and variables. Inventory modeling assures that the appropriate amount of inventory required for an organization is available at all times.

Linear programming is a mathematical planning tool that helps the organization project for the future by analyzing its practices and deciding the next steps to take to maximize profitability and minimize expenditures. The queuing theory involves the use of mathematical tools to analyze systems where a service is performed under conditions of randomly varying demand and where holding patterns or queues may occur, due to lack of control over the demand or the amount required or both. Simulations are usually based on the systems approach and utilize groups to practice analytical skills in making managerial decisions. The participants are challenged to utilize quantitative processes to make such decisions as future pricing, marketing, product development, or capital investment.

Modern management theory turns the tables on organizational management from top down to bottom up. The pyramid becomes inverted as managerial layers are flattened. A new appreciation arises for an organization's most precious asset: the employee. Efforts are extended to develop and utilize the talents of a diverse work force. The new management gurus, such as Deming, Juran, and Senge, are dynamic personalities who proposed a shift in the focus of the organization from quantity to quality.

W. Edwards Deming placed emphasis on quality instead of quotas in production. Deming stressed the importance of organizational missions and the need to disperse the essence of the mission to all employees. The vision was to be communicated to the employee and modeled by management. His quality improvement model is to plan, do, check, and act (PDCA). Many variations on the quality cycle exist, but the core processes remain the same.

Joseph M. Juran summarized some of his quality ideas to incorporate the concepts of quality planning, improvement, and control. His management focus was on management training to control quality. He believed that upper management's responsibility was to control organizational strategic positioning. Middle management should handle the day-to-day operational tasks of the workforce, and the workforce was then responsible for the getting the job done. Effectively done, this can result in workforce reduction.

Peter Senge has had a major influence on modern business management, especially through his idealistic theories involving corporate flexibility and adaptation to change. Flexibility promotes a learning organization. Senge developed five areas of organizational discipline: systems thinking, personal mastery, mental models, shared models, shared vision, and team learning. Decentralization of organizational leadership, corporate development, and appreciation for the contributions of individual employees are keys to success.

## Impact on the Organization, the Manager, and Employees

Management theory impacts organizations because it impacts people. Through the years, paradigms have shifted and the focus has changed from a hierarchal pyramid of management structure to a flattened, inverse pyramid model. It is no longer enough to manage employees. To be a successful manager, one must now be a successful leader. The successful workforce follows dynamic leaders who lead through example and share a corporate vision.

In his book, *The Essential Drucker,* Peter Drucker wrote, "Management's concern and management's responsibility are everything that affects the performance of the institution and its results  whether inside or outside, whether under the institution's control or totally beyond it."[47] He also wrote that "in a traditional workforce the worker serves the system; in a knowledge workforce the system must serve the worker."[48]

Today's corporate systems have evolved into thinking and learning organizations to survive in an increasingly competitive market. Obstacles become challenges; challenges become opportunities. Flexibility is crucial to successfully accept change. Competitive organizations utilize strategic planning to position themselves effectively in the market.

The workforce is recognized as an integral key to company success by the contributions of those who operate at the ground-level who participate in performance improvement. The realization that processes can be improved by consulting with those who perform the tasks has led to the formation of diverse work groups that combine members with different sets of talents, collaborating to achieve a shared mission. All of this has occurred because individuals existed in history who challenged the status quo. The individuals discussed in this chapter were instrumental in the evolutionary process of management theory, but they did not do it alone. The quest for change and better methods has carried management theory from productivity to quality.

# Endnotes

1   Dhamee, Y. (1995). *Adam Smith and the division of labor. The Victorian Web Home Page.* Retrieved August 1,2006 from: http://www.victorianweb.org/economics/division.html

2   Smith, Adam. An Inquiry into the Nature and Causes of the Wealth of Nations. Library of Economics and Liberty. Retrieved September 16, 2006 from the World Wide Web: http://www.econlib.org/LIBRARY/Smith/smWN1.html

3   Pugh, D.S. & Hickson, D. J. (1997). *Writers on organizations (5th edition).* Thousand Oaks, California: Sage Publications.

4   The history of management. *Management Guru* Retrieved August 5, 2006 from: http://www.mgmtguru.com/mgt301/301_Lecture1Page5.htm

5   Micklethwait, J. & Wooldridge, A. (1996). *The witch doctors making sense of the management gurus.* p. 65. New York: Times Books.

6   Price, B. (1989). Frank and Lillian Gilbreth and the manufacture and marketing of motion study, 1908 – 1924. Business and Economic History, 18. Retrieved August 6, 2006 from: http://www.h-net.org/~business/bhcweb/publications/BEHprint/v018/p0088-p0098.pdf

7   Marlow, J. (1979). *The great women.* New York, New York. Galahad Books.

8   Moorehead, G., Griffin, R.W. (2001). *Organizational behavior: managing people and organizations, (6th edition).* Boston, MA: Houghton Mifflin Company.

9   Fayol, H. (1949). General and Industrial Management. Trans Storrs, C. Mashfield, MA: Pitman Publishing.

10  Hofstede, G. (1997). *Cultures and organizations: software of the mind*, p.146. New York, N.Y. McGraw-Hill.

11  Fayol, H. (1949). General and Industrial Management. Trans Storrs, C. Mashfield, MA: Pitman Publishing.

12  Weber, M. (1947). The Theory of Social and Economic Organization. New York: The Free Press.

13  Hofstede, G. (1997). *Cultures and organizations: software of the mind*, p. 147. New York, N.Y. McGraw-Hill.

14  Yukl, G. (2002). *Leadership in organizations (5th edition)*, p.241. Upper Saddle River, N.J.: Prentice-Hall International, Inc.

15  None. Robert Owen. (2001). *World of sociology.* 2 vols. ¶ 7. Gale Group. Reproduced in *Biography Resource Center.* Farmington Hills, Mich.: Retrieved Aug.1,2006 from: http://galenet.galegroup.com

16  Ferris, G., Buckley, M. (1996). *Human resource management: perspectives,context, functions, and outcomes (3rd edition),* p. 151. Englewood Cliffs, N.J: Prentice-Hall.

17  Mary Parker Follett. *Mary Parker Follett Foundation.* Retrieved August 8, 2006 from: http://www.follettfoundation.org/mpf.htm

18  Barnard, C.I. (1938), The *functions of the executive.* Cambridge, MA: Harvard University Press.

19  Barnard, C.I. (2001). *The functions of the executive,* p. 296. Cambridge, Massachusetts: Harvard University Press.

20  Katz, D. & Kahn, R.L. (2003). *The social psychology of organizations.* USA: John Wiley & Sons.

21  Burrell, G., Morgan, G. (2001). *Sociological paradigms and organizational analysis,* p. 148. Burlington, Vermont: Ashgate.

22  Mayo, E. (1933). The Human Problems of Industrial Civilization. New York: Viking Press.

23  Lombard, G.F. Elton Mayo. ¶ 8.*Dictionary of American Biography, Supplement 4: 1946-1950.* American Council of Learned Societies, 1974. Reproduced in *Biography Resource Center.* Farmington Hills, Mich.: Thomson Gale. 2006. Retrieved July 31, 2006 from Academic Source Premiere.

24  Simons, J. Irwin, D.B. & Drinnien, B.A. (1987). Psychology – The Search for Understanding. New York: West Publishing Company.

25  Hofstede, G. (1997). *Cultures and organizations: software of the mind*, p. 147. New York, N.Y: McGraw-Hill.

26  McGregor, D. (1960). The Human Side of Enterprise. New York: McGraw-Hill.

27  Argyris, C. (1957). Personality and Organization. New York: Harper & Row.

28  Argyris, C. & Schon D. (1978). *Organizational learning: a theory of action perspective,* Reading, MA: Addison Wesley.

29  Schwandt, D. & Marquardt, M.J. (2000). *Organizational learning from world-class theories to global best practices.* Boca Raton, Florida: St. Lucie  Press.

30  Salvatore, D. (2004). *Managerial economics in a global economy (5ᵗʰ edition)* p. 652. Mason, Ohio: Thomson South-Western.

31  Schultz, S.(2005). Waiting for practicality: After 20 years, one IE discovers that queuing theory really can be used in the real world. *Industrial Engineer 37*.10  31(5).

32  Barnard, C.I. (1938). *Functions of the executive.* Cambridge, MA. Harvard University Press.

33  Fiedler, F.E. (1967). A Theory of Leadership Effectiveness. New York: McGraw-Hill.

34  Dunham, R.B. (1984). Organizational Behavior. Homewood, Illinois: Irwin.

35  Weisbord, M. (1987). *Productive workplaces organizing and managing for dignity, meaning. and community.* San Francisco, CA.: Jossey-Bass.

36  Gift, R. & Kinney, C. (1996). *Today's management methods a guide for the health care executive.* USA: American Hospital Publishing, Inc.

37  Deming, W.E. (1982). Out of the Crisis. Cambridge, MA: MIT Press.

38  Pande, P.S., Neuman, R.P. & Cavanagh, R.R. (2000). *The Six Sigma way how GE, Motorola, and other top companies are honing their performance.* New York.: McGraw-Hill.

39  Juran Institute Home Page. Retrieved from the World Wide Web: http://www.juran.com/lower_2.cfm?article_id=21

40  Joseph M. Juran: a quality life. Retrieved July 28, 2006 from: http://www.skymark.com/resources/leaders/juran.asp

41  Morgan, R. & Smith, J. (1996). *Staffing the new workplace selecting and Promoting for quality improvement.* Milwaukee, Wisconsin: ASQ Quality Press.

42  Schwandt, D. & Marquardt, M.J. (2000). *Organizational learning from world-class theories to global best practices.* p. 39. Boca Raton, Florida: St. Lucie.

43  Pugh, D.S. & Hickson, D. J., (1997). *Writers on organizations (5ᵗʰ edition).* p. 182. Thousand Oaks, California: Sage Publications.

44   Galagan, P. A. (1991). The learning organization made plain. *Training & development* 37, (8) 45.n10 ¶ *Professional collection.*

45   Pugh, D.S. & Hickson, D. J. (1997). *Writers on organizations (5ᵗʰ edition).* p. 182. Thousand Oaks, California: Sage Publications.

46   Schwandt, D. &Marquardt, M.J. (2000). *Organizational learning from world class theories to global best practices.* p. 39. Boca Raton, Florida: St. Lucie.

47   Drucker, P. (2001). *The Essential Drucker.* New York: Harper Collins Publishers, Inc. p. 94

48   Drucker, P.F. (2002). *Managing in the Next Society.* New York: Truman Talley Books St. Martin's Press. pp. 124-125

# CHAPTER 3 — The Functions Of Management

## MEASURABLE LEARNING OBJECTIVES

1. Define the management functions of planning, controlling, organizing and leading and differentiate a manager's tasks in each function.

2. Identify steps in the planning process and identify management actions taken in each step.

3. Distinguish between effectiveness and efficiency.

4. Summarize the differences of an organization's short term and long term goals.

5. Discuss the strategic planning process and the manager's role in the process.

6. Describe the operational planning process and the manager's role in the process.

7. Elaborate on the importance of the management function of controlling to organizational learning.

8. Identify the steps in the control process and identify management actions taken in each step.

9. Identify the different structures which an organization may have.

10. Discuss different types of corporate governance.

11. Identify current issues that are of concern to managers within the management function of organizing.

# Introduction

Planning, a crucial function of management, is setting goals for specific results and determining how to achieve those results. Planning must take into account the uncertainty that the future holds by considering not only anticipated events but also those that are unexpected. Planning requires formulating the future actions of the organization. As corporations plan for future events, they have a wealth of tools available to help plan and mitigate unknown variables that may arise. The goal of planning is to anticipate as many future events as possible in order to successfully plan the course a company will pursue, increase revenues, and satisfy owner requirements; however, it is virtually impossible for a corporation to plan for and conceive of every future event that it may encounter. Planning is considered an indispensable tool for organization's of all sizes. Why Plan?

When taking a cross-country trip by car from New York to San Francisco—a distance of approximate 2900 miles—one does not hop in his or her car, begin driving, and hope to see signs that will lead him or her to the destination. Most likely, such an unplanned trip would cause the traveler to spend more money, time, and personal stress than he or she would have wished to expend. In planning such a trip, one would normally consult maps to determine the routes to travel, determine the budget for the trip, make hotel reservations—to help stay within his budget—and maybe even plan some time to explore some side roads along the way. The traveler should also plan for contingencies, such as ensuring that the car has a spare tire, tire jack, lug wrench, and the skill to change the tire in case of a flat. In addition, the road maps will ensure that one is on the right path to San Francisco. If while driving along an individual regularly checks the route on which he or she should be and finds that a wrong turn was taken, he or she is able to correct the mistake with minimal upset to plans.

The same applies to planning within an organization. Effective planning will help an organization save time and money, decrease stress, and ensure that actions taken by personnel throughout the organization will work together, so the organization can meet its goals. The impact of planning on an organization includes the following:

- Planning gives the organization direction by looking ahead into the future. Effort throughout the organization is coordinated because all levels of the organization understand where the organization is headed and what it will take to get there.

- Planning decreases uncertainty. With planning, managers have already anticipated problems which may arise and are ready to respond.

- Planning ensures that an organization is progressing toward the goal. At any time a manager can check actual progress toward the goal and determine if the organization is on track toward meeting the goal. If the actual progress does not align with the goal, then . . .

- Planning allows the organization to take corrective action.

- Failing to plan is planning to fail.[1]

## *The Basic Planning Process*

The basic planning process starts with knowing where the company wants to go and determining how to achieve that objective. "Basically, the planning process includes planners working backwards through the system, starting from what they want the system to produce."[2] Managers decide what needs to be produced and then plan how to achieve the objective. There are numerous steps to the basic planning process, including establishing the overarching goal, establishment of smaller goals, development of strategies to achieve the goals, identification of essential resources needed to attain results, and implementation and monitoring of the plan. Fundamentally, managers need to develop a goal and then prepare the strategy and determine the resources needed to implement that particular goal. The accomplishment of a larger goal is almost always through utilizing smaller corporate goals. Smaller, short-term goals help to ensure that employees and management do not become overwhelmed in accomplishing a large goal. Though no easy task, by developing and utilizing the basic steps involved in the planning process, managers can take into account planned and unplanned variables that may arise in the accomplishment of a goal.

The formal planning process consists of six steps: situational analysis, generation of alternative goals and plans, evaluation of goals and plans, selection of goals and plans, implementation of the chosen goals and plans, and monitoring and controlling of the goals and plans.

### *Conduct a Situational Analysis*

Although planning is primarily future oriented, effective planning begins by conducting a situational analysis that assesses and evaluates an organization's current status. In order to make successful decisions about the future direction of an organization, a manager should take an inventory of all critical areas to create an accurate profile of the current condition of the organization. A situational analysis is concerned with evaluating the current condition of an organization and its capabilities in order to ascertain the plausibility of future plans and strategies. Performing a situational analysis lays the necessary groundwork and is fundamental to the entire planning process. In order to successfully plan for present and future goals and events, an organization must have a fundamental understanding of the local and global climate in social, political, and environmental concerns. A situational analysis consists of evaluation of an organization's strengths, weaknesses, opportunities, and threats—a SWOT analysis.

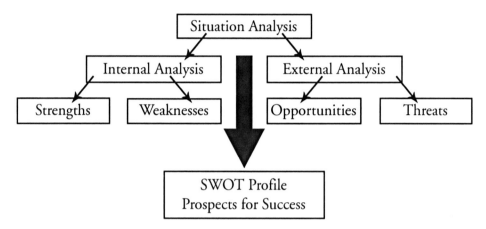

*SWOT*

The situational analysis performed by most organizations is a SWOT analysis. A SWOT analysis is a simple framework to help answer the question, "What are the prospects for success?" The approach recognizes that any project should be examined for both positive and negative influences from internal and external perspectives. A SWOT framework prompts a manager to look in detail at both sides of a situation.

A SWOT analysis is a subjective tool that is simple to use and can be used in conjunction with other analysis tools. Strengths and weaknesses are from the internal perspective of the organization, while opportunities and threats are those matters external to the organization. A SWOT analysis helps an organization see and plan for future events that may occur outside of the company's normal control. These factors help an organization highlight areas for improvement and help determine the course of action for the future.

*External Areas—Opportunities and Threats.* A SWOT analysis examines the numerous external influences that affect an organization, such as new competitors, strikes, new government regulations, a changing political landscape, improvements in technology, public opinion, and wars. Companies must address all external factors that have the possibility of affecting the organization. A strike by a competitor may allow a forward thinking company—aware of external factors affecting the business—to capitalize on the temporary loss of a competitor. A business that is able to accurately assess the effects of external factors, such as a strike against their own organization, will be better prepared for such threats. If an organization does not assess current and potential opportunities and threats, the organization may suffer financial loss trying to develop compliance to such a measure as a new regulation or a failed opportunity.

A lack of a thorough review of external influences may result in a devastating financial loss for a company. For this reason, the threats and opportunities that may affect a corporation would be crippling, if not reviewed and assessed during a SWOT analysis.

*Internal Areas—Strengths and Weaknesses.* Internal areas of a SWOT analysis are the organization's internal strengths and weaknesses. Numerous variables effect a company's strengths and weaknesses, such as research and development, purchasing, distribution, human resources, management, financial analyses, manufacturing processes, and operating budgets. A company's goal is to ensure that strengths do not become weaknesses and to evaluate the weaknesses that must be improved. Each of these areas must be carefully assessed in order for an organization to properly plan. A SWOT analysis provides the necessary tool, though not an all-inclusive assessment, of areas that function well or not so well within the corporation. A company must be willing to recognize the internal influences of a corporation in order for a company to remain successful. Weaknesses can be turned into advantages once they are identified and a plan is developed to rectify the weakness, turning an internal problem into a corporate asset. An example would be if a company discovered that there was a weakness in the distribution process of a product. The company can utilize that information and determine the best course of action to correct the weakness. The company may find that by utilizing a different transportation method to distribute the product, the weakness may become a strength and give the company a competitive advantage. As an organization's leaders assess internal strengths and weaknesses, they must be willing to recognize and adapt to ever-changing internal conditions within the corporation.

*Develop Alternative Goals and Actions.* After performing the situational analysis, the next step in the planning process is to develop alternative goals and actions. One of the key elements in planning is deciding upon which goals the organization will pursue. A company's leaders cannot pursue every goal that is brought before them; rather, they must choose sensible steps to ensure alignment with the company's mission. The business environment is not static but operates in a state of flux and constant change; therefore, alternative goals must also be determined to ensure that the business is prepared to meet a variety of future scenarios. The ability to accurately predict the future environment is not realistic, but planners can forecast possible or probable scenarios and determine how the organization will respond under varying circumstances and environmental conditions. "A manager must generate a set of feasible alternative courses of action in response to the opportunity or threat. Management experts cite failure to properly generate and consider different alternatives as one reason why managers sometimes make bad decisions."[3]

Managers must be equipped to properly identify and react to all plausible scenarios that they may encounter. Successful planning will ensure that they are able to determine and help mitigate a situation before a crisis develops and an organization suffers financial loss.

*Evaluate Alternative Goals and Plans for Organizational Fit.* While it is crucial to develop alternative goals and actions, not all of the goals under consideration are of equal weight in either their profitability or plausibility, which necessitates that they be evaluated. Evaluation of alternative goals and plans is an essential phase in the planning process, because while individual goals may seem appropriate, if they are not evaluated in light of the organization's competencies and capabilities, they are likely to lead the business into failure. Therefore, leadership must be cognizant of the organization's capabilities and resources, so that leaders can select goals and plans that are compatible with the organization's goals. The objective is to select those goals that are most compatible with organizational capabilities to generate and achieve optimal results.

Selecting the best goals and plans requires choosing between a variety of options, giving careful consideration to each, weighing the advantages and disadvantages of each in a variety of scenarios. In ascertaining which goals to choose, the alternatives can be evaluated according to their potential for bringing forth the anticipated results and are ranked accordingly.

## Select Specific Goals and Plans

Once the alternative goals have been prioritized, the organization must implement the goals and plans selected. The value of going through a rigorous planning process is that the probability of making good decisions increases, because each step of the planning process serves as a filtering mechanism that eliminates inferior and incompatible ideas and enables superior goals and plans to stand out.

Prior to the final selection, goals must be scrutinized as to their legality, conformity to ethical standards, fit with the organization's culture, and other such criteria. One cannot assume that every plan will be successful, but the ability to adapt and plan for all variables will help an organization to succeed.

*Implement the Selected Goals and Plans*

Implementation determines the practical direction, objectives, goals, and plans of the organization. This is the phase where many plans fail—in that they do not go beyond the realm of the idea stage and are never implemented. In fact, less than 10 percent of intended strategies are successfully implemented.[4] The chosen plans must be integrated into the daily actions of the organization. When implementing a goal a company must consider two important steps. "There are two things to always consider during implementation: time frame and assignment of responsibilities."[5] A manager must determine who will be responsible for what and the time frames for implementing a given task. There is little room for ambiguity as an organization strives to implement goals and a strategy that will guide the organization towards their intended path.

*Monitor Results and Use Information to Control the Process*

Implementing a plan is necessary to attain desired goals; however, simply implementing a plan is insufficient to achieve optimal results. How can an organization determine if its goals are being attained or if performance levels are where they were intended to be? The answer is that an organization must monitor results. The results must be monitored so that actions can be adapted, adjusted, and assessed as to the actual progress against the planned progress toward a goal. While those in charge of the planning process intend to produce plans that are ideal, unanticipated changes often occur, new ideas are gleaned from benchmarking, or new technologies emerge, thereby necessitating changes and alterations in the organization's plan. Monitoring the results provides the feedback necessary to know how the plan is working. The information gathered from monitoring the difference between the actual progress and the plan provides the necessary signals as to when a plan is working or if it needs to be modified or adjusted. A manager must be willing to make changes to the plan that will guide the company towards the most productive path.

Organizations often make decisions without taking the time to carefully consider the analysis already performed and the scenario plans already in place. A successful planning process will give leaders assistance when faced with difficult decisions. In an interview, Paul Nutt, author of *Why Decisions Fail: Avoiding the Blunders and Traps that Lead to Debacles,* stated the following:

> A very widespread error is the rush to judgment, or committing to a course of action prematurely. Executives got seduced by it. But the research shows that only one in ten decisions is urgent, and only one in one hundred is a crisis. You have time to reflect, usually. But decision makers feel they must hurry.[6]

# Effectiveness/Efficiency

While organizations differ in goal specifics and scope, two goals are universal and common to all organizations. Effectiveness and efficiency are a crucial part of any organization that wishes to remain competitive. Effectiveness is a measure of achieving organizational goals, whereas efficiency is using resources wisely to get the most output for the least amount of input. Managers must assure that they are truly working towards organizational efficiency and effectiveness:

> It is fundamentally the confusion between effectiveness and efficiency that stands between doing the right things and doing things right. There is surely nothing quite as useless as doing with great efficiency what should not be done at all. Yet our tools—especially our accounting concepts and data—all focus on efficiency. What we need is (1) a way to identify the areas of effectiveness (of possible significant results), and (2) a method for concentrating on them.[7]

Today's business environment is highly competitive; and while there are a number of ways that a business can gain a viable advantage, achieving greater levels of effectiveness and becoming more efficient are two sure performance enhancers. Efficiency and effectiveness are companion goals that are ongoing, complementing and enhancing other goals being pursued. Being competitive entails ongoing continuous improvement in performance, while efficiency includes improving processes to reduce costs and streamline processes.

## *Strategic planning*

Strategic planning is the process by which an organization's top managers envision the future and develop action plans to make that future a reality. A strategic vision is the organization's overarching goal, which guides management as they make plans and conduct business. An essential element of strategic planning is the ability of an organization's leaders to be able to forecast and adapt to the future of the organization.

### *Establish Mission/Vision/Goals*

The first step of strategic planning involves preparing for the strategic planning process. The planning process will be a roadmap for what the company is going to accomplish through the establishment of a mission statement, vision statement, and goals.

The mission statement is the reason that the organization exists and should be a succinct statement about the purpose of the organization.  Instead of being a slogan, a mission statement is a "precise statement of purpose.  Words should be chosen for their meaning rather than beauty, for clarity over cleverness."[8]  The best mission statements are those that clearly communicate to all shareholders what drives the organization.  "A mission statement is like an introductory paragraph: it lets the reader know where the writer is going."[9]  The mission statement is the crucial first step of establishing the future direction of the corporation.

The vision statement is a picture of an organization's preferred future that works to build commitment for the organization's goals.  An effective vision statement becomes the blueprint of the organization that leaders want to build.  This vision serves as a guideline for organizational changes.  Each change is designed to add up to that end point.  It explains to staff where they are going and why near-term changes—the steps along the way—are worthwhile.  A vision statement motivates change by saying "the bar is raised.  Maybe we were OK by past standards; but compared to this vision, we must change."[10]

While a number of issues must be addressed in assessing readiness, the determination essentially comes down to whether an organization's leaders are truly committed to the effort and whether they are able to devote the necessary attention to the "big picture."[11]

*Benchmarking*

Benchmarking is the process by which an organization compares its performance against not only its competitors but also other high performing organizations.  Though many debate which method of benchmarking is most effective, The Spendolini Benchmarking Model is based upon common elements of twenty-four benchmarking models and is comprised of five unique steps:

1.  The first step of benchmarking consists of determining what to benchmark.  Planning who will use the information and what will be benchmarked must be determined prior to beginning the process.

2.  Step two is to form a team of knowledgeable individuals to work on the benchmarking project.

3.  In step three, sources that a company will use to collect information must be identified.

4. Step four consists of collection and interpretation of the collected information. Team members must be willing to read the information they collect and analyze the significance of the information. An essential element to this process is being able to accurately analyze the results of the benchmarking study.

5. The final step in the benchmarking process is to take action. A company must be able to act on the information that they have received as a result of their benchmarking and be able to use it to improve the organization.[12]

Benchmarking provides an organization with information that will provide momentum toward improving processes.

*Strategy Formulation—Corporate Level (Concentration, Vertical, Concentric, Conglomerate)*

An organization's leaders base the overall strategy of the organization on their belief of growth and stability within the industry or market and the industries or markets with which the organization competes. An organization's chosen strategy will determine the industry, business, or market in which the organization will operate and how the products or services will be distributed. There are four distinct strategies: concentration, vertical integration, conglomerate diversification, and concentric diversification:

- Concentration strategies focus on the organization operating a single business. Growth occurs through increasing product sales or production capacity.

- An organization practices vertical integration by acquiring or organizing businesses that provide it with materials or services or businesses that will provide distribution channels for the organization's products or services.

- An organization employing conglomerate diversification will add new products or businesses that are unrelated to any of the organization's products, markets, or businesses.

- Utilizing the strategy of concentric diversification, organizations add new products or businesses that produce similar products and services to the organization's current products or businesses.

To formulate a strategy, an organization's leaders determine which strategies to follow and then modify those strategies so that they are a precise fit for the organization's needs.

*Implementation*

Strategic plans must be fully implemented for an organization to meet its mission. There are numerous reasons for failure to execute a strategic plan, including lack of communication, mixed messages, lack of clarity, lack of perseverance, and lack of focus.[13] Companies must overcome these obstacles and follow through with implementing the corporate strategy; otherwise, the corporation has wasted money, time, and resources for very little gain. The importance of implementing a strategy cannot be stressed enough as a corporation continues to work towards setting a strategy to help meet future goals.

## Operational Planning

Strategic plans cascade downward from the top of the organization, through the tactical level. Tactical plans provide the foundation upon which operational plans are formed . There are numerous components of an operational plan, such as action plans, purpose, products, and outcomes. These individual components help an organization focus on the operational goals, which help the organization attain tactical goals. At the operational level, an integral part of the planning process consists of specific details—to whom, what, when, and how— and includes operational areas within the organization, such as marketing, finance, and distribution. When all work together, these components allow the organization to achieve the overall strategic goal.

*Policies*

A policy outlines actions to be taken, given certain events and what is acceptable and not acceptable within the workplace.[14] Each organization sets different policies, based upon organizational needs. One organization may have a policy in place that another will not need. The development of policies is specific to an individual organization. Depending upon an organization's current and changing situations, the leaders may find a need to update old policies or develop new.

A policy sets forth guidelines to be followed and what steps are to be pursued, given a deviation from the given policy. As new policies are developed, an organization must recognize that a policy is not an all inclusive approach to outlining every possible action in every situation. Although a policy may attempt to cover many scenarios, managers must understand that the interpretation of many policies is subjective.

*Procedures and Rules*

An organization's procedures and rules set forth specific guidelines for employees to follow. A procedure establishes a baseline by setting forth the steps to be taken by employees to ensure success in the completion of a specific task.[15] This baseline ensures that all employees are taking the same actions to complete a task and eliminates confusion within the project. Procedures can be developed for any given event and may delineate the actions that are to be taken in case of certain events—such as when reporting sexual harassment or operating a copy machine. An organization's managers must determine what procedures must have official written operating procedures.

Procedures must be documented and should be written in a manner so as to clearly communicate the specifications for compliance. A well-written policy can be described as follows:

- Clear and concise—getting directly to the point and avoiding wordy sentences. Standard operating procedures should be communicated in the fewest possible words, phrases, and paragraphs.

- Complete—containing all the necessary information to perform the procedure.

- Objective—containing facts, not opinions.

- Coherent—showing a logical thought process and sequentially listing all steps necessary to complete the procedure.[16]

Rules outline the steps that employees are to take in performing their job. Rules help an organization to ensure that the workforce understands the boundaries in which they must operate to secure a productive and successful workforce. An example of a workplace rule may be that all lunches must be taken between 11:30 a.m. and 12:30 p.m. Managers must be willing to develop realistic rules that give employees the ability to complete jobs without undue constraints. In order to be enforced, rules must apply to all members of the organization; otherwise, legal ramifications may surface.

*Budgets*

Managers use budgets to determine how to utilize organizational resources. Budgets help provide a financial plan for an organization throughout a fiscal or calendar year. Typically, upper management sets budgets for each specific department and then allows the departmental managers to decide how to allocate the budgetary resources. Managers use numerous methods to allocate the budget—depending largely on the goal(s) of the organization.

*Project Management*

"Project management is a methodical approach to planning and guiding project processes from start to finish."[17] A project is a one-time set of events to accomplish a specific goal. A project manager must apply the management tools, skills, and knowledge of a project team to successfully meet the project's requirements.

Project management includes planning, scheduling, and ensuring the team is maintaining the scheduled progress toward the project's end. Planning is an important aspect of project management and the first step in successfully accomplishing the planned results of the project. A project manager should forecast future events as they relate to the project and plan for all aspects of a given project—both those that are expected, and especially those that would not normally be expected.

In the construction industry, project managers work with all aspects of the designing, planning, and construction of a project. The project manager will work with architects and the customer to design the project. They will then work with contractors and employees to develop a plan to complete the project within the customer's given specifications. Finally, the project manager will oversee the construction of the project to ensure successful completion. Though companies employ project managers to ensure that the project is completed in a manner specific to the company's interests, they also serve as an advocate for the customer, making sure the project meets all specifications. A project manager supervises every aspect of a given assignment to ensure project accomplishment.

Projects can begin to falter anywhere in the implementation process. A project manager must determine whether to attempt to save a project and get it back on track or recommend termination, since the project will not meet its goals. A project manager must go through ten steps to determine whether to continue a project or let it die.

1. Stop the project. This is a drastic step, but it stops all processes and allows all stakeholders to see the gravity of the situation.

2. Bring in an outside assessor. Someone who does not have a stake in the project will assess the situation without partiality.

3. Assess the status of the project. Determine where the project stands and reevaluate the strategic importance of the project. The assessor should investigate the possibility of bad news by speaking with members of the project team.

4. Evaluate the team. Does the team have the necessary knowledge, skills, and abilities to successfully complete the project?

5.  Redefine minimum goals. A project that is focused on activities rather than on outcomes can falter. Ensure that only the essential goals are being pursued.

6.  Determine whether minimum goals can be achieved. Once it is determined that the minimum goals can be met, all project stakeholders must agree to those goals and revise resource and time budgets.

7.  Rebuild the team. Once a project has been halted, the team may become demoralized and will need to be invigorated to accomplish the project requirements. In addition, make sure team members have the knowledge, skills, and abilities required for the project.

8.  Perform a risk analysis. All stakeholders should participate in identifying potential problems and the likelihood that each problem could occur. Armed with this information the team must then perform scenario planning for the most serious potential problems.

9.  Develop a plan. Armed with the information gathered by the outside assessor and the team, a new plan must be created.

10. Implement an early warning system. Implementing a warning system will ensure that the project does falter again. "Collect metrics, periodically review project status, define red flags, and create procedures for corrective action and follow up."[18]

The project can be permanently halted after any of these steps—if the outside assessor finds that the project cannot be saved. Although these steps are meant to review a project in trouble, an astute project manager can also utilize these steps to ensure project success.

## Scenario Planning

Scenario planning is an awareness of potential risks and developing plans for possible future conditions. Scenario planning is a method companies use to plan ahead and predict how certain future events will affect the corporation. This planning is particularly useful for a corporation as it attempts to mitigate risks in certain ventures. Scenario planning acknowledges that an organization's leaders cannot stop catastrophic events from occurring, but they can plan for those events.

One method an organization can employ to conduct scenario planning is computer simulation and models. For example, an architect can test the design of a building against a hurricane by using computer simulation. This important piece of scenario planning provides managers the means to see into the future. Organizations employ scenario planning—both as a risk assessment tool and a training aid—to help corporations plan for an uncertain future. Every leader should apply the following five lessons to better understand and control risk:[19]

1. Turbo-charge the imagination. Since it had happened before, the idea of a plane crashing into the World Trade Center was obvious. However, although it was a realistic potential threat, what had not been considered was the threat of a combination of two large planes, both with full fuel tanks, which would jar the fireproofing from the Towers girders.

2. Build scenarios. Shell Oil makes its scenario planning exercise public (www.shell.com/scenarios). These scenarios "identify some significant events, main actors and their motivations, and they convey how the world functions."[20]

3. Think in probabilities. Each scenario should be assigned a probability that the event will occur, either in relative terms (1%, 50%) or in relation to the occurrence of other events.

4. Use the power of markets. Markets, such as InTrade.com offers contracts on events that affect a wide variety of businesses. There are real people betting on the likelihood of an event taking place. Such sites are good places to research possible future scenarios.

5. Create a culture that insists on facing reality. Change happens at a fast pace, and there are many events for which an organization will simply not be prepared. "A tendency to avoid reality, to minimize bad news, is embedded deep in corporate culture. But while most cultural change must start at the top…this change can start most anywhere."[21]

The ability to predict the future and change as that future unfolds is an essential part of an organization's goal to increase profits for its shareholders. A manager must ensure that scenario planning includes all aspects of an organization that will be affected by future events: strategic, financial, operational, reputational, and regulatory.

# Controlling

The control process is an important managerial function and is directly linked to the planning function. "When you decide to make adjustments to what, how, when, or by whom the work gets done, you are performing the controlling function."[22]

The Control process gives managers the tools needed to effectively monitor progress towards an objective. Managers utilize various types of the control functions to ensure corporate achievement.

Monitoring individuals within the control process is only one aspect of controlling; one must look at every aspect of the organization to see if objectives are being met and what can be done to improve the process. As a result of the constant need for assessment to improve an organization's processes, the control process is cyclic and without end. In the control process, managers measure performance and consider feedback to tweak processes, which improves performance.

Controlling is an essential piece to organizational learning. An organization must be able to anticipate and react to problems when they occur. "Control is both anticipatory and retrospective. The process anticipates problems and takes preventive action. With corrective action, the process also follows up on problems."[23] An after action review is one tool that an organization can utilize in the control process to gauge effectiveness.

An after action review "is a discussion of a project or an activity that enables the individuals involved to learn for themselves what happened, why it happened, what went well, what needs improvement and what lessons can be learned from the experience."[24] An after action report is helpful to managers because it will contain both positive and negative aspects of a procedure and help managers make a decision on how to improve the process. The ability not only to understand what works well in an organization but also to anticipate and learn from mistakes is a vital tool that managers use to effectively administer the organization's resources and prevent future problems. The military makes extensive use of after action reports to help gauge the effectiveness of training, which prepares soldiers for real combat situations. The constant improvement of the training and learning process has ultimately saved millions of lives in combat.[25]

## Types of Control

Managers within an organization utilize a litany of techniques for measuring processes. Though various types exist, most processes are within the general categories of external or internal processes. External controls exist outside of the organization, while internal controls exist within the organization's boundaries. Managers utilize both internal and external means to ensure that they are implementing an effective control process.

*Internal Controls*

Internal controls are those controls that are internal to the organization that help to achieve an objective; it is broadly defined as a process, affected by an entity's board of directors, management and other personnel, designed to provide reasonable assurance regarding the achievement of objectives in the following categories: effectiveness and efficiency of operations, reliability of financial reporting, compliance with applicable laws and regulations.[26]

Internal controls generally can be classified into two categories: preventive or detective. "Preventive controls are designed to discourage errors or irregularities. . . . Detective controls are designed to identify an error or irregularity after it has occurred."[27] Examples of internal controls include policies, procedures, organizational design, receipts, taking an inventory of merchandise for sale, accounting records, and internal audits.

Five inter-related components of internal control should be fully integrated into the management process. These components are (a) control environment, (b) risk assessment, (c) control activities, (d) information monitoring, and (e) communication monitoring.[28]

1. The control environment is the foundation for all other components of internal control and set the tone of the organization toward the control process. Environmental factors in the control process include "integrity, ethical values and competencies of the entity's people."[29]

2. Risk assessment is the mechanisms that are in place to identify and deal with risk.

3. Control activities are the actions that are taken to address risk that may affect an organization's ability to achieve its objectives. These activities include "a range of activities as diverse as approvals, authorizations, verifications, reconciliations, reviews of operating performance, security of assets, and segregation of duties."[30]

4. Information and communication are important to the control process because information must not only flow effectively throughout the organization, but relevant information must be recognized, summarized, and conveyed in a format and within a period of time that allow the workforce to perform their responsibilities.

5. Monitoring activities are an important part of the controlling process. Monitoring assesses performance over time and determines whether the planned goals are being met by the current activities.

These mechanisms are an essential part of the organization's infrastructure; and when working seamlessly, they allow for effective control and process review within a corporation.

### External Controls

Controls that are external are largely out of an organization's control. An outside accounting firm handling all accounting for an organization would be an example of an external control. This would allow an outside observer to objectively view and comment on a company's accounting processes. Additionally, a consulting firm hired to view an organization's processes would be another example of an external control. An organization would not be able to control the consultant's impartial observation of policies and regulations and would be able to receive an objective view of the organization.

## Control Systems and Tools

Control systems and tools are utilized to keep employees motivated and focused. The goal of every organization is to increase the levels of efficiency and effectiveness. Companies utilize various tools, such as discipline systems, the Management By Objectives process, and information controls. An organization cannot afford to make the mistake of focusing only on information controls and neglecting other control tools. All aspects of an organization—assessing performance objectives, ensuring employee discipline systems are in place, assessing the profitability of certain business ventures, and checking inventory and purchasing procedures—must be included in the control process.

### Management by Objectives

Management by Objectives (MBO) is "effective planning [which] depends on every manager having clearly defined objectives that apply specifically to his or her functions. Each objective must also contribute to the objectives of higher management and of the organization[sic] as a whole."[31]

Peter Drucker first introduced the concept of MBO, which emphasizes the relationship between manager and employee. There are three steps involved in the management by objectives process:

1. Step one involves organizational leaders setting goals. In this step, top management sets specific goals which then cascade throughout the

organization, and each division/department area sets targets to meet the broad objectives.

2.  Step two involves each supervisor and subordinate meeting to develop appropriate goals for the subordinate (which align with the organization goals).

3.  Step three is an objective view of the goals that were previously set. In this step, managers and subordinates meet to evaluate the progress that has been made towards reaching the previously developed goals. Normally, performance based incentives are linked to this final process and employees are rewarded for making significant progress towards the goals that were established for the employee.[32]

### Employee Discipline Systems

Employee discipline systems are in place to ensure that employees are performing the job in an effective manner and are following company guidelines in the performance of an employee's pre-established duties. "Conduct problems typically stem from employees who fail to comply with the written and unwritten rules of the workplace such as coming to work on time, obeying orders, protecting government property, and in general supporting."[33]

Numerous techniques and different discipline systems address employee misconduct, but most follow the same process of preventing misconduct, addressing the conduct problem, and formal discipline.

1.  Preventing misconduct is accomplished by ensuring a clear channel of communication, which establishes expectations and guidelines for performance. Standards of performance must be understandable, objective, obtainable, and measurable.

2.  Addressing a conduct problem is usually carried out by a manager prior to any formal discipline taking place. The supervisor should discuss performance problems or wrongdoing directly with the employee and develop a plan for improvement which includes specific actions and dates. Consequences for not meeting the expectations outlined in the plan for improvement should be clearly outlined. Feedback should be given at regular intervals.

3.  Each organization determines its own formal discipline—the process of discipline and what the discipline entails—and usually formalizes the regulations that are available in employee handbooks. Formal discipline can include reprimand, suspension, and even termination.

*Information and Financial Controls (Ratio and Breakeven Analysis)*

An organization's leadership utilizes numerous financial controls in order to achieve maximum profitability. Financial controls can help managers determine the correct financial steps to take to ensure increased profits. Breakeven analysis and ratio analysis are two tools that are financial controls.

Breakeven analysis is a calculation of the point at which total sales revenues equal total costs and helps determine when an organization will be able to cover all of its expenses and begin to make a profit.[34] Managers utilize breakeven analysis to determine if a new product or service will be profitable. Fixed costs, variable costs, and the selling price of the product or service are all taken into consideration when determining a breakeven point. The Harvard Business School has a breakeven analysis toolkit available for download at: http://hbswk.hbs.edu/archive/1262.html.

Financial controls are also available in the form of ratio analysis. Ratios are utilized to analyze trends—to determine an organization's financial numbers over a period of time. An organization's ratios can be used as benchmarks against other organizations within a region or industry. Such comparisons can be found in Dun & Bradstreet's publication of key business ratios, The Almanac of Business and Industrial Financial Ratios, and publications from the Risk Management Association.[35] The following are a few types of ratio analysis:

1. Current ratio: current assets ÷ current liabilities

2. Quick ratio: current assets (less inventories) ÷ current liabilities

3. Inventory turnover ratio: cost of goods sold ÷ average value of inventory

These tools help to determine the financial health and profitability of an organization.


*Operations Management and Control*

Operations management deals with the efficient transformation of an organization's input into the output of a product or service and the controls that ensure maximization of efficiency in operational areas, such as purchasing and inventory.

Inventory control ensures that the size of the inventory is adequate to meet the needs of the organization; it involves managing the inventory that is already in your warehouse, stockroom or store, that is, knowing what products are "out there," how much you have of each item, and where it is. Inventory management involves determining when to order products and how much to order, as well as identifying the most effective source of supply for each item in each stocking location. Inventory management includes all of the activities of forecasting and replenishment.[36]

Many inventory control systems are automated to maintain optimal levels of inventory. Just in time ordering describes a process where inventory is scheduled to arrive "just in time" to be utilized or sold.

Purchasing controls help to ensure that organizations are ordering the correct amount and kind of materials and are getting the best value for their money. Purchasing controls can help determine if it is better to stock materials and buy in bulk or purchase materials "just in time." Most organizations centralize purchasing so that purchasing managers can work with a few suppliers to negotiate preferred service and special contracts. This is a win–win situation for both customer and supplier, because costs are lower for the customer and the supplier gains an exclusive contract.

## Steps in the Control Process

Assessing employee performance is designed to measure employee progress toward organizational objectives and to ensure that an employee's individual level of performance is aligned with the organization's goals. The control function consists of four cyclical steps that are utilized to both assess and motivate employees: responsibility for establishing objectives, measuring performance, comparing results, and taking corrective action. These steps detect any discrepancy in employee output from the set standards.

### Establish Objectives and Standards

The goal of management is to establish standards by which the organization will reach organizational objectives. Management uses these overarching standards to establish standards of performance for individual positions within the organization. "A standard is the level of expected performance for a given goal. Standards are performance targets that establish desired performance levels and motivate performance and service as benchmarks against which to assess actual performance."[37] An organization's leaders must set goals, objectives, and standards that are not only in line with strategic objectives but also specific, realistic, measurable, and have a timeline for completion. Performance standards can be set for increasing sales volume (10 percent increase in sales for the upcoming quarter), decreasing defects (documents prepared with have zero defects), decrease in variable costs (decrease labor expenses by 5 percent in the next fiscal year), or improve customer service (increase by 25 percent the number of customers who rate a cashier as friendly or very friendly).

*Measure Actual Performance*

Once specific, measurable, realistic, and timely standards are set and communicated to employees, managers can ascertain if the standards have been met, exceeded, or fallen short of the intended goals. Documentation of actual performance can be determined by review of written reports—sales information or expense reports.

*Compare Results with Objectives and Standards*

In the third step, managers evaluate the actual performance of the subordinate against the standard. Results of the evaluation must be scrutinized by the manager to determine if deviations from the expected outcomes are significant or if deviations are within acceptable ranges. Immediate action is taken for those performances that fall outside of acceptable ranges.

*Take Corrective Action*

Finally, effective control requires immediate corrective action to correct deviations from the standards. A manager must understand the problem through proper appraisal of the issue and then take quick action and implement the appropriate steps to ensure that the problem does not continue.

# Organizing

"Organizing can be viewed as the activities to collect and configure resources in order to implement plans in a highly effective and efficient fashion."[38] When a manager is performing the management function of organizing, this individual is coordinating resources—human, financial, time, raw materials, etc.—to work collectively to accomplish the goals and objectives of the organization.

Organizing the structure of an organization begins by arranging individuals into specific units and illustrating the structure on an organization chart. An organization chart is a pictorial representation of the formal organization, which clearly illustrates the following:

- formal reporting structure—who reports to whom

- official lines of communication

- levels of management (strategic, operational, tactical)

- units that report to a shared manager

- work responsibilities—shown by positions and titles[39]

Informal structures show the informal working relationships of an organization and how informal communication flows among peers, subordinates, and managers. The informal structure includes the friendships and relationships that people who work together have outside of their professional relationship—perhaps through their children or church activities.

In an informal structure, the spread of information and feedback occur quickly. The informal structure can be utilized because the informal channels of communication provide a conduit for managers to understand employees' reaction to news or events. On the other hand, the informal channel of communication can also work against the organization, because people can easily spread gossip and untruths within an organization. Misinformation can be spread throughout the company, either maliciously or unintentionally. Management cannot control the information flow within the informal structure, and this loss of control could lead to confusion and loss of production among the employees. Management understands that when an organization establishes a formal structure, an informal structure will develop. Management must effectively control the communication flow to ensure that the informal structure does not overpower the formal structure and that employees understand the formal structure already in place.

## Structures

Since the advent of scientific management, an underlying principle of management reveals that specialization leads to expertise in a specific job. This specialization produces an organizational structure that groups workers into departments that are connected in a way that best serves the needs of the organization. These structures can take on a variety of different forms, dependent largely on the organization and the task that the group of workers is trying to accomplish.

### Traditional Structures

Traditional structures are generally associated with large corporations and are most commonly used to perform a task or group of tasks. These structures have been time tested and proven to work effectively within certain organizational cultures. Traditional structures are functional, divisional, and matrix structures.

*Functional Structure.* In a functional structure, employees who perform comparable duties are organized into a formal work group. "A functional structure is … composed of all the departments that an organization requires to produce its goods and services."[40]   Functions of a large organization can include logistics, operations, production, marketing, finance, and human resources.  Each functional area within an organization fulfills specific needs and will vary depending upon the needs and goals of the organization.  In other words, Lockheed Martin may have a completely different organizational structure than Microsoft.

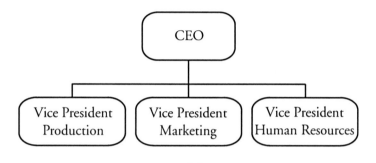

Functional Structure

A functional structure has several advantages:

- Economies of scale with efficient use of resources

- Task assignments consistent with expertise and training

- High-quality technical problem solving

- In-depth training and skill development within functions

- Clear career paths within functions [41]

Disadvantages of the functional system include problems with communication and problem-solving across the functions.  Problems within the functional system may take longer to resolve because the formal lines of communication do not travel horizontally; therefore, employees often push problems up rather than solve them within the same horizontal level of the organization.  The formal functional organization divides people within different functions into an "us" and "them" mentality; when in reality, all should be working toward the same goals and for the success of the organization.

*Divisional Structure.* A divisional structure is an organizational structure in which employees are grouped according to the product or service that they produce or by their geographical location.  This structure allows flexibility by focusing on specific customers, products, or regions.  General Motors is an example of a divisional structure. Several divisions—such as Buick, Chevrolet, and Cadillac—are autonomous groups within the larger corporation. These different car divisions are separate entities within the respective division, but they belong and report to a larger organization. In the case of General Motors, each individual division is responsible for a car class and expected to compete against rival companies in that class, such as Cadillac in the luxury car class. In a large company such as General Motors, a divisional configuration allows managers to break up similar but unique tasks within a corporation into smaller entities, thus making the divisions more manageable.[42]

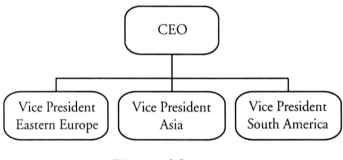

Divisional Structure

*Matrix Organization.* "The matrix is a coordinative structural device which constructively blends the program orientation of project staffs with the specialty orientation of functional personnel in a new and synergistic relationship."[43] Personnel from functional areas throughout the organization are assigned to a project team. Each team member belongs to two formal reporting groups: the functional group and the project group. As a result, these members report to bosses from both the functional group and the project group.

The advantage of such a structure is that each member brings different areas of expertise and experiences to the project group, creating synergy for the decision making process. The disadvantage to the matrix organization is found in reporting to two bosses, who may provide contradictory information or involve the subordinate in power struggles. Multi-manager chaos "can be blamed on many things: empire builders (whoever has the biggest team wins), glory seekers (anything touched can be taken credit for), and ubiquitous leaders-in-training (potential and potentate are close enough)."[44]

The matrix approach is successful if communication is central to the project structure. Without proper communication, the project may experience failure, due to confusion among project members. Because of the integrated approach to accomplishing a task, the matrix structure allows for flexibility between the teams.

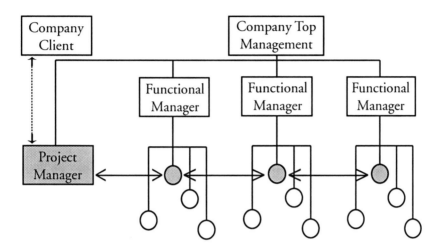

Matrix Organizational Chart of Arabize Computer Services Ltd.

## Contemporary Approaches to Structure

Successful organizations must constantly adapt to an ever changing world and utilize different approaches to structuring employees. The twenty-first century has ushered in a new era of advances that allow companies to explore organizational structure options beyond traditional management. These new and innovative approaches are often referred to as contemporary approaches to management. Contemporary approaches to structuring employees allows for flexibility when conducting specialty projects and the most efficient use of resources.

*Boundaryless organization.* Technological advances have allowed companies to challenge the traditional structure of an organization. Communication can now take place via fax, phone, computer, and video teleconferencing, minimizing the need for face to face interaction. Informational technology has challenged traditional methods of business and given managers creative ways to reduce expenses, while increasing efficiency within an organization. Utilizing information technology, which requires little physical interaction between employees or employees and customers to conduct business, is known as a boundaryless organization.

*Team structure.* More traditional structures are giving way to the use of teams. A team is not just any group working together. Committees, councils, and task forces are not necessarily teams. Groups do not become teams simply because that is what someone calls them. A team is a small number of people who have complementary skills who are committed to a common purpose, set of performance goals, and approach for which they hold themselves mutually accountable.[45]

The performance of teams is a result of the collective work of the team's members. Collective works represent the joint contribution of the members and the result of synergy, in which the team members produce more than they could individually.

Teams are composed of personnel from different line and staff functions within an organization. Team members come together to work on typical day-to-day tasks, solve a problem, or work on a project.[46] The advantage of teams is that they break down the barriers between different departments or divisions and allow for horizontal communication across the organization chart. Disadvantages of a team include sacrificing one's time to be a part of a team and a willingness to trust one's fate to teammates.

*Network structure.* A network structure is a central organization that works together with assorted independent companies, as if they were a single operation. Some refer to these organizations as virtual corporations.[47] The organization maintains the most crucial elements of the business model, with all other services provided through strategic alliances or outsourced. Utilizing a network structure, organizations may utilize contractors—such as an accounting firm—to complete business records or enter into a strategic alliance with a distributor to sell their product.

An organization that maintains its core competencies by utilizing the network structure reduces costs by streamlining operations. However, networked organizations can become very complicated because of the multiple contracts and relationships. A manager must be able to control activities that are not under his direct supervision. Organizations experience many problems with outsourcing. A recent article by Judy Artuinian has named, "The Seven Deadly Sins of Outsourcing:"

1. Feeble governance. Governance must provide feedback not only about how the relationship is working but also about the work that is being done. The costs of managing outsourcing contracts should be built into the budget.

2. Overblown expectations. Ensure that decisions are based upon an evaluation of capabilities rather than a marketing pitch.

3. Blindly banishing projects. Projects that are outsourced offshore cost more to manage than those projects that are sent to local or national organizations. Administrative costs for offshore outsourcing may be 20–25 percent greater than those outsourced domestically.

4. Dumbly disowning projects. Don't provide so much information that the contractor knows as much about the organization, its industry, products, and customer as the management of the organization for which they provide the product or service.

5. Bad Assumptions. Because of constantly changing technologies, contracts should be written so that they provide flexibility for change without penalties.

6. Sloppy Service Levels. Poor service levels are never acceptable, which also holds true for contractors. Service levels should be clearly spelled out in the contract and include severe penalties for missed service levels.

7. End Game Myopia. The contract should clearly spell out the contractors responsibilities at the end of the contract.[48]

Organizations that utilize the network structure must take great care in planning and controlling the contract and performance of contractors and strategic alliances.

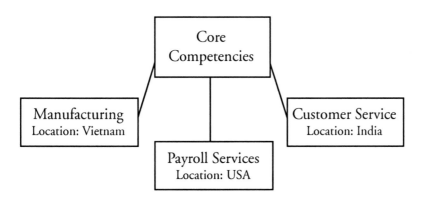

System-thinking and inter-relatedness of all systems within an organization.

To be effective, all components of an organization must fit together; leaders must examine how the inputs, transformation process, and outputs all interact with and impact the internal and external environments. Managers must understand the complexity of the inner-relatedness between systems—how a decision to utilize an input will affect not only the transformation process and the output but also the cost of raw materials and the environment.

## *Corporate Governance*

"Corporate governance is about promoting corporate fairness, transparency and accountability."[49] Corporate governance entails the management function of control, in which a monitoring system is implemented to ensure accountability of top management.  In light of recent corporate scandals involving deceptive management practices and fraudulent accounting schemes, it is imperative that each member of a board of directors provides corporate governance to keep close watch on financial records and assess strategy.  Cases such as Enron and World Com have shown the devastating results of irresponsible corporate leadership.  Millions of people can be negatively affected by the greed of a few managers.  Following standards of corporate governance also provides a monetary payoff. "Corporations practicing good corporate governance outperform those companies whose processes and procedures are unsound."[50]

Rather than rubber stamp all decisions made by top management, a member of the board of directors is expected to take an active role in ensuring that the organization is run ethically, top management is held accountable, and the organization is acting in a socially responsible manner.  Organizations must police themselves to avoid governmental, political, or social backlash for irresponsible behavior.

### *Chain of Command*

Introduced by Henri Fayol, the Scalar chain of command is the unbroken vertical authority in the organization that clarifies who reports to whom.  It follows the line of authority and responsibility from the lowest levels of an organization to the top manager.  A chain of command outlines the structure of responsibility within an organization.

A chain of command takes excessive time for an idea to make its way up through all the levels to one who can make a decision.  One company, Gore (maker of Glide Dental Floss), decided to do away with organizational layers and has been extremely successful.

The $1.84 billion company's flat organizational structure makes it exceptionally nimble. "If someone has an idea for a new product, they don't have to go up a hierarchy to find some boss to approve it. . . . Instead, they have to find peers in the organization who support the idea and will work with them. That open style of communication allows ideas to come up from the bottom."[51] However, a chain of command allows for a clear understanding of where an employee fits within an organization and ensures that efforts are coordinated across the organization.

*Span of Control*

Span of control refers to the number of workers who report directly to a supervisor or manager. Different organizations have different requirements, so not every organization will utilize the same span of control structure. The number of subordinates reporting to any one manager depends upon many factors.

The concept of span of control was popularized in 1922 by Sir Ian Hamilton, a British general who said the experiences of centuries of military leaders have shown that a leader can directly control no more than three to six persons . . . Supervising three people who interact daily, for instance, might be harder than supervising six who rarely cross paths . . . An executive should supervise no more than four or five people.[52]

A narrow span of control builds a tall organization, while a wide span of control builds a wide organization. The following conditions reveal when a span of control should be wider:

- When the work of subordinates is clearly defined.

- When highly trained subordinates have access to information that they need to successfully complete their tasks.

- When the manager is considerably competent.

- When the subordinates all perform a similar job and the performance measures are similar.

One company may find that the optimal number of direct reports to a manager is fifteen to one. Other companies or areas within the same company may find a five to one ratio the ideal number of employees to report to a manager. Managers need to be able to adapt to changing conditions and different requirements within the business to determine optimal span of control.[53]

*Delegation and Empowerment*

Delegation is assigning a task or duty to a subordinate beyond their normal job description that normally would be done by the manager. A manager that delegates tasks must follow through to ensure that the tasks are getting completed and to maintain responsibility for the delegated duties. "Delegation will require you to set goals, direct your staff, keep them on track, be accessible for questions, and boost their spirits should they need it."[54] Delegation does not give the employee permission to take a management role but gives him or her the opportunity to move beyond traditional positional roles within an organization to learn new skills. Delegation can help motivate employees to take a more active role within the organization and work beyond general job descriptions, giving the employee a greater sense of job accomplishment.

Empowerment is the authority a subordinate has to make decisions without asking for guidance.[55] One example of empowerment would be a manager giving an employee the ability to order supplies for the office, without having to seek management approval. Empowerment allows employees to experience autonomy within their job and gives them the ability to help shape the organization with their decisions.

### Centralization/Decentralization

Centralization in an organization refers to decisions being made at the higher levels of the organization. In a centralized organization, upper management has control over how the organization operates. Upper-level managers develop a strategy and make all decisions related to the organization, giving middle- and lower-level employees very few choices in the operation of the organization. Decisions involving the utilization of all resources—human, financial, time, raw materials, technology, etc.—are made at the upper levels of the organization. Centralized authority has the advantages of less work duplication and uniform work procedures, which promote an organization's consistency. An example of a centralized organization is McDonald's. A hamburger ordered at a McDonald's in California is the same as a hamburger ordered in New York.

Decentralization allows for power to be distributed throughout middle- and lower-levels of management, giving those at lower levels of management the ability to make decisions. Power is distributed throughout the organization instead of being concentrated at the top with a few key individuals. This is advantageous for a corporation because it allows those closest to a problem to make decisions on how to fix or improve a problem or process. Depending on the size of an organization, upper management may not fully understand all variables that encompass a problem or allow those with the most experience to fix the problem.

Ultimately an organization must decide what method works best for the business. A company may decide to centralize certain aspects of the corporation, while decentralizing others. Whether an organization utilizes a centralized or decentralized method of management, management must be willing to adapt and change as situations arise.

### Downsizing—Doing More with Less Staff, etc.

Downsizing refers to the planned reduction of staff and is done for a variety of reasons. A company may downsize to cut costs associated with employees, such as salaries, pension, or health care. Downsizing has both positive and negative aspects. One positive element to downsizing is that an organization may be able to significantly reduce overhead costs, which allow it to free up valuable resources for other company objectives.

A downsizing effort has far-reaching effects on employees. Employees are forced to complete more tasks with fewer personnel, which challenges and frustrates many employees. This reduction of personnel normally increases the stress level of employees, as they not only complete more work with less staff but also question the security of their own jobs.

# Conclusion

Planning, controlling, and organizing are three of the four major functions of an organization. Managers utilize each of these functions to run an effective and efficient organization. An essential element to an organization is to plan the goals towards which the organization will strive. Lastly, managers must organize the organization in a manageable fashion, based on the needs and nature of the business. No one step has greater importance over the others, but all pieces work together to ensure success as the business implements different functions into the corporation. If a manager fails to properly balance the three functional areas, then the business will not be successful in a free market society. A manager must be willing to adapt and change within the three functional areas to meet the ever changing business environment needs.

### *Brief Summary of Major Points for Planning, Controlling, and Organizing*

The planning phase refers to the need for an organization to plan the direction an organization will take. This is accomplished through the planning and eventual implementation of carefully considered plans. Managers use various tools to ensure successful plans, such as the SWOT analysis and benchmarking. These tools, coupled with a plethora of other planning strategies, help managers to decide the best direction for an organization to take.

Organizations, such as Microsoft and Wal-Mart, successfully utilize business plans. These organizations and others like them understand the need for strategic planning. General Motors' strategic plan in 1908 involved producing a million cars a year and becoming the industry leader. "Yet in 1908 when the industry produced only 65,000 machines in the United States, Mr. Durant looked forward to a one-million car year to come."[56] A manager's ability to develop a sound business plan could lead to an organization's dominance of a particular industry. Leaders must be willing to develop primary and alternative goals, implement and assess the goals, and monitor the goals to ensure success.

The function of organizing refers to the structure a manager will utilize to effectively manage the organization's employees. Managers use traditional and nontraditional structures, employing various techniques based on the requirements of an organization.

A manager must be able to understand the nature of the organization and the most effective way to manage employees. Whether or not businesses develop a successful organizational structure could determine the survival of the organization.

Controlling refers to the need for a manager to effectively develop and implement a plan within the organization. A leader must understand the process by which an organization will successfully accomplish its objectives. Techniques, such as management by objectives, give a roadmap to managers on how to increase effectiveness and efficiency within an organization, which are major goals of an organization's leadership.

A manager must focus on increasing profits and decreasing costs as he seeks to be competitive. A manager that does not recognize faulty finances because of a lack of financial controls leads the way to unethical business practices. A manager must recognize the resources and controls necessary to monitor and improve processes.

## Impact on the Organization, Manager, and Employees

A manager must be willing to accept risk and understand the consequences of both internal and external factors–as in seeking to plan the organization's future. This planning phase affects every stakeholder—whether the manager is successful or unsuccessful in predicting future events. An organization that lacks leadership in the planning phase will most likely not meet stakeholder expectations.

The importance of managers being able to motivate and challenge employees, while simultaneously seeking to increase profits, is essential to a company's well being. A manager must properly consider all organizing techniques and select the best technique for the company. Would a traditional structure work best in the business environment? What helps the manager provide direction without stifling creativity? The correct answer to these questions has positive implications, whereas the wrong answer could spell disaster for an organization.

# Endnotes

1    Lakein, A. (1973). *How to Get Control of Your Time and Your Life*. New York: New American Library.

2    McNamara, C. (1999). *One perspective on the basic planning process,* ¶ 1 . Retrieved July 26, 2006 from http://www.managementhelp.org/plan_dec/gen_plan.htm

3    Jones, G. R. (2006). Contemporary Management (4th ed.), p. 235. Boston: McGraw-Hill.

4    Mintzburg, H. (1994). The Rise and Fall of Strategic Planning. New York: The Free Press.

5    WISC. (n.d.). *Community Planning Resource,* ¶ 3. Retrieved July 21, 2006 from http://planning. lic.wisc.edu/CPR/implement%20tasks.dwt

6    Fisher, A. (2005). The secrets of great decision making. Money.Com Home Page. Retrieved from the World Wide Web on September 29, 2006 from: http://money.cnn.com/2005/06/23/news/economy/annie/fortune_annie062305/index.htm

7    Drucker, P.F. (2006). What executives should remember. Harvard Business Review, 84, (2). February 2006.

8    Leader to Leader Institute Home Page. (n.d.) Retrieved September 30, 2006 from the World Wide Web: http://leadertoleader.org/leaderbooks/sat/mission.html

9    Meyer, N.D. (July 26, 2005). Mission, vision and value statements. CIO.com. Retrieved September 30, 2006 from the World Wide Web: http://www.cio.com/leadership/buzz/column. html?ID=9311

10   Alliance. (2003). *What are the basic steps in the strategic planning process,* ¶ 4. Retrieved July 23, 2006 from http://www.allianceonline.org/FAQ/strategic_planning/what_are_basic_steps.faq

11   Ibid.

12   Spendolini, M.J. (1992). The Benchmarking Book. New York: ANACOM. p. 48.

13   Tearle, R. (n.d.). *Why strategy implantation fails,* ¶ 1. Retrieved July 24, 2006 from http://www. changedesigns.co.za/why_strategy_implementation_fails.htm

14   American Heritage Dictionary. (2005). *The American Heritage Dictionary of the English Language (4ᵗʰ ed.).* Houghton Mifflin Company: New York, NY.

15   Chaneski, W. (1997). *Competing Ideas: Writing Standard Operating Procedures,* ¶ 4. Retrieved August 12, 2006 from http://www.mmsonline.com/articles/0498ci.html

16   Ibid.

17   SMB.Com Home Page. Retrieved October 7, 2006 from the World Wide Web: http://searchsmb.techtarget.com/sDefinition/0,,sid44_gci951200,00.html

18   Bennatan, E.M. (2006). Catastrophe *Disentanglement: Getting SoftwareProjects Back on Track.* (Addison- Wesley Professional, 2006)

19   Colvin, G. (2005). An executive risk handbook., *Fortune,* 152, (7).

20   Shell Oil Home Page. Retrieved on October 7, 2006 from the World Wide Web: http://www. shell.com/home/Framework?siteId=royal-en&FC2=/royal-en/html/iwgen/our_strategy/scenarios/ what_are_scenarios/zzz_lhn.html&FC3=/royal-en/html/iwgen/our_strategy/scenarios/what_are_ scenarios/what_are_scenarios_14082006.html

21   Colvin, G. (2005, October 3). An executive risk handbook., *Fortune,* 10/3/2005, Vol. 152, Issue 7.

22    Thompson Rivers University Open Learning Agency. (2002). *Role of the Supervisor,* ¶ 6 . Retrieved August 12, 2006 from http://openet.ola.bc.ca/WKPL_minicourse/functions.html

23    Erven, B. (n.d.). *Controlling,* ¶ 5. Retrieved July 3, 2006 from, Ohio State University Extention, Department of Agriculture Economics Web site: http://www.ag.ohio-state.edu/~mgtexcel/ Control.html

24    National Library for Health, Knowledge Management Home Page. Retrieved October 7, 2006 from the World Wide Web:  http://www.nelh.nhs.uk/knowledge_management/km2/aar_toolkit. asp

25    *Texas Army MARS* (n.d.). *After Action Reports,* ¶ 2. Retrieved July 3, 2006 from: http://www. txarmymars.org/oplanp24.htm

26    American Institute of Certified Public Accounting Committee of Sponsoring Organizations (n.d.). *Internal Control-Integrated Framework,* ¶ 3. Retrieved July 3, 2006 from: http://www.coso. org/Publications/executive_summary_integrated_framework.htm

27    McNeeley, K. (2003). *Internal Controls,* ¶ 3. Retrieved July 3, 2006, from Indiana University Web site: http://www.indiana.edu/~iuaudit/controls.html

28    COSO (n.d.). *Internal Control-Integrated Framework,* ¶ 1. Retrieved July 3, 2006 from: http:// www.coso.org/Publications/executive_summary_integrated_framework.htm

29    Ibid.

30    Ibid.

31    Kow, L.Y. (1991).  Management by objectives for better management effectiveness in the SAF Journal of the Singapore Armed Forces, 25, (4).  Retrieved October 2, 2006 from the World Wide Web: http://www.mindef.gov.sg/safti/pointer/back/journals/1999/Vol25_4/6.htm

32    Drucker, P.F. (1982). The Practice of Management.New York:  Harper Collins.

33    National Institute of Health, Office of Human Resources Home page.  Retrieved October 7, 2006 from the World Wide Web: http://hr.od.nih.gov/ER/Empl-Disc/Emp-Disc-Overview.htm

34    United States Small Business Administration Home Page.  Retrieved October 7, 2006 from the World Wide Web: http://www.sba.gov/starting_business/financing/breakeven.html

35    American Express, Small Business Home Page.  Retrieved October 7, 2006 from the World Wide Web:  http://www133.americanexpress.com/osbn/tool/ratios/ratioarticle.asp

36    Schreibfeder, J. (2002).  The First Steps to Achieving Effective Inventory Control Retrieved on October 7, 2006 from the World Wide Web:  http://download.microsoft.com/download/b/f/3/ bf334d7f-ad07-458e-a716-fdf46a0cf63c/eimwp1_invcontrol.pdf#search=%22inventory%20con trol%22

37    Bateman, T. S. & Snell, S.A. (2004).  Management: The new competitive landscape. Boston: McGraw, Hill Irwin. p. 491.

38    McNamara, C. (1999). *Management Function of Organizing,* ¶ 1. Retrieved July 3, 2006 from http://www.managementhelp.org/orgnzing/orgnzing.htm

39    Chandler, Jr. A.D. (1988).  Origins of the organization chart. Harvard Business Review, 66, (2). pp. 156-157.

40    Jones, G. R. (2006). Contemporary Management (4th ed.), p. 343. McGraw-Hill: Boston, MA.

41    Schermerhorn, Jr. J.R., (2006).  Management.  Hoboken, N.J.: John Wiley & Sons, Inc.

42    Sloan, Alfred P. (1990). My Life with General Motors. Currency-DoubleDay: New York, NY.

43    Vishwanath, P. (2006, July 10). *Surviving the Matrix,* ¶ 3. Financial Times Business Line.

44    Sandburg, J. (2005). Office democracies: How many bosses can one person have? The Wall Street Journal, (246), 111. p. B1.

45    Katzenbach, J.R. & Smith, D.K. (1993, Mar-Apr). The Discipline of teams. Harvard Business Review. 71, (2). pp. 111-120.

46    Mohrman, S.A., Cohen, S.G., & Mohrman, Jr., A.M. (1996). Designing team-based organizations. San Francisco: Jossey-Bass.

47    Byrne, J.A. (1993). The virtual corporation. Business Week, 3304  pp. 98 – 102.

48    Artunian, J. (2006). The seven deadly sins of outsourcing. Computer World. 40, (19).  pp56 – 58.

49    Wolfensohn, J. (1999, June 21). *What is Corporate Governance,* ¶ 7. Retrieved August 12, 2006 from http://www.encycogov.com/WhatIsGorpGov.asp

50    Eisenhoffer, J. (2005, September 23). *Corporate accountability Report,* ¶ 8. Retrieved August 12, 2006 from http://www.issproxy.com/pdf/CorporateAccountabilityReport.pdf.

51    Kiger, P.J. (2006). Small groups big ideas. Workforce Management, 85, (4). pp. 22- 27.

52    Henrichs, M. (2001, January). Span control. Entrepreneur,

53    Theobald, N. (2005). *The many faces of span of control.* Administration & Society, Vol. 36, No. 6, pp. 648-660.

54    IOMA. (2005, October). Strategic Planning in the Payroll Department: Delegate More To Keep Your Staff Engaged With Payroll Challenge, ¶ 3. Payroll Manager's Report.

55    Mitsfiner, D. (1995). *Empowerment.* Retrieved August 12, 2006 from http://www.kon.org/ leadership/empowered.html

56    Sloan, A. P. (1990). My Life with General Motors, p. 3. Currency-DoubleDay: New York, NY.

55    Mitsfiner, D. (1995). *Empowerment.* Retrieved August 12, 2006 from http://www.kon.org/ leadership/empowered.html

56    Sloan, A. P. (1990). My Life with General Motors, p. 3. Currency-DoubleDay: New York, NY.

## MEASURABLE LEARNING OBJECTIVES

1. Explain the nature of leadership.

2. Discuss the different styles of leadership.

3. Discuss the Trait theories of leadership and identify their impact on modern management.

4. Discuss the Behavior theories of leadership and identify their impact on modern management.

5. Discuss the models of leadership and identify their impact on modern management. Identify the contributions of Fiedler, Hersey-Blanchard and Vroom-Jago.

6. Distinguish between transformational and transactional leadership.

7. Discuss the concept expounded by Jim Collins in Good to Great.

8. Explain the nature of Servant Leadership.

9. Discuss the theory of leadership proposed by Stephen R. Covey; Principle-Centered Leadership.

10. Discuss change and change leadership.

# Leading

All managers desire to lead a successful organization. The greatest opportunity to achieve that success is if all employees are working towards accomplishing the organization's goals, Accomplishing goals requires a manager to influence employees. The study of leadership is a tool that managers can utilize to help the organization attain its goals. A leader can develop many styles, theories, and concepts: "there are almost as many definitions of leadership as there are persons who have attempted to define the concept."[1] Although often used interchangeably, the terms manager and leader are not the same. In *Managing People is like Herding Cats,* Warren Bennis distinguishes between a leader and a manager:

- The manager administers; the leader innovates.
- The manager is a copy; the leader is an original.
- The manager maintains; the leader develops.
- The manager focuses on systems and structure; the leader focuses on people.
- The manager relies on control; the leader inspires trust.
- The manager has a short-range view; the leader has a long-range perspective.
- The manager asks how and when; the leader asks what and why.
- The manager has his eye on the bottom line; the leader has his eye on the horizon.
- The manager imitates; the leader originates.
- The manager accepts the status quo; the leader challenges it.
- The manager is the classic good soldier; the leader is his or her own person.
- The manager does things right; the leader does the right thing.[2]

To become a leader, a manager must develop an understanding of the nature of leadership along with the importance of vision, power, influence, and ethics.

Developing a unique leadership style is also important. Depending on the type of working environment, a manager could choose between autocratic, democratic, and laissez-faire styles of leadership. Investigating trait and behavioral theories can give a manager an idea of how his or her personal inherited or behavioral characteristics can influence his or her leadership abilities.

The different models of leadership can also be reviewed to give insight into how a particular leadership style and different environments can affect relations with employees. Leading is multi-dimensional and requires that managers understand their leadership abilities to help an organization achieve its goals. The achievement of those goals ultimately leads to the success of a leader and the success of an organization.

## *The Nature of Leadership*

Leadership is easily defined, but the nature of leadership depends on the effectiveness of a leader. The most competitive organizations are those that have the most effective leaders. Leadership is the fundamental component to an organization's success. Kouzes and Posner define leadership as "the art of mobilizing others to want to struggle for shared aspirations."[3] This definition acknowledges that those being led must want to exert effort to meet the expectations and goals of a motivating, inspirational leader. One should remember that it is essential to distinguish between the different aspects of leadership: the person, the position, and the processes.

The person who is fulfilling a leadership responsibility is the individual who has authority and exerts influence over others—to meet organizational goals. Leaders have an immense responsibility to build upon interpersonal relationships and implement activities that are for the greater good of the organization and its stakeholders. To achieve success, leaders must fine-tune their personal leadership style to effectively influence others. Such a leader will be better prepared to deal with adverse situations or circumstances that involve adapting to change.

One of the most important leadership skills is effective communication. Communication is vital in any work environment, especially in the relationship between a subordinate and superior.

> Communication is not one of the skills, or tools, of leadership; it is the very process by which leadership itself is exercised. Without communication leaders nor leadership would exist. Viewing leadership as communication and perceiving the currency of its realm to be symbolic interaction have important ramifications for leaders and those whom they seek to lead.[4]

Leaders utilize communication to persuade another to support a message.

### *Vision*

To be an effective leader, one must have vision for what the organization should become. Leaders look to the future, chart the course for the organization, and attract, retain, motivate, inspire, and develop relationships with employees, based on trust and mutual respect. Leaders provide meaning and purpose, seek innovation rather than stability, and impassion employees to work together to achieve the leader's vision.[5]

Leaders constantly struggle to find new ways to remain competitive. They know that vision is not merely a dream but a certainty that will come to fruition. Vision drives toward the goal. "A leader motivates, drives, and inspires other members of the organization, and often those outside of it, to believe in the vision. That motivation and creation of belief must translate into effort in pursuit of the vision."[6] An organization's vision should cascade down from top-management throughout the entire organization. Vision without action is meaningless.

*Power and Influence*

Leaders must take the responsibility of influencing, motivating, and generating dedication and compliance among subordinates. French and Raven first identified the different types of power that are used to influence employee behavior: reward, coercive, legitimate, expert and referent.[7]

*Reward Power.* Reward power is the belief that an employee will comply in exchange for rewards controlled by the superior. In addition to a pay check, anything that is desirable can be considered a reward. Pay raises and bonuses are rewards, but anything that an individual values can be utilized as a reward.

*Coercive Power.* Another form of influence is coercive power, through which the employee obeys, but only because of the presence of threats. Coercive power bases a relationship between a subordinate and a leader on fear, which could hinder the subordinate's desire to willingly follow the leader.

*Legitimate Power.* Legitimate power is the power found in a position. A leader has the authority of his or her position providing power. Individuals do not follow the individual, but the position.

A common trap that people in such roles can fall into is to forget that people are obeying the position, not them. When they either fall from power or move on to other things, it can be a puzzling surprise that people who used to fawn at your feet no longer do so.[8]

*Expert Power.* Expert power is the result of specialized skills, knowledge, or abilities. Subordinates comply not only because they can learn from the leader but also because of the understanding that the leader has specialized knowledge, skills, and abilities that are valuable to the organization.

*Referent Power.* Referent power is associated with charisma – people identify with and have a high level of respect for those with this type of power.

Leaders utilize power to get things done. Expert and referent power are the more influential types of power, but reward, coercive, and legitimate power may be more productive at times. The way that leaders express power will determine its probability of success.

*Ethics*

Leadership is effective only if carried out in an ethical manner. Ethics are the values, morals, and basic principles that an individual uses to decide between right and wrong.[9] Ethical behavior is dependent upon the leader's integrity even when no one is looking. [10]

Organizations should have a written code of ethics that all employees follow, regardless of position. A written code of ethics will let all stakeholders know what behaviors are acceptable. This code should be made available to employees in organizations of all sizes. The following are the guiding principles upon which a code of ethics should be based:[11]

1. Focus on business practices and specific issues. Issues to include: "conflicts of interest to avoid, accuracy of financial statements, sexual harassment, workplace safety, environmental standards, and rules and regulations specific to your industry and company."[12]

2. Customize it to fit the organization. Each organization will have a unique code of ethics; therefore, while codes of ethics from other organizations can be reviewed, they should never be copied for use. The code of ethics must flow from the organization's mission and vision.

3. Include employees in its development. Not only will employees be more accepting of a code of ethics which they helped to develop, but those employees will know more about what ethical issues and dilemmas they face.

4. Train employees to be ethical. Training classes, seminars, or workshops—to convey the code of ethics in a user-friendly format—must be done to ensure that employees understand the code and be able to apply it to everyday activities.

5. Post the code and implement a reporting system: This may include both open-door policies and anonymous reporting.

6. Appoint a compliance officer. These individuals are "responsible for their company's ethics, compliance, and business conduct."[13] These officers are knowledgeable in the organization's internal code of ethics. In larger organizations, they are also familiar with SEC governance and mandates set forth in the Sarbanes-Oxley.

7. Follow up on any ethics violations that are discovered. Failure to enforce the code of ethics will make it powerless. Penalties for violations and an appeal process should be included in every code of ethics. Employees must be held accountable for violating the code.

8. Live it throughout the organization—from top down. There should never be the appearance that any one person is above the code. Even those within the highest echelons must adhere to the code and become role models for the rest of the organization.

Executive managers are expected to be role models of ethical behavior for the entire organization. But that behavior does not suddenly occur when one reaches the pinnacle of a career. One must exhibit personal ethical decision making and integrity from the earliest stages of a career "long before the strenuous tests of the business world arrive."[14] Transparency in all business dealings is required, but that transparency extends outside of the business environment. A leader must "be prepared to open all your books at any time."[15]

## Leadership Styles

Each individual has a different approach to the way he or she leads. The environment, a specific situation, or the skill level of subordinates can affect the way that someone leads. Leaders may choose to focus on developing a friendly relationship with a subordinate or choose to focus principally on a subordinate's production. The behaviors and actions of leaders shape their leadership style. These styles can be classified into three major categories: autocratic, democratic, and laissez-faire leadership.

### Autocratic

The autocratic leader—also know as authoritarian style—employs a domineering approach to leadership, which dictates job processes to subordinates. The autocratic leader makes unilateral decisions and then announces those decisions to subordinates. If overused, autocratic leadership could lead to passive resistance from subordinates. Although the autocratic style seems to have negative overtones, it does serve a purpose. Some situations call for immediate or critical action, such as on a battlefield or in an emergency. In such cases, this type of leadership is best.

The autocratic style of leadership mirrors McGregor's Theory X with its strict rules, system of rewards and penalties, and a more centralized control within the organization. Leadership places less emphasis on creativity and self-direction and more emphasis on completing an assignment, in accordance with the leader's direction.

### Democratic

A democratic leader will make decisions after gathering input from subordinates. A democratic leader maintains control but allows subordinates to offer input. Open lines of communication will help democratic leaders gather vital information from subordinates to ensure optimal decisions. A good democratic leader values openness and group participation but does not lose sight of his or her ultimate leadership of the group.

### Laissez-Faire

Under the laissez-faire form of leadership, a leader makes no decisions. This type of leader results in subordinates exhibiting negative attitudes and lower performance.[16] A laissez-faire leader disassociates from the subordinates that he or she leads, which means that the group may not be able to obtain all resources required for completion of a project.

There are a few instances when the laissez-faire management style can be effective. Having skilled and/or experienced workers allows leaders to have minimal influence on the decisions of the team. Skilled workers have this sort of freedom because they have proven themselves as competent, which gives employees a feeling of empowerment and can lead to increased job satisfaction.

## Trait Theories

Many researchers believe that specific personality characteristics and physical and social traits set leaders apart from followers. Trait theories assume that individuals are born with traits that are suited to leadership and that the right combination of traits will make a good leader. According to trait theory, one that is born with the proper traits could be an effective leader in almost any situation. Six traits are often associated with successful leaders:

- Drive—a high desire for accomplishment
- Desire to lead
- Honesty and integrity
- Self-confidence
- Intelligence
- Job-relevant knowledge[17]

Studies on trait theories of leadership concluded that researchers had not proven the likelihood that all good leaders had inherited traits but that successful leadership might be dependent upon a combination of traits that work well in specific situations.

These traits, combined with acquired skills, could potentially develop an individual into a quality leader. Many believed that the traits gave an individual the best opportunity to become an effective leader. These traits do not necessarily mean that only leaders have these qualities. Situational, behavioral, and environmental factors could positively influence an otherwise incapable individual into a superior leader.

## Behavior Theories

The behavior theories of leadership attempt to understand what makes a leader effective by determining what combination of skills, behaviors, and traits leaders possess. Behavior theories support the idea that individuals can be trained to be leaders. There are two classic studies regarding leadership behaviors: The University of Michigan Leadership Model and the Ohio State Leadership Model.

In the late 1940s at the University of Michigan, Rensis Likert led a team that interviewed managers and their subordinates. The researchers determined that there were two forms of leadership styles: task centered and people centered. The task-centered leader focuses more on the job at hand, and his or her concern deals with efficiency and effectiveness. People-centered leaders are concerned with employee satisfaction.[18]

The leadership model proposed by Ralph Stogdill—in the Ohio State Leadership Model—included two major dimensions of leadership behavior: initiating structure and consideration.[19] In the initiating structure, leaders exhibit behaviors that organize and define the activities of subordinates. Conversely, the leadership behavior of consideration communicates with subordinates in a friendly, supportive environment.

Behavior theories only reflect the tendencies of a leader; they do not account for external influences, such as the environment in which the leader operates or the subordinate being led. Therefore, researchers began to develop new models that measure leader effectiveness by analyzing the leader, the subordinate, and their environment. These new models came to be known as the contingency models of leadership.

## Contingency Models of Leadership

As researchers studied the basic trait and behavior models of leadership, they began to discover that additional factors beyond a leader's natural traits and tendencies impacted his or her leadership effectiveness. The basic trait and behavior models focused primarily on internal characteristics of the leader and did not account for external influences on leadership ability. This directed researchers to discover how a leader's traits and behavior within a given situation would impact leadership effectiveness, commonly referred to as the contingency models of leadership.[20]

One of the first contingency models—Fiedler's Contingency Model—studied the characteristics of a leader and the situation in which they were leading. House's path-goal theory focused on what leaders should do to motivate subordinates to achieve expected results. The Hershey-Blanchard situational theory focused on matching a leader's style of leadership with the maturity of subordinates in a given situation. Finally, the Vroom-Jago leadership-participation model focused on which leadership decision–making procedures would be most effective in various situations.

### Fiedler Contingency Model

Fred Fiedler and his associates were among the first to develop a contingency model of leadership. Fiedler utilized the Least Preferred Coworker (LPC) scale to determine the inclination of a leader to exhibit task-motivated behaviors or relationship-motivated behaviors. The concept that a leader is either task or relationship-motivated was important, because Fiedler believed that those orientations were fixed and difficult to change. The key to contingency leadership is to put the leader's style in situations where the style is the most effective—the best fit. His model evaluated traits and behaviors of a leader (leadership style) to determine the effectiveness of specific leadership styles in various situations. This model asserts that just because an individual is a good leader in one situation does not mean he or she could effectively lead in another.

Because a leader could not change styles, Fiedler sought to determine the success of leaders given various situations, which resulted in three situational characteristics. He branded these three situational characteristics task structure, position power, and leader-member relations.

Task structure (high or low) measures the degree to which tasks, procedures, and goals are clear and unambiguous. Task structure refers to the ability of the leader's subordinates to understand what needs to be accomplished and the steps needed to get the job done. Leading is favorable when the task structure is well defined. When people know their proper positions and assignments and have the tools necessary to successfully complete the task, leading will be easy. When leaders do not define task structure, confusion exists and people do not know their positions and assignments. This lack of task structure will sometimes cause people to begin making their own decisions, which may not be in the best interests of the organization.

Position power (strong or weak) is determined by the ability of a leader to dispense rewards and punishments. Position power refers to the three types of power a leader possesses, based on the individual's position within the organization. The legitimate power of leaders is greatly strengthened when all employees have a clear organizational chart with job responsibilities, which removes ambiguity.

The degree to which subordinates accept and support a leader is based upon leader-member relations. A good relationship, built on trust, loyalty, and respect, will create an environment favorable for leading. Leaders must recognize that their success largely depends on the efforts and support of their subordinates.

Fiedler's model categorizes a leader's effectiveness from favorable to unfavorable by taking their leadership style and applying it in various situations. Neither the task-oriented nor the people-oriented leader is effective in all situations.

- High control or low control situations are where the task-oriented leader will be most successful.
- Situations of moderate control will be successful for the relationship-oriented leader.

### Fielder's Contingency Model

| Leader-Member Relations | Situations | | | | | | | |
|---|---|---|---|---|---|---|---|---|
| | Poor | | | | Good | | | |
| Task Structure | Unstructured | | Structured | | Unstructured | | Structured | |
| Position Power | Low | High | Low | High | Low | High | Low | High |
| | Task | Relationship | | | | | Task | |

### Hersey-Blanchard Situational Leadership Model

The Hersey-Blanchard situational theory seeks to match leadership style with the maturity of the subordinates:

Situational Leadership is based on an interplay among (1) the amount of direction (task behavior) a leader gives, (2) the amount of socio-emotional support (relationship behavior) a leader provides, and (3) the "readiness" level that followers exhibit on a specific task, function, activity, or objective that the leader is attempting to accomplish through the individual or group.[21]

The Hersey-Blanchard model was developed on the premise that a leader should have the ability to adapt different leadership styles to different situations.[22] In addition, the model encompasses the development level of the subordinate, and that level should determine the leader's style.

This leadership model determined the leadership style needed for the following:

- Task behavior—the extent to which a leader engages in one-way communication by explaining what each follower is to do, as well as when, where, and how tasks are to be accomplished.
- Relationship behavior—the extent to which a leader engages in two-way communication by providing socio-emotional support, "psychological strokes" and facilitating behaviors.
- Readiness—the ability and willingness of a person to take responsibility for directing their own behavior in relation to a specific task to be performed.[23]

As the subordinate increases in readiness to accept responsibility and skills and technical knowledge—in terms of accomplishment of a specific task—the leader can begin to reduce task behaviors and increase relationship behaviors. Leaders make this transition by moving from the Telling and Selling leadership behaviors to those of Participating and Delegating.

Telling leaders closely supervise and direct subordinates by giving specific instructions and assignments. Telling leaders also possess decision-making power and do not rely on subordinate input. This style of leadership is most often applied when the subordinate is highly immature in task competence and commitment, forcing the leader to employ an autocratic style of leadership.

Selling leaders define subordinate assignments and provide direction but they rely heavily on training and seek to pass their knowledge and skills on to the subordinate. Leaders maintain decision-making power but communicate the decision-making process with subordinates. This style of leadership is most often applied when the subordinate is slightly immature in task competence and commitment.

Participating leaders facilitate and establish overall direction, but they allow subordinates to conduct daily operations by taking a more participative rather than direct roll in their subordinate's efforts. This style of leadership is most often applied when the subordinate is moderately mature in task competence and commitment.

The delegating style of leadership is most appropriately applied when subordinates are highly mature in task competence and commitment. Leaders relinquish control to subordinates, who then decide when the leader will be involved in a decision or process.

As with the leader's style, the development level of the subordinate is also situational. The model established four levels of development, determined by a combination of task competence and commitment. For example, the developmental levels were labeled as D1 through D4. A D1 subordinate lacks task competence and commitment (immature), meaning they lack the skills, confidence, and motivation required to complete the task. The D4 level describes a subordinate who is highly competent and committed (mature), meaning they were experienced at the task and had the drive to work independently.

The Hersey-Blanchard Situational Leadership Model is based upon the responsibility of the leader to adapt his or her leadership style to the developmental level of the subordinate. Once the leader adapts to the subordinate's maturity level, tasks get accomplished, relationships grow stronger, and the development level of the subordinate increases.

Hersey Blanchard Situational Leadership Model

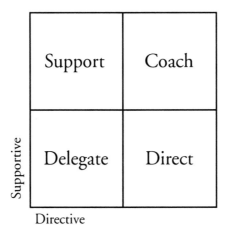

*House Path-Goal*

The path-goal theory, proposed by Robert House, is considered a contingency model of leadership, because it proposes that an effective leader will clarify paths by which subordinates can achieve both personal- and job- related goals.[24] This theory suggests that effective leaders motivate subordinates along those paths and remove any obstacles over which a subordinate may stumble, providing rewards for task accomplishment. The level of definition provided in goal obtainment, the extent to which obstacles are removed, and the type of rewards offered depend upon the nature of the subordinate and the working environment. Leaders should be adaptable and move freely among four leadership styles: directive, supportive, achievement-oriented, and participative.

Directive leadership involves the establishment of specific objectives and clear rules, including giving detailed job assignments, providing comprehensive training, and a well-defined operational structure.

Supportive leadership involves the creation of a pleasant working environment by forecasting the needs of the subordinates. This leadership style is particularly beneficial in high stress situations because it emphasizes the personal well being of the subordinate over task completion.

Participative leadership involves subordinates in the decision-making process, as leaders and subordinates share information freely. When subordinates are part of decision making, group members establish a sense of belonging. This belonging creates momentum by allowing everyone to be a part of the team.

Achievement-oriented leadership focuses on setting challenging goals and standards of high performance, while expressing confidence in subordinate abilities.

Good leaders should have the ability to determine which leadership style or behavior is appropriate in a given situation. Unlike Fiedler's model, which suggests that leader behaviors cannot be changed, the path-goal theory suggests that leaders should be able to adapt different behaviors to different situations. A proper balance of leader behavior, based on a given situation, will lead to effective leadership.

The House path-goal theory led to the recognition that substitutes for leadership do exist.[25] These substitutes, which can decrease the need for a leader's involvement, are found in the characteristics of the work environment and the individuals involved. Substitutes for leadership include subordinate, task, and organizational characteristics. Subordinate characteristics include ability, experience, and independence. Task characteristics include regularity of tasks and the availability of feedback. Organizational characteristics include clear, concise plans and formal rules and procedures. When these substitutes for leadership are present, managers should not duplicate them but focus attention on more important things.

## Vroom-Jago Decision-Making Model

The Vroom-Jago model was developed to assist leaders in determining what method of decision making best fits the problem that is being confronted. Should the leader make a unilateral decision or involve a group, and to what extent should a group be involved?[26] The model's premise is based upon the amount of participation that subordinates have in decision-making. Through a series of questions, a determination can be made on the correct leadership style to be used for making a decision. There are five decision-making options that a leader can make, depending upon the outcome of the series of questions:

- Autocratic—the leader comes to a decision and communicates that decision to subordinates.
- Individual consultation—the leader shares the problem with subordinates, gathers input individually, and then makes the decision.
- Group consultation—the leader assembles the group, shares the problem, gathers input from all present, and then makes the decision.
- Facilitation—the leader assembles the group, shares the problems, and then facilitates discussion. After which, the group makes a decision.
- Delegation—the leader assembles a group and delegates the decision-making authority to the group to make a decision.

The decision-making style utilized is ascertained after the leader asks the following seven yes/no questions:

1. Is a good solution critical? (Is this a situation where having several equal options is not acceptable?)
2. Do subordinates and other team members have to accept the decision for it to work?
3. Is enough information available so that the leader can make a good decision on his or her own?
4. Are there clearly defined and recognized solutions to the problem?
5. Will the group accept the leader's decision?
6. Is disagreement likely among group members in reaching a decision?
7. Are group members and the leader working toward the same goals?

The validity of this model has not been proven, but it is consistent with empirical findings regarding situational leadership.

None of these decision-making methods is considered superior to the others. Leaders should identify the problem and situation at hand and apply one of the decision-making styles to make an effective decision. Organizations favor the leader-centered methods of decision making when the leader has the personal expertise to solve a problem, there is little time to make the decision, and others will accept the decision. Organizations prefer the subordinate-centered methods of decision making when the leader lacks the personal expertise to solve a problem, there is adequate time to make the decision, and acceptance of and commitment to the decision by subordinates is necessary.

## *Transformational vs. Transactional*

Transformational and transactional leadership are two very distinct paths that can ultimately determine the overall morale within an organization. The transformational method proves to be the more dynamic approach to leadership with a focus on individuals within the organization. This method attempts to go beyond the corporate goal of productivity to focus on the health of the organization, as well as the individual. Transformational leadership believes that by improving employees' quality of life, the organization will benefit in the long run. By focusing on the individual, each employee feels valued and knows that his or her contributions to the company matter, which causes them to work more efficiently for the company.

In contrast, the transactional method of leadership is more rigid. Workers are rewarded for their good work and chastised for sub-par performances. This method can be a motivator for greater production but does not necessarily persuade the employee to personally invest in the company. This greater production only continues as long as the employee feels obligated to complete his or her tasks. Organizations can demonstrate both methods of leadership by ensuring that the organization's vision is communicated to all within the organization, focusing on employee morale, and rewarding hard work.

In 1962, a small discount store opened in Rogers, Arkansas with the purpose of driving down prices paid by the consumer for everyday goods. The store was Wal-Mart, and the owner was Sam Walton. Wal-Mart has grown to be the nation's largest discount chain, overshadowing other discounters. By 1985, Sam Walton had achieved the title of America's Wealthiest Man. What set Walton apart was his ability to connect with individuals of differing backgrounds. Walton's vision of Wal-Mart was about others, not just himself. The following is a glimpse into what made Sam Walton such a transformational leader:

> We're all working together; that's the secret. And we'll lower the cost of living
> for everyone, not just in America, but we'll give the world an opportunity to
> see what it's like to save and have a better lifestyle, a better life for all. We're
> proud of what we've accomplished; we've just begun.[27]

A common trait of the transformational leader is charisma. A charismatic leader is able to paint the organization's picture of success and inspire followers to get there. This trait is essential for motivating employees.

The transformational leader is a leader who communicates a vision—the idea of giving employees something larger than themselves of which to be a part. The following are behaviors which are common among transformational leaders:

- Develop and share inspirational visions of the organization's future.
- Model exemplary, personal behaviors to bring out the best in subordinates.
- Show genuine concern and respect for others.
- Continual investment in both self-development and the development of others.
- Development of a collaborative culture; change is welcomed as an opportunity rather than a threat.
- Recognition that leadership is a trait that is not limited to managers but can be demonstrated by everyone involved in the organization.[28]

By contrast, the transactional leader utilizes multiple leadership models and applies those models in an organized fashion to achieve goals. "Transactional leaders . . . recognize subordinates' needs and wants and clarify how [those needs] will be satisfied . . . By changing leadership methods and approaches, to include adjusting tasks and locating rewards, one is implementing the transactional leadership model."[29]

These two leadership methods are drastically different. One method involves embracing change and investing in employees, while the other involves little change and rewarding employees only after they have earned it.

## Collins' Good to Great Concept on Leading

In *Good To Great*, Jim Collins discusses how normal, everyday companies transition to become hugely successful organizations.[30] Collins attempted to pinpoint the deciding factors in what causes organizations to turn from mediocrity to become standouts. Collins identifies five concepts that organizations must recognize and accept in order to achieve greatness:

- Level 5 Leadership—Leaders who operate at the level of greatness want the organization to continue successfully, even after that leader has departed. These leaders make the organization the focus rather than themselves.
- First Who, Then What—In Good to Great organizations, the leader builds a strategic team with the right people and then figures out how to obtain greatness.
- Confront the Brutal Facts—Great leaders accept brutal truths about the organization and work through those hard times until the organization can succeed.
- Hedgehog Concept—A leader cannot focus on the organization being the best; he or she must focus on doing what the organization does best.

- Building the Organization's Vision—Leaders of great companies recognize that although operating practices and business strategies may constantly change, the organization's core values must not change.[31]

"Every good-to-great company had Level 5 leadership during the pivotal transition years."[32] Level 5 leaders must balance a high level of personal humility with an intense will for the organization to succeed. When a leader is focused solely on personal ambition, the organization will be led with that goal in mind, leaving gaps in the strategic goals once that leader is gone. The Level 5 leader desires for the company to be successful long after he or she leaves, structuring and organizing its successor accordingly.

Those gifted with humility are not afraid of putting others first. It is sometimes difficult to spot those who practice genuine humility, because they never try to put themselves in the spotlight. When individual recognition is due, these leaders often pass it on to others around or below them, even though they themselves probably deserve it the most. When failures occur, the Level 5 leader looks inward first to find out what went wrong. The underlying principle characteristic of the Level 5 leader is "it's not about me." Instead, they lead to further the organization and make it successful.

Level 5 leaders are a study in duality: modest and willful, humble and fearless. To quickly grasp this concept, think of United States President Abraham Lincoln (one of the few Level 5 presidents in United States history), who never let his ego get in the way of his primary ambition for the larger cause of an enduring great nation. Yet those who mistook Mr. Lincoln's personal modesty, shy nature, and awkward manner as signs of weakness found themselves terribly mistaken, to the scale of 250,000 Confederate and 360,000 Union lives, including Lincoln's own.[33]

The concept of leading an organization goes far beyond the personal characteristics of the top individual. Those in leadership, no matter how good a leader they are, must at some point rely on others for assistance in guiding the organization:

The old adage "people are your most important asset" is wrong. People are not your most important asset. The right people are. . . . Whether someone is the "right person" has more to do with character traits and innate capabilities than with specific knowledge, background, or skills.[34]

Just placing people in seats is not an effective way of staffing an organization. An effective leader needs to find people that practice the utmost integrity and have a superb work ethic; to do otherwise would undermine the work of the leader, no matter how great. Individuals with adequate skills are not too difficult to find; however, individuals with adequate skills, who will put the organization above their own personal needs, require more searching.

## Servant Leadership

First proposed in the early 1970s by Robert Greenleaf, servant leadership "supports those who choose to serve first and then lead. . . . encourag[ing] collaboration, trust, foresight, listening, and the ethical use of power and empowerment."[35] Servant leadership is looking at leadership as stewardship rather than ownership.

Greenleaf believed that most organizations were performing below what was possible and believed it was because the leaders of those organizations had lost sight of their responsibility to serve others. The test of a servant leader is based upon the growth of his or her followers. Do those whom the leader serves "become healthier, wiser, freer, more autonomous, more likely themselves to become servants?"[36]

Greenleaf believed that servant leadership would be successful if organizations would restructure from the hierarchical format found in most organizations to an executive team lead by *primus inter pares* (first among equals). In such an organization, ultimate authority would rest with the board of directors, which would have to make an almost total commitment to the organization. Such a board would serve as a protection against abuses of power by an organization's executives.[37]

## Principle-Centered Leadership

Stephen Covey's leadership theory is based on the concept that "natural laws, based upon principles, operate regardless of our awareness of them or our obedience to them."[38] Success is built upon the principles of character, competency, and trust. These principles can only be changed from the inside out and those changes often come after breaks with traditional ways of thinking or paradigm shifts.

Principles are not based upon a person, organization or society, but are irrefutable truths that don't change and are practiced from the inside out on four levels:
- Personal – the relationship that one has with himself or herself.
- Interpersonal – the relationship and interactions that one has with others.
- Managerial – the responsibility one has to get a job done with and through others.
- Organizational – the responsibility to recruit, train, compensate, build teams, solve problems, and create aligned structure, strategy, and systems.[39]

Covey proposes eight characteristics of principle-centered leaders:
1. Continuously learning. They learn from others and their own experiences. They work to expand their competencies and knowledge through training, classes and development of new skills.

2.  Service-oriented.  They think of others and each day are prepared to serve others.  Principle-centered leaders understand the importance of service in their areas of stewardship.

3.  Radiate positive energy. Positive energy, exuded by principle-centered leaders, is viewed as an optimistic and upbeat attitude with an enthusiastic and believing spirit.  Those who exhibit this characteristic can neutralize the negative attitudes and spirits of others.

4.  Believe in others.  Rather than feel built-up when they notice a weakness in others, principle-centered leaders will choose to believe in the unseen potential and refuse to stereotype.  In addition, belief in others requires compassion and forgiveness of all offenses.  By believing, a leader is creating a climate that will promote opportunity and growth.

5.  Lead a balanced life. Principle-centered leaders read not only to keep up with current issues, but also for enjoyment.  In addition, they keep socially and physically active and take time to have fun.  Leading a balanced life precludes the need for name-dropping, materialism, titles, and bragging about past achievements.  These leaders are genuinely happy for the successes of others.

6.  Life is an adventure.  For a principle-centered leader, security comes from within; thus, their security comes from initiative, creativity, willpower, courage, stamina and resourcefulness.  Those who exhibit this principle are interested in others, ask questions, get involved, and are good listeners.

7.  Practice Synergy.  Synergy is when the whole is more than the sums of the parts.  A principle-centered leader is a change catalyst who improves any situation in which they are involved.  They work smart and hard and are productive.  Synergetic leaders easily delegate and when in a difficult situation can easily separate the person from the problem.

8.  Exercise for self-renewal.  The four dimensions of the human personality—physical, mental, emotional, and spiritual—are regularly exercised by principle-centered leaders.

## Change Leadership

In a never-ending pursuit for continual improvement—called kaizen by the Japanese—change must occur. Since leadership is about coping with change, leaders need to motivate and inspire subordinates to overcome the normal resistance to change.

Kurt Lewin described change as a three-step process; unfreezing, change, and refreezing.[40] Unfreezing is the stage in which management must overcome inertia and disassemble the existing attitudes, beliefs, and behaviors of the organization's workers. Leaders need to reduce barriers to change, and workers must be motivated to accept the change.

Workers are provided with the tools for change during the change step. Leaders should provide role models and training.

Refreezing involves integrating change into the work environment, which becomes the 'normal' way of doing things.

John Kotter has proposed eight steps to leading organizational change, which closely correspond with Lewin's three-step change process. [41]

Kotter's Steps for Successful Change

| | Steps to successful organizational change | |
|---|---|---|
| Unfreezing | Establish a sense of urgency | Create a compelling reason for the need for change. |
| | Create a guiding coalition | Cross-functional, cross-level groups are formed with members who have the power to lead change. |
| | Develop a vision and strategy | Creation of a vision and strategy will direct the change process. |
| | Communicate the vision for change | A communication strategy must be created and implemented to ensure the new vision and strategy are shared with all change stakeholders. |
| Change | Empower broad-based action | Eliminate all barriers to change, encourage risk taking and creative problem-solving. |
| | Generate short-term wins | Recognize and reward workers that are a factor in this step. |
| | Consolidate gains and produce more change | Credibility from short-term wins is utilized to create more change. |
| Refreezing | Anchor change in the organization's culture | Changes are reinforced. |

# Conclusion

A discussion of leadership involves not only an analysis of authority, power, and influence, but also the personal characteristics that lead to proper and effective decision making. Two defining traits of an effective leader are high ethical standards and the ability to hire and manage the right people. Leaders that lead with integrity assure the longevity of an organization, because their focus is on the welfare of the organization and its employees, not their own interests. The decisions are made with only the company's well-being in mind.

Many businesses suffer from blindness. Blindness is the inability to see what needs to be done for the welfare of the organization. An organization must find the right people and weed out those detrimental to the company.

## *Brief Summary of Major Points*

An individual in a leadership role must take responsibility for the organization by building relationships with employees. The nature of leadership not only involves the person but also must take into account the position, whether supervisory, managerial, etc. The type of leadership is dependent upon the position held, as well as the process that is being undertaken to express this leadership.

The effective leader must cast vision for an organization in such a way that employees feel the need to take on the vision and work to make the vision a reality. This type of motivation serves as an example of the type of power and influence that a leader must hold and exert over an employee. Of course, this influence must be exerted in an ethical manner, compliant with a defined code of ethics, by which a leader must abide.

Many different leadership styles can be found in an organization. The autocratic style employs a domineering approach to leadership that, when used correctly, can be effective if a good relationship exists between the leader and the subordinates. A democratic leader makes decisions based on the consensus of the team, which allows for open lines of communication. However, in this style of leadership, the leader must always keep the ultimate goal of the team in sight. Last, under the Laissez-faire form of leadership, the leader gives control to the group, which can either detract from efficiency or lead to empowerment, depending on the situation.

Some researchers have determined that effective leaders possess traits and skills that others do not have. These can include intelligence, maturity, integrity, and honesty. Other researchers propose that there are situational or environmental characteristics that determine whether a person will make a good leader. Whether these traits are inherited or gained through experience, many propose that certain traits are common among good leaders.

Since researchers have found that additional factors beyond a leader's natural traits impact the effectiveness of a leader, models were created to illustrate those theories. Fiedler's Contingency Model takes a leadership style and determines its effectiveness in various situations. The Hersey-Blanchard situational theory seeks to match leadership style with the maturity of the subordinates. The House path-goal theory matches the steps a manager should take to motivate subordinates with the characteristics and responsibilities of the subordinate. Finally, the Vroom-Jago decision-making model determines how leadership behavior and group participation relates to decision making.

The transformational leader provides vision while the transactional leader operates in the present.

In the book *Good to Great*, Collins attempts to pinpoint the deciding factor that causes good companies to turn from mediocrity to standouts among their competitors. The Level 5 Leader performs a balancing act by achieving a high level of personal humility, as well as an intense will for the organization to succeed.

## *Impact on the Organization, the Manager, and Employees*

An effective leader has a good understanding of vision, power, influence, and ethics. When a leader displays these qualities, an organization has the tools necessary to succeed, both in monetary terms and in employee goodwill. Results will include low employee turn-over, good communication, and an overall positive tone throughout the office environment.

When a manager exercises good leadership in an organization, both the organization and its employees benefit. When employees have a good leader, there is a sense of belonging, a sense of being understood, and the sense that he or she is working toward a worthy goal. Power and influence, correctly employed by a leader, can help direct employees to achieve the goals set before them.

The impact of leadership trickles down through the entire organization. When a leader exercises good leadership traits that are either inherited or learned, the employees will respond to this and work toward the goals set before them by the leader. When the leader and the employee are working together to meet a unified goal, success is attained.

# Endnotes

1   Stogdill, R.M. (1974). Handbook of leadership: A survey of the literature, New York: Free Press.

2   Bennis, W. (2000). *Managing People is Like Herding Cats.* Provo, Utah: Executive Excellence Publishing.

3   Kouzes, J. & Posner, B. (1987) The leadership challenge. 3rd ed. Jossey-Bass.

4   Vickrey, J. (n.d.). *Symbolic leadership: The symbolic nature of leadership.* Retrieved July 20, 2006, from http://www.au.af.mil/au/awc/awcgate/au-24/vickrey.pdf

5   Jones, G.R., & George, J.M. (2006). *Contemporary management* (4th ed.), p. 496. New York, New York: McGraw-Hill Irwin.

6   American Library Association. (2005). *Leadership and vision.* Retrieved July 19, 2006, from http://www.ala.org/ala/nmrtbucket/leadvision/leadvision.htm, ¶ 5

7   French, J. P. R. Jr., and Raven, B. (1960). The bases of social power. In D. Cartwright and A. Zander (eds.), *Group dynamics* (pp. 607-623). New York: Harper and Row.

8   Changing Minds.org Home Page. Retrieved October 11, 2006 from the World Wide Web: http://changingminds.org/explanations/power/french_and_raven.htm

9   Cornett, Z.J., & Thomas, J.W. (1995). *Integrity as professionalism: Ethics and leadership in practice.* Retrieved July 26, 2006, from http://www.fs.fed.us/eco/eco-watch/ew960123.htm, ¶ 36

10  Ibid, p. 1.

11  Wuorio, J. (n.d.) Put it in writing: Your business has ethics. Retrieved October 13, 2006 from the World Wide Web: http://www.microsoft.com/smallbusiness/resources/management/leadership_training/put_it_in_writing_your_business_has_ethics.mspx

12  Ibid.

13  Ethics and compliance officer association home page. Retrieved from the World Wide Web on October 13, 2006 at: http://www.theecoa.org/

14  Sundvick, H. Ethics and Spirituality in the Workplace Conference, February 2006. http://www.yale.edu/faith/esw/business_conference.htm

15  Ibid.

16  White, R. & Lippitt, R. (1960). Autocracy and democracy: An experimental inquiry. New York: Harper & Brothers.

17  Kirkpatrick, S.A. & Locke, E.A. (1991). Leadership: Do traits really matter? Academy of Management Eecutive, 5, (2) pp 48-60.

18  Likert, R. (1961). New Patterns of Management. New York: Mc-Graw Hill.; and Likert, R. (1967). The Human Organization. New York: Mc-Graw Hill.

19  Schriesman, C.A. & Bird, B.J. (1979). Contributions of the Ohio state studies to the field of leadership. Journal of Management, 5 (2). pp. 135-145.; and Shartle, C.L. (1979). Early years of the Ohio state university leadership studies. Journal of Management, 5, (2) pp. 127 - 134.

20  Fiedler, F.E. (1954). Assumed similarity measures as predictors of team effectiveness. Journal of Abnormal Psychology, 49, (3). pp. 381- 388.

21  Schermerhorn, Jr., J.R. (!997). Situational leadership: Conversations with Paul Heresy. Mid-American Journal of Business, 12, (2). pp. 5 – 12. Retrieved from http://www.bsu.edu/web/majb/

22  Hersey, P. & Blanchard, K.H. (1988). Management and Organizational Behavior. Englewood Cliffs, NJ: Prentice-Hall.

23  Schermerhorn, Jr., J.R. (1997). Situational leadership: Conversations with Paul Heresy. Mid-American Journal of Business, 12, (2). p. 6. Retrieved from http://www.bsu.edu/web/majb/

24  House, R.J. (1971). A path-goal theory of leader effectiveness. Administrative Science Quarterly, 16, (3). p. 321, 19p.

25  Howell, J.P. & Dorfman, P.W. (1986). Leadership and substitutes for leadership among professional and nonprofessional workers. Journal of Applied Behavioral Science, 22. pp. 29-46.

26  Vroom, V. H. & Jago, A. G. (1988). The new leadership: Managing participation in organizations. Englewood Cliffs, NJ: Prentice-Hall.

27  Scott, R.V. & S.S. Vance. (1994). Wal-Mart: A History of Sam Walton's Retail Phenomenon. New York: Twayne.

28  Banger, A. (2005). *Transformational Leadership*. Retrieved August 9, 2006, from http://www.teamtechnology.co.uk/transformational-leadership.html

29  Bass, B.M. (1985). Leadership: Good, better, best. Organizational Dynamics, 13, (3), pp. 26-40, 15p.

30  Collins, J. (2001). *Good to Great*. New York: HarperCollins.

31  Collins, J. (2006). *Laboratory: Leadership*. Retrieved August 9, 2006, from http://www.jimcollins.com/lab/buildingVision/index.html, p. 1.

32  Collins, J. (2001). *Good to Great*. New York: HarperCollins. p. 39.

33  Collins, J. (2006). *Laboratory: Leadership*. Retrieved August 9, 2006, from http://www.jimcollins.com/lab/level5/p2.html#, p. 1.

34  Ibid.

35  Greenleaf Center for Servant Leadership Home page. (n.d.). Retrieved from the World Wide Web on October 14, 2006: http://www.greenleaf.org/leadership/servant-leadership/What-is-Servant-Leadership.html

36  Ibid.

37  Greenleaf, R.K. (1977). Servant leadership. New York: Paulist.

38  Covey, S. (1991) Principle-centered leadership. New York: Simon & Schuester. p. 17.

39  Ibid, p. 31.

40  Lewin, K. (1951). *Field Theory in Social Science*, Harper and Row, New York.

41  Kotter, J.P. (1996). Leading change. Boston, MA. Harvard Business School Press.

# CHAPTER 5 — Effective Communication

## MEASURABLE LEARNING OBJECTIVES

1. Identify the elements of interpersonal communications.

2. Summarize the communication process.

3. Identify the different issues within the communication process.

4. Summarize how to make a professional presentation.

5. Discuss the proper way to run a professional business meeting.

6. Explain proper business protocol as it relates to office etiquette, the rumor mill, office politics, dress codes, office layout, proxemics.

7. Distinguish between formal and informal office norms.

# Interpersonal Communication

Communication is a process that is vital to transmitting and understanding information.[1] It is the means by which information, in the form of verbal or non-verbal cues, is transmitted via an encoded message by a sender to a receiver who fully understands. Essentially, interpersonal communication refers to communication between a speaker and listener. "Interpersonal communication is defined as person-to-person conversation; it's an exchange that occurs through dialogue between two people or through discussion among several, with participation by everyone involved."[2] In order for interpersonal communication to exist, the essential elements of communication must be present.

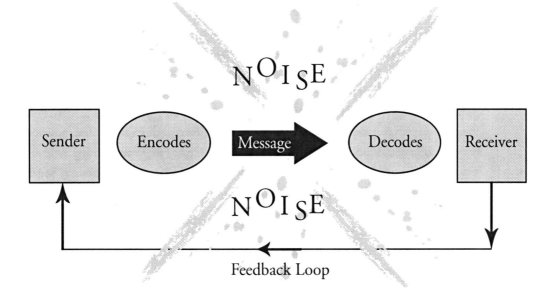

## Communication Process—Sender, Receiver, Meaning, Encoding, Message Transmittal, Channel, Decoding, Interpreting, Feedback

The first component of the communication process is the sender. The sender has to be aware of the desired meaning of a message and to whom the message is being sent, prior to encoding the message and transmitting the message through a chosen channel. The sender may choose to speak, write, or utilize gestures as a means of transmitting or sending a message.[3]

A sender encodes information into meaningful verbal and/or nonverbal symbols that will be understood by the receiver. The message is then sent through a communication channel to the receiver who interprets the meaning of the message, which may or may not match the sender's intended message. Feedback is the process whereby the receiver returns the message to the sender to ensure proper decoding. A person can communicate a message in three ways: oral, written, and nonverbal.

Oral communication is the primary method of conveying messages because of the quick feedback. In an informal setting, oral communication is usually chosen for one-on-one encounters and gatherings of teams. In contrast, formal settings, such as performance appraisals or employee handbooks, require oral communication to be accompanied by written communication to ensure that each person receives the same message and is able to confirm the message's receipt. Formal written communication is tangible and should be verifiable—well thought out, logical, and clear. Non-verbal communication may reflect emotion and is not as clear as written or oral communication. Non-verbal cues may include body movements (kinesics), physical distance (proxemics), facial expressions, and voice intonations. Channels used to convey messages include the spoken word, written word, symbolic gestures, visual images, and multimedia.

Using previous experiences with and knowledge of the receiver helps the sender determine how to encode the message and the channel necessary to convey the message. The sender chooses the channel that will be most receptive to the receiver. The channel needs to be free of any noise that might distract the receiver. The clarity of the message, based on feedback from the receiver, determines the effectiveness of the chosen channel.

Once the message is acquired, the receiver decodes the message. Decoding is interpretation of the message. Feedback is the final step in the communication process and determines how successful the sender was in transferring the message as originally intended. A receiver might misunderstand a message for many reasons. Those reasons are often referred to as barriers to or issues in effective interpersonal communication.

## *Barriers to Communication*

Because of barriers in the communication process, achieving clarity in inter-personal communication is a challenge to both the sender and the receiver of a message. In order to achieve clarity, the sender must be clear in his or her mind regarding the idea to be communicated, deliver the message succinctly, and ensure that the message has been correctly understood.[4] The sender must also be aware of the receiver's background. The sender can think that a message was clear and concise, but the receiver can think otherwise. As a sender considers ways of communicating effectively, he or she must examine issues that prevent clarity.

### *Noise*

Both the sender and receiver must utilize skill and effort in the two-way communication process. Noise is anything that causes interference in a message's true intent and interferes with effective communication.[5] Noise can include physical distraction, being hard of hearing, or having poor eyesight. For example, two people may be in a restaurant having a dialogue. As they are conversing, the waitress begins to ask questions, other restaurant patrons are talking loudly, and the manager makes an announcement over the intercom. In each case, these noises are likely to distract the two people having the dialogue, causing them to misinterpret the original intent of the messages being transmitted.

Another example of noise is interruptions. Interruptions stop the flow of conversation and may cause the communication to lose focus. Interruptions shift the focus of a conversation. Parents who try to engage in conversation with another adult may find themselves interrupted by a toddler desiring attention.

Noise can also occur in the medium chosen for the message transmittal. Communication sent via email may be difficult to decipher because such communication is usually written and sent without much thought. The sentence structure, words chosen, or absence of punctuation or capitalization may cause the receiver to misinterpret the sender's intended meaning.

### *One-Way vs. Two-Way*

Without sufficient feedback in the communication process, a message will not be very clear. Interpersonal communication is a dialogue—not a monologue. One-way communication creates a barrier because it lacks feedback to ensure the recipient received the intended message. Though one-way communication is fast and non-threatening, it has a very high probability of being misunderstood. Two way communication requires more time, but it fulfills the requirements of the communication process.

### Perception

Perception affects the transference and understanding of a message's meaning. In a conversation, each person has a set of wants, needs, and attitudes that can distort the original intent of a message. The sender may have wants, needs, and attitudes that favor offering a job to a certain applicant; however, the receiver, who has different wants, needs, and attitudes may oppose the job offer. How does the advocate convey a message that persuades the adversary to change positions on the issue?

Beliefs, personalities, emotions, values, and other personal characteristics also affect the sender's encoding or the receiver's decoding of a message. Beliefs have a profound affect on perception. Each person in a conversation makes inferences based upon his or her belief system. Personality can affect the sender's or receiver's perception of a message. An optimist is likely to view a message from a positive aspect, while a pessimist will likely interpret a message with skepticism.

Perception can be observed in a person's emotional state. Emotional responses indicate the receptiveness of the sender's message. How the receiver feels at the time of communication will influence how he or she interprets the message.

In a typical conversation, the difference in individual values may lead the sender to place a higher level of importance on a decision than the receiver. The decision may be concerning employee pay raises. The sender tries to convey the message that raises need to reflect a cost of living raise as well as a length of service raise. The receiver may have a difficult time understanding the importance of including both types of raises in the budget proposal. The sender and receiver clearly have their values prioritized differently.

### Filtering

Filtering is "a sender's purposely manipulating information so that the receiver will see the information more favorably."[6] Filtering allows a sender to select which information to encode and is able to dictate what is received by controlling the message sent.

Filtering is a major issue in the business community. Important information can be purposefully left out of a conversation so that the receiver can view the sender favorably. A manager requests a written report from a work group; the group selects a writer who can write the report in a believable and favorable way. However, unfavorable news may be hidden in the details.

*Non-Verbal*

"Verbal communication consists of sharing thoughts through the meanings of words, while nonverbal communication shares thoughts through all other means."[7] Nonverbal communication includes any form of expression that does not utilize written or spoken words. Body language is the most common form of nonverbal communication, but all senses can be utilized for non-verbal communication.

Attentiveness of the receiver or the sender when communicating in person is determined by the distance between the two and may also be indicated by direct eye contact. Communication norms, such as the desirability of eye contact or the acceptable distance between sender and receiver, are determined by cultural norms. A person from the southern part of the U.S. will smile at a stranger with the tacit understanding that the smile be interpreted as being friendly. Northerners, in contrast, will smile in private social settings but may become suspicious of a cordial smile in public.

Body posture is one form of nonverbal communication that can indicate the emotional state of a sender or receiver. The body posture can be displayed as sitting erectly versus slouching in a chair. Sitting erectly is translated as showing interest in the topic being discussed. Slouching in a chair can be interpreted as having no interest and may be perceived as rudeness.

Hand movements are a form of nonverbal communication that can have multiple meanings. When a sender makes the "V" sign with the fingers, the receiver may think that the "V" stands for peace or victory. The correct interpretation depends upon the traditions of the host country where the "V" is used. For an American, the "V" stands for peace, while the European knows the "V" stands for victory.

Nonverbal language is not limited to eye contact, standing position, facial expressions, body posture, hand movements, or mannerisms. Nonverbal language includes squirms, gestures, tone of voice, puffs, whistles, and such vocalized non-words (*segregates*) as the "mm" response to somebody's troubles or "mm-*mm!*" over a bowl of steaming gumbo.[8] In the example of the vocalized response to somebody's troubles, the receiver's tone will be quite different from the tone vocalized in response to a good meal. The same words were used in both examples, but the message was different.

Research purports that up to 70 percent of communication may be based upon gestures alone.[9] Since gestures are not part of the electronic communication process, care must be taken to write electronic messages in a clear, concise manner—so that errors in decoding the message will not take place.

*Mixed Messages*

Mixed messages occur when the sender says one thing, but actions, body language, or personal appearance communicate another. In a meeting, a person who does not agree with the discussion may cross her arms over her chest. One who is fighting with a coworker may sit next to him or her but lean in the opposite direction. Nonverbal messages alert others that the verbal message has not been received warmly or positively, transmitting a strong message in itself.

## *Professional Presentations*

Over a million business presentations are given every day.[10] Business leaders use presentations to communicate to colleagues, customers, and stakeholders in an effort to clearly convey relevant information. The clarity and delivery of a presentation is instrumental in determining whether the audience is able to connect with the speaker and understand the information presented. For the sales and marketing professional, the presentation is an extension of the product's package and can make or break a sale.

For millions of American managers, the thought of giving a presentation can invoke fear and anxiety. Surveys consistently show that the fear of public speaking is one of the top phobias in the US.[11]

A recent online poll of 382 executives found that over half of the respondents gave one or more presentations per month. Of those respondents, 36 percent found presenting data to the board or senior management tedious, with a further 24 percent stating that they dread it each time it comes around.[12] To ease fears of public speaking, managers benefit from practicing a presentation.

In *The Shortcut to Persuasive Presentations*, the words of Pericles 2,500 years ago are quoted: "A person who can think but cannot express what he thinks, places himself at the level of the person who cannot think."[13] Are the qualities that make an individual a dynamic speaker in-born traits? While it is true that some personality types are more comfortable with public speaking, almost all speakers experience a certain degree of apprehension prior to addressing a group. Any manager can improve his or her presentation skills and ability to captivate an audience with the proper knowledge and preparation.

While many models provide detailed guidance for developing and giving a successful presentation, each model adheres to some common tenets. The common tenets include strategy, substance, structure, style, support, and supplement—each of which is important in conveying the message. Proper use of each principle will ensure that the speaker effectively communicates the intended message. Understanding the basic tenets is vital to developing a successful presentation.[14]

## Strategy

A specific communication strategy should be devised for each audience to whom a topic is presented. One should know the makeup of the individuals in the audience and prepare the presentation to match their level of knowledge on the subject matter. The use of technical jargon or complex data will only confuse an audience not familiar with the lingo.

Detailed planning and preparation is crucial. Individuals must identify the theme or main point and spend a considerable amount of effort preparing the presentation. The intent of the presentation could be to provide information, offer various alternatives, or provide a solution to a problem. A successful strategy engages the audience, persuading them to accept the main point.

## Substance

Substance consists of the speaker's knowledge of the subject matter being presented. A speaker can ensure that he understands all facets of a subject and is ready to respond to the audience's questions by utilizing what some speakers refer to as "murder board."[15] The purpose of the murder board is to ensure the presenter can answer probing questions regarding the subject matter. The presenter lists all potential questions about the topic and composes, then practices a response to each. The rehearsal allows the presenter to gain confidence by proactively anticipating tough questions.

## Structure

A presentation must be structured so that the topic is presented in such a manner that allows the audience to logically follow the speaker's message. A presenter should always adhere to the cliché—yet proverbial presentation truth: begin by introducing what you are going to tell them, tell them; and conclude by telling them what you told them. The format should be sequential, logical, and allow the audience to stay focused on the main topic at hand.

## Style

"Style, the passion and [energy] of the speaker, includes the use of [symbolic] devices . . . voice inflection . . . eye contact . . . and positive body language."[16] Style is the art of public speaking. Video recording a rehearsal presentation can help a speaker practice and develop the fundamentals involved in style. Since audiences tend to listen to a speaker with whom they are comfortable and connect, one must recognize that style can be as important as substance.

### Support

A speaker must support his presentation with accurate data. One should never play with the facts, because a presenter's credibility will be at risk. Once credibility is lost, the audience will no longer be interested in what the presenter has to say. Visual aids, such as a well-constructed PowerPoint slideshow or an old-fashioned butcher board, can be instrumental in allowing the presenter to disseminate relevant, accurate data.

Significant evidence suggests that people retain more data visually than audibly. According to the Department of Labor's OSHA website, "Three days after an event, people retain 10% of what they heard from an oral presentation, 35% from a visual presentation, and 65% from a visual and oral presentation."[17] However, care must be taken that the visual aids are appropriate to the audience; faulty visual aids which are too flashy, illegible, or inappropriate will distract from the presenter's message.

### Supplement

Finally, the speaker should supplement the message by providing informed responses that support the ideas presented. At the end of each presentation, Apple CEO Steve Jobs adds to the drama by stating the following:

"And one more thing." He then adds a new product, new feature, or sometimes introduces a band. He approaches each presentation as an event, a production with a strong opening, product demonstration in the middle, a strong conclusion, and an encore–that "one more thing!"[18]

### Presentation Taboos

Managers are often evaluated based upon their skill at giving effective presentations. Most managers learn through experience the skills required to stand in front of a group of people and communicate a message. A good starting point is an understanding of what should be avoided. Ten things must be avoided when giving a presentation:

1. Reading from notes.
2. Not making eye contact.

3.  Dressing down—dress like a leader, and a little bit better than everyone else.

4.  Swaying back and forth, jiggling coins, and fidgeting with your hands.

5.  Failure to rehearse.

6.  Standing at attention.

7.  Reciting bullet points.

8.  Speaking too long.

9.  Failing to grab the audience's attention.

10. Ending on a flat note. Presentations should not end with an inspiration deficit; the attendees should be prepared to act on the points given in the presentation.[19]

## *The Perfect Presentation*

Now that the reader has been given a list of what not to do, several things should be included in a great presentation. The following is a step by step guide for putting together an effective presentation:[20]

1.  Incite, don't inform. Effective presentations end with the audience taking action. It is the presenter's responsibility to convince them to act.

2.  Don't talk to strangers. "You should know as much as you can about those to whom you're speaking. . . .What are their expectations? Where are they positioned on the issue? What is their knowledge level? What are their demographics and cultures?[21]

3.  First and last impressions are everything. The audience is going to remember the first thirty and last fifteen seconds of a presentation and determine within that first 30 seconds if they are going to pay attention to the speaker. A presenter can also create positive feelings by finishing the presentation early.

4.  Simpler is better. "Too many presentations are too long, too slick, and too convoluted. . . .[Consensus says] to make . . . presentations shorter and more candid."[22]

5.  Perform, don't present. In a typical presentation, the audience will be influenced by how you look (55 percent), how you talk (38 percent), and what you say (7 percent). If you look and speak with authority and knowledge, the audience will listen to what you have to say.

6.  The show must go on. Because so much technology is involved in presentations, ensure that a back-up plan exists. If the projector bulb burns out and cannot be replaced, alternative plans should be in place, allowing the presentation to proceed.

7.  One exists in every crowd; how should a hostile audience member be handled? One suggestion is to answer the question, "but don't address the questioner directly—speak to the entire audience instead."[23]

8.  Practice. As with most other things, the only way to improve presentation skills is to practice. Practice can take place in front of coworkers or recording for later review and assessment. One should practice new presentations a minimum of six times—even previous presentations should be practiced twice prior to the event.

## Meetings

People in most organizations view meetings from a negative viewpoint. This reaction is partly the result of personal experiences with poorly planned, misdirected, or poorly executed meetings. In today's workforce, no one has time to waste, but according to recent studies, "the average number of meetings at work more than doubled in the second half of the 20th century, and time spent in meetings keeps growing."[24]

However, Google appears to have perfected the science of meetings. Marissa Mayer, vice-president of search products for Google, holds over seventy meetings a week and acknowledges that the structure of her meetings has lead to some innovative advances in technology.[25] Mayer believes in six keys to running a successful meeting:

1.  Set an agenda that outlines what will be discussed and makes the optimal use of the allotted time. An agenda serves to focus the participants on what they wish to achieve in a meeting.

2.  Appoint a note taker. "A Google meeting features a lot of displays. On one wall a projector displays the presentation, while right next to it, another projector shows the transcription of the meeting. . . . An official set of notes [captures] inaccuracies and inconsistencies . . . immediately."[26] Transcribed notes are sent to those who missed the meeting, allowing attendees to review notes to determine what actions were assigned or what decisions were made.

3.  Carve out micro-meetings. Mayer reserves large blocks in her schedule—from which she carves short meetings. Google staff can schedule a ten-minute "micro-meeting" almost immediately, instead of having to wait weeks for the next thirty-minute opening.

4.  Hold office hours. Every day, beginning at 4:00 p.m. and lasting for ninety minutes, Mayer holds office hours. Employees can schedule an appointment by adding their name to a board that sits outside her office—on a first-come, first-serve basis. Mayer averages seven minutes per employee, but Google

News, Google Reviews, and Google Desktop were all pitches first made during these office hours.

5.  Discourage politics, use data. Ideas, designs, or projects chosen should be assessed using a metrics. The option chosen should be based upon how well it performs on those metrics. Decisions should be made based upon evidence, not relationships.

6.  Stick to the clock. "Google gatherings often feature a giant timer on the wall, counting down the minutes left for a particular meeting or topic. . . .[It] runs off a computer that is projected to be 4 feet tall."[27] Keeping a schedule proves very important, but the schedule must be utilized with great care.

While these guidelines may not be appropriate in all situations, they may be a starting point for transforming meetings normally considered a waste of time, compared to productive, effective meetings that benefit the organization.

An effective meeting requires strong leadership to ensure that the agenda is addressed and attendees focus on making productive plans, which will result in action and advancement of the organization's goals. The following reveal some guidelines for strong meeting leadership:

•   Begin meetings on time. When attendees know that a meeting will not start promptly, they will begin showing up late. Such tardiness leads to the start time of each meeting being pushed back, while everyone waits for the late arrivals. All attendees should be extremely prompt for meetings. Since showing up late shows a lack of responsibility and respect, no one should be allowed to enter after the meeting begins.

•   The entire agenda should be covered prior to discussing any new business. However, the leader should insured that issues raised will be addressed at the next meeting.

•   A meeting should never be dominated by one attendee; therefore, inputs from all participants must be encouraged. The leader must watch for discussions that are off-topic and redirect conversations back to the subject at hand.[28]

In addition to meeting leaders, meeting participants also have responsibilities. Before speaking, a participant should ask himself or herself if the comment contributes to the understanding of an issue and if the comment is relevant. If one answers "no" to those questions, then the attendee should continue to listen to the discussion without interjection.

Successful meetings are structured events. A meeting should be called for a defined objective and allow for resolution of routine matters and a quick address of the agenda. The roles of all meeting participants should be clearly spelled out prior to the meeting and should, at a minimum, include a leader, recorder, and timekeeper. A meeting outline should assign the amount of time that will be spent on each agenda item. "During the course of the meeting the leader should insure that everyone precedes through the agenda items, summarizing agreed on action items and decisions as they are made."[29] At the end of the meeting, the leader should summarize the agenda, make plans for follow up meetings, and thank all attendees for their participation.

# Business Etiquette

Business protocol is a major aspect of today's corporate world. Business leaders are expected to fully understand office etiquette, email etiquette, etiquette utilized in dining, and etiquette utilized in meeting business contacts outside of an office setting. Business etiquette ranges from how early to arrive for a business appointment to the appropriate ways to utilize email.

## *Email Etiquette*

Electronic communication has become an excellent way to correspond with those both inside and outside of one's organization; however, one must be cautious about how email is utilized. "People who are not familiar with email etiquette risk alienating potential clients and customers."[30] A breach of etiquette occurs when one hits the "reply all" function when they should have hit the "reply" function. This sends the email to everyone—even those who should not have received it or did not need to receive it. Another breach of email etiquette is attaching documents to email; such attachments can carry computer viruses that infect the recipient's computer. Therefore, make sure others are willing to accept attachments prior to actually sending them.

One should keep the following general guidelines in mind when using email:[31]

1. Include a subject line with your messages. This allows the recipient to know that the email is not junk mail. Sending out an email without a subject line shows lack of respect for your recipient's time.
2. Check and double check the intended recipient's address before you click on send. You do not want to risk sending an email to the wrong person.
3. NEVER WRITE IN ALL CAPS. This makes your message difficult to read. In cyber world, this is tantamount to screaming at the recipient.
4. Never forward a "chain-letter" email, which is never appropriate in an office environment.

5.  Don't expect immediate replies to an email.  Don't send an announcement for a meeting to be held at 3:00 pm at noon the same day.  Someone may be out of the office for the afternoon or in a meeting.

6.  Never send email when you are angry.  Once you send the message you can never get it back.  While writing down your thoughts may be therapeutic, sending these thoughts can be a disaster.

7.  Be cautious when using sarcasm and humor.  Without facial expressions and tone of voice, they do not translate easily through email.

8.  Write well, using proper grammar and punctuation.

## *Phone Etiquette*

Phone etiquette is very important for a leader's image. The ubiquitous nature of cell phones has made understanding etiquette especially important.  However tempting, cell phone calls should never be answered during a meeting, whether that meeting is with a boss, a subordinate, a peer, or a group. This also holds true for text messages, which should not be read or answered when meeting with an individual or a group—whether a client(s), boss(es), or subordinate(s).  Such interruption not only distracts the person who received the call but implicates that the person on the phone is more important than the person(s) present.

A great tool that comes with most phones is the ability to put someone on "speaker."  The speaker function allows one to have both hands free to comb through papers or type notes.  However, managers must take care that speakerphones are not utilized unless everyone near the phone is participating in the phone call. In this case, the person(s) at the other end of the call should be notified that they are on the speaker, and those present should introduce themselves.

## *Dining Etiquette*

Dining with business associates is an important part of the business culture.  It is important to follow proper etiquette while dining with business associates. Approximately "half of all business transactions are finalized over a meal."[32]  Etiquette for business dining includes all of the basic, straightforward table manners, such as not speaking with a full mouth and not waving utensils around to emphasize a point.  In addition to knowing what fork to use and when, business dining requires one to understand that he or she is still in a business environment and should act appropriately:

- Never ask for a doggy bag when a guest at a business meal; taking home leftovers should be saved for informal situations.
- Since drinking too much is one of the most disliked behaviors, do not order alcoholic beverages.
- Do not smoke.
- Do not season food before tasting—many view this as making a decision prior to having accurate information.[33]

## Office Etiquette

In a competitive work environment, understanding and practicing good office etiquette can lead to professional and personal success. Office etiquette has changed in recent years because most offices now have shared office spaces, shared copiers, and staff kitchens—to store and heat meals. In addition, an office is no longer populated by traditional nine-to-five workers because of flex-time, part-time, and contract workers. Therefore, office etiquette allows everyone to work in a congenial environment.

- When fixing a meal, think twice about foods that have strong odors—remember coworkers will have to smell that meal all afternoon.
- If choosing food for a meeting, offer healthy options for those who may be trying to cut back on sugar, fat, or salt.
- One should always clean up a meeting room or the kitchen after using the facilities.
- While cubicles allow easy access, don't borrow from other people without asking for permission.
- Play music on headphones—musical tastes vary too much to assume that everyone will want to hear a personal collection of bluegrass CD's.
- Visual privacy afforded by a cubicle does not mean that all habits are secret. Do not practice personal hygiene in a personal office space.
- Fill the copy machine with paper when making a lot of copies.[34]

## Introductions

When one introduces himself or herself or is being introduced by a coworker, he or she should project self confidence, friendliness, and interest. Handshakes should be firm, and one should look into the eyes of the person being introduced and smile.

The protocol for introductions is that the person to whom someone is introduced will be older or more senior in rank than the person being introduced. Introduce a junior employee to a senior employee or manager and introduce a fellow employee to a client. Do not use first names unless the person to whom one is being introduced suggests it.[35]

## Rumor Mill

The rumor mill, an informal channel of communication, is inevitable in an office environment of three or more people. "Rumors are totally natural. . . . It is the group trying to make sense of something that is important to them."[36] When employees produce a lot of rumors, it is an indication that leaders need to regularly explain company actions—and not just when major changes occur. If a rumor is circulating that is correct (most of them are), then leaders need to present the facts. This courtesy should be given especially in the case of imminent layoffs.

## Office Politics

Success in the work environment and the resulting promotion up an organization's ranks is dependent upon how well a job is done and how well one gets along with colleagues. "When people talk about office politics, they usually mean something dirty or underhanded. . . . But nobody exists in an atmosphere where everybody agrees. Politics is the art of trying to accomplish things within organizations."[37]

> Many people believe the end always justifies the means—and they'll do anything to win the prize—while the rest of us wrestle with the trade-offs. We view politics as conniving end-runs and backroom deals perpetrated by power hungry self-promoters willing to step on anyone to get ahead.[38]

Organizational politics don't have to be negative; they are a means by which things get accomplished. Since approximately 80 percent of the grapevine is business related, one should always be alert to the rumor mill but not believe everything that is said.[39] The following points reveal the five ways to utilize office politics in an ethical manner:[40]

1. Set up win–win situations. Rather than the best idea, it is most often the best packaged idea that is chosen. Political skills involves, "pulling people toward your ideas and then pushing those ideas through to other people. . . . It comes down to personality and positioning."[41]

2. Ask for opinions, but be ready to change them, because you cannot change someone's mind if you don't know their opinion on a matter. You can also create a groundswell of support as you are testing ideas.

3.  All favors are personal, and most people expect reciprocity. Your budget may not be large, but even people who work in small departments have "currencies" with which they can barter. Given the opportunity, most people want to back projects that support the organization's mission and goals. Building relationships with others who want to make a difference and a chance to earn recognition is a great way to recruit project supporters. Share credit and be sure to thank supporters, and the relationships will extend beyond the current project.

4.  Some can view success as a threat and become the opposition. Success may bring extra work to some, or the high profile of the one leading the project may threaten those not involved. One must be prepared for opposition—communicate openly and be prepared for creative input from others.

5.  Develop a strategy for success. Once the work is done to complete a project, it should be understood what resources will be needed for the project to continue.

Politics are more likely to surface when an organization's resources are declining and/or changing and when opportunities arise for promotions. When organizations downsize to improve efficiency, people tend to engage in political actions to safeguard their territories. When promotion time comes around, the evaluation period encourages employees to compete for limited resources and to try to positively influence the outcome of the decision. Leaders can work to decrease negative politicking by ensuring that a high level of trust exists between subordinates and management. If subordinates know that leaders will do the right thing, political maneuvering in an organization will decrease.

*Norms*

While almost every large company has a written code of ethics, often the real ethical fabric of a company can be measured by the unwritten rules in the form of norms. Norms define the limitations of acceptable and unacceptable behaviors and are the standards by which the appropriateness of behaviors, beliefs, perceptions, and feelings are measured. Relevance of a norm is determined independently within each organization."[42] Groups tend to enforce norms for four different reasons:[43]

•   The first reason norms are enforced is to facilitate group survival. It may be the norm not to discuss internal problems of the group with outsiders because that information could be utilized against the group at a later date.

•   Groups use norms to clarify member behavior. In a meeting where a proposal is given, do group members really want feedback or is the presenter merely going through the motions?

- Norms are used so that group members avoid embarrassing situations. The norms in such a case would include not discussing romantic involvements or dominating a discussion.
- Norms expand on what is unique about a group and are enforced to show the strength of a group.

Just because a group behavior is the norm does not mean that the behavior is in the best interest of the organization. One of the toughest challenges for a leader is to determine which norms within the organization are positive and which ones are negative. Positive norms should be reinforced, yet negative norms must be identified and changed. A manager must understand group dynamics to determine why certain norms exist. A norm on a factory floor may be to only produce goods at a certain rate—even though the technology is available and the skill of the worker would allow production at a much faster rate. A leader must identify informal leaders and communicate effectively the objectives of the company or the work unit. In many instances, a policy or procedure may be misunderstood, requiring the manager to provide insight into the policy's intended purpose.

## Groupthink

First identified by Irvin Janis, groupthink takes place when a group's "strivings for unanimity override their motivation to realistically appraise alternative courses of action."[44] Symptoms of groupthink manifest in three different ways: overestimation of the group's power, closed-mindedness, and pressure toward uniformity. The more the symptoms are manifested, the worse the quality of the decision that is made.

One of the worst cases of groupthink was the decision to launch the Challenger from Kennedy Space Center in January 1986.[45] Even though engineers had warned that the flight was risky, the decision-makers ignored the warnings and allowed the mission to continue. Groupthink can occur in eight specific ways:[46]

1. An illusion of invulnerability. If it has always worked in the past, it will surely work this time—a strong, optimistic belief that "we never fail."
2. An unquestioned belief in the group's inherent morality—even if that morality has shifted. Group members believe in the "rightness" of their cause and may ignore the moral or ethical consequences of their decisions.
3. Collective efforts to rationalize in order to discount warnings. No one will introduce information that may go against the group's rationalizing efforts because they may be ostracized as a result.

4. <u>Stereotyped views of the opposition</u>. Group members may look down upon those outside of the group as unintelligent because they are providing information contrary to the beliefs held by group members.

5. <u>Self-censorship</u>. Group members may offer opinions rather than make strong recommendations that are against the group consensus.

6. <u>A shared illusion of unanimity</u>. Silence may be interpreted to mean agreement.

7. <u>Direct pressure on any member who expresses strong disagreement</u>. Pressure may be put on those who dissent directly through threats of job loss or indirectly through group pressure. It is believed that dissent would never come from a loyal group member.

8. <u>Emergence of self-appointed mindguards</u>. These are members who work to prevent anyone within the group from hearing information that may disrupt the group's complacency regarding their decision-making process.

### Dress Codes

In the past, dress codes for work were more basic and predictable—men wore three-piece suits and women wore skirts. Today, work attire has become more casual and relaxed, causing many companies to enforce a dress code to prevent employees from dressing inappropriately, or in some cases, to ensure the safety of the worker. Although clothing policies have become more casual in many work settings, the casual dress for work seems to be less exhibited in office environments. In a BizRate study conducted in 2005, researchers found that only 26 percent of office employers allowed casual apparel to be worn at work.[47]

Even unexpected organizations, like the NBA, have begun requiring a dress code to present a more professional image. Business casual has become a very popular trend. In these places of business, women wear dresses, skirts, and slacks, and men wear khakis and long-sleeved shirts—with or without a tie. Businesses with established dress codes often have a policy where employees are expected to dress in an appropriate manner. This policy, however, can have a wide range of meanings and can be read differently by different workers. Opinions of what is meant by appropriate dress can lead to accusations of gender or religious discrimination. For instance, an employee of the Department of Work and Pensions in the UK took his employer to court because of a dress code that required men to wear a collar and tie but had no stipulations for women.[48]

Despite the uncertainty of dress codes that have no clear guidelines, businesses generally agree that the way an employee dresses should reflect the type of work they do and the company's image. Simply focusing on a job's characteristics can help employees to decide what would be appropriate to wear. Many suggest that workers observe the style of clothing their coworkers and employers display. Paying attention to the styles of those in the work environment can be very helpful when one is uncertain about what to wear, reducing the chance of being addressed about one's personal style.

When deciding on a dress code, employers should avoid being insensitive to the religious requirements or gender of their personnel. Employers can reduce confusion and avoid disputes by revealing the exact specifications in the dress code and applying the code to both genders. Dress codes should also include safety clothing, such as steel-toed boots, that should be worn to prevent injury.

## Office Layout

Poor workplace layout and design are major factors contributing to workplace injuries. This can result in an increase in risk of sprain, strain, and occupational overuse injuries (OOS). Bad workplace layout and design can cause collisions, trips, and falls—in addition to difficulty dealing with emergency situations.[49]

To compel office workers to move around during their shifts, the copier, printer, and fax should be located in a separate part of the office, because all workers should be encouraged to move frequently throughout the day. To meet this goal, employees should mix standing and sitting tasks and have bookshelves and file cabinets located away from desks, so that employees must move from their work stations to reach them.

As well as causing physical injuries, bad workplace layout and design can lead to increased stress levels. Poor workplace design could have a worker near noisy equipment, which can increase the risk of hearing loss. Numerous factors need to be considered when assessing workplace design and layout. These include not only the physical layout of the workplace but also lighting, temperature, and ventilation.[50] Leaders should consider the following layout features of the workplace:

1. Are desks, benches and chairs suitable for the people using them and for the tasks being performed? Poorly designed chairs, which cannot be adjusted for height, may lead to back problems. Desks that are not ergonomically designed and adjustable to accommodate a range of heights can also cause discomfort and increase the risk of OOS and other injuries.

2. Are all passages, exits and entrances, clear from clutter? Accidents can be caused by poor housekeeping.

3. Is equipment with dangerous moving parts properly guarded? Unguarded equipment is a frequent cause of workplace injuries and fatal accidents.

4.  Are electrical cords out of the walkway? Are cords kept away from places that may get wet?

5.  Are suitable lifting and carrying devices supplied, such as hoists, trolleys, and back-support belts?

6.  Are items which must be manually lifted and carried stored and worked on at a suitable height? Well designed storage areas and work areas can significantly reduce the amount of bending, twisting, and lifting that employees need to do to carry out their tasks.[51]

Ergonomics is arranging the work environment to fit the worker. "When ergonomics is applied correctly . . . visual, musculoskeletal discomfort, and fatigue are reduced significantly."[52] By following ergonomic principles—available from the Center for Disease Control or Occupational Safety and Health Administration Web sites—employers can reduce not only workplace stress but also potential injuries associated with overuse of muscles and repeated tasks. Through the careful consideration of the design of tasks, work space layout, lighting, and equipment, these injuries and stresses can be prevented.

## *Proxemics*

Proxemics is the use of distance—the arrangement of the physical space that surrounds the people who occupy the space. The proximity of people to one another when interacting in a business environment and the configuration of a work area sends a message to workers and visitors alike.

To effectively communicate spatially, people must first become aware of the effects of proxemics, understanding the messages they and others send not only through the way they enter or use space but also through their preferred meeting environment and office.[53]

Consciously and unconsciously, humans have a desire to defend territory, even when two friends go to lunch, they instinctively draw a line down the middle of the table to establish their own space. This line represents a boundary line, and neither person will cross the line nor invade the other's territory. In America, the personal zone extends from one's face out about twenty inches. However, to someone from Latin America or the Middle East, this distance shrinks down to approximately eight to ten inches.[54]

The location and size of furniture in a work area are potential indicators of a person's status. The way that a person has his or her office organized implies an individual leadership style. For example, chairs placed in front of the desk, forcing visitors across from the occupant, imply an autocratic style. In such instances, communication tends to be formal. A manager who prefers informal management techniques may place chairs on either side of his or her desk. Managers who have a collaborative leadership style remove their desks all together and prefer to conduct business with visitors in a circle or arrangement of chairs and tables. The following are suggestions for dealing with proxemics:

1. Observe and be aware of others' personal space. Determine the best way to use distance and space to communicate more effectively.

2. No space arrangement alone will make a leader more or less powerful or a better communicator.

3. Study others' workspace to see if it implies the message that they would like.

4. Include nonverbal and spatial elements into persuasion plans.[55]

# Conclusion

Communication is extremely important in the world of business, because each business or organization interacts with internal and external customers on a daily basis. To be productive and maintain a competitive edge in corporate America, organizations must correspond with customers in a manner that is beneficial to both the organization and customer.

People constantly communicate, but an astounding number of errors can occur in both transmitting and receiving messages. The childhood game of whispering a statement into one child's ear and having them individually share it with classmates clearly illustrates the potential for miscommunication. Rarely does the last child in the sequence receive a message that is remotely close to the original.

One cannot overstate the importance of effective communication for the aspiring manager or business leader. Effective communication skills, both written and verbal, are high on the list of managerial job skills. A survey conducted in 1995 by the National Association of Colleges and Employers (NACE) asked 259 employers to rank the importance of a list of skills employers seek in college graduates. Employers rated the skills in the following order: oral communication, interpersonal, teamwork, analytical, flexibility, leadership, written communication, proficiency in field of study, and computer skills.[56]

For the business leader, first-rate communication skills are a prerequisite to success. Business presentations, employee counseling, coaching, and instructions to subordinates are only a few examples of the daily requirements for effective communication. Leaders in organizations stress that college graduates must be able communicate effectively and succinctly.[57] Knowledge or information that is not effectively communicated may be useless. As wisely stated by United States Marine Corp General Alfred Gray, "Communications without intelligence is noise; intelligence without communications is irrelevant."[58]

In meetings, managers have the opportunity to convey messages through several methods of communication, such as handouts, speeches, and presentations. Managers must ensure that they choose the method that will be the most receptive and effective.

Employees practice corporate culture, whether consciously or subconsciously. Consciously, employees observe other employees—particularly the employees who have been with a company for a long time. Employees are conditioned to understand the expectations of office etiquette. Employees also learn about office politics through firsthand observation or secondhand information. Secondhand information, which can usually be accepted as fact, is a part of the rumor mill.

Subconsciously, managers and employees display behaviors that can be interpreted differently by different observers. Behaviors and non-verbal communication, such as standing position, eye contact, hand movements, and facial expressions reveal a lot. In order to direct and lead employees effectively, managers have to be conscious of their non-verbal communication behaviors. Employees must also be aware of preconceived ideas that others reveal through non-verbal communication.

Successful managers understand the importance of interpersonal communication. Businesses are constantly trying creative methods to convey messages. From corporate culture to business etiquette, each business has standards concerning dress codes, office layout, informal norms, and office politics. To be effective in conveying messages, businesses have to go through the communication process and require feedback. Feedback allows for clarity and ultimately results in improved efficiency.

# Endnotes

1    Arnold, V. (1987). The concept of process. *Journal of Business Communication, 24*(1), pp. 33-35.

2    Arredondo, L. (2000). *Communicating effectively.* New York, NY: The McGraw-Hill Companies, p. 6.

3    Bovee, C.L., & Thill, J.V. (1992). Business Communication Today. New York: McGraw-Hill.

4    Heller, R. (1998). *Communicate clearly.* New York: DK Publishing, Inc, p. 7.

5    Hogan, K. (2000). *Talk your way to the top: Communication secrets to change your life.* Louisiana: Pelican Publishing Company, Inc, p. 74.

6    Robbins, S. (2000). *Essentials of organizational behavior,* (6th ed.). New Jersey: Prentice-Hall, Inc., p. 124.

7    Penrose, J.M., Raspberry, R.W., & Myers, R.J. (2004). *Business communication for managers: An advanced approach.* Ohio: South-Western. p. 20.

8    Plotnik, A. (1996). *The elements of expression.* New York: Henry Holt and Company, Inc. p. 35.

9    McNeill, D. (1992). Hand and mind: What gestuers research about thought. Chicago: University of Chicago Press.

10   Abrams, R. (2006, February 7). To succeed, polish your presentation. *The Times Union.,* 3rd Edition, Business; p. E1.

11   Tracy, L. (2002). The Shortcut to Persuasive Presentations. Ebook.

12   Meyerhoff, R. (2006, June 15). Business objects survey shows executives suffer from presentation burn out. *Business Wire News.* Retrieved from: http://news.moneycentral.msn.com/ticker/article. asp?Symbol=US:BOBJ&Feed=BW&Date=20060615&ID=5798176

13   Tracy, L. (2002) The shortcut to persuasive presentations.North Charleston, SC., Imprint Books.

14   Ibid.

15   Ibid, p. 36.

16   Ibid, p. 22.

17   U.S Department of Labor Website. *Presenting effective presentations with visual aids.* p. 1 Retrieved from: http://www.osha.gov/doc/outreachtraining/htmlfiles/traintec.html

18   Gallo, C. (2006, April 6). How to wow 'em like Steve Jobs. *Business Week.* Online Retrieved from: http://www.businessweek.com/smallbiz/content/apr2006/sb20060406_865110. htm?chan=search

19   Gallo, C. (n.d.) The ten worst presentation habits. Businessweek online. Retrieved October 14, 2006 from: http://images.businessweek.com/ss/06/02/mistakes/index_01.htm?link_position=link1&campaign_id=nws_smlbz_Mar1

20   Matson, E. (1997). Now that we have your complete attention. Fast Company, 7. Retrieved on October 14, 2006 from: http://www.fastcompany.com/online/07/124present.html

21   Ibid.

22   Ibid.

23   Ibid.

24   Burnfield, J., Leach, D. & Rogelburg, S. (2006 February). Scientific study finds meetings at work decrease employee well-being, but not for everyone. Journal of Applied Psychology, 91(2), 1. Retrieved from: http://www.eurekalert.org/pub_releases/2006-02/uonc-ssf022406.php

25   Gallo, C. (2006). *No one wastes time searching for a purpose at Marissa Mayer's meetings—even five-minute gatherings must have a clear agenda. Business Week Online (Sept 27)*. Retrieved on October 16, 2006 from the World Wide Web: http://yahoo.businessweek.com/smallbiz/content/sep2006/sb20060927_259688.htm

26   Ibid.

27   Ibid.

28   Kepcher, C. (2004). Carolyn 101 business lessons from the apprentice's straight shooter. New York: Fireside.

29   Business.Gov Website. Retrieved from: http://www.business.gov/phases/managing/

30   Small Business Association Retrieved October 18, 2006 http://www.sba.gov/idc/groups/public/documents/nc_charlotte/nc_rpnewsmar06.pdf

31   Denair Unifed School District Web Page. Retrieved October 23, 2006 from: http://dusd.k12.ca.us/District/Technology/Email_Netiquette/default.mgi

32   Paige Riley, D. as quoted in Black Enterprise, August 2004. http://www.findarticles.com/p/articles/mi_m1365/is_1_35/ai_n6148221

33   Ball State Career Center. Retrieved October 18, 2006 from: http://www.bsu.edu/students/careers/students/interviewing/dinetips/

34   Haworth Home Page. Retrieved October 18, 2006 from: http://sourcebook.haworth.com/websourcebook/content/items/document/e1062.pdf

35   Ibid, p. 404.

36   Voigt, K. (n.d.). Making the rumor mill work for you. *The Wall Street Journal* Online. Retrieved on July 8, 2006, from http://www.careerjournalasia.com/myc/officelife/20050128-voigt.html

37   Warshaw, M. (1998). Thee good guys (and gals) guide to office politics. Fast Company., 14. Retrieved October 23, 2006 from http://www.fastcompany.com/online/14/politics.html

38   King, D. (2000, April 30). http://print.jobfind.com/news/career_connection/king04302000.htm

39   Ibid.

40   Warshaw, M. (1998). Thee good guys (and gals) guide to office politics. Fast Company., 14. Retrieved October 23, 2006 from http://www.fastcompany.com/online/14/politics.html

41   Ibid.

42   Feldman, D.C. (1984). The development and enforcement of group norms. Academy of Management Review, 9, (1). pp. 47-53.

43   Ibid.

44   Janis, L. (1982). Grouthink. (2nd ed.). Boston: Houghton Mifflin. p. 9.

45   Griffin, Em. Groupthink. McGraw-Hill Inc., 1997.

46   Janis, L. (1982). Grouthink. (2nd ed.). Boston: Houghton Mifflin.

47   Armour, S. (2005). Dust off those ties and pumps: Dress codes gussy up. Retrieved July 17, 2006, from: http://www.keepmedia.com/pubs/USATODAY/2005/10/26/1062139?ba=a&bi=0&bp=7

48   Wiper, C.(2003) Employee Alert; Dress Codes at Work. Retrieved July 19, 2006 from http://www.close-thornton.co.uk/news/dress-code.htm

49   Australian Government Department of Employment & Workplace Relations. Retrieved July 23, 2006, from: www.nohsc.gov.au/OHSInformation/NOHSCPublications/factsheet/layou1.htm

50    Ibid.

51    Ibid.

52    Center for Disease Control Web Page.  Retrieved October 23, 2006 from: http://www.cdc.gov/
      od/ohs/Ergonomics/ergodef.htm

53    Preston, P. (2005). Proxemics in clinical and administrative settings [Electronic version]. Journal
      of Healthcare Management, p. 151 (4).

54    Ibid.

55    Ibid.

56    Business-Higher Education Forum. (1997). *Spanning the Chasm: Corporate* Force on High-
      Performance Work and Workers: The Academic Connection Retrieved from: http://www.chass.
      ncsu.edu/ccstm/CONNECTIONS/chasm.html

57    National Association of Colleges and Employers. (1995). Survey of 239 Employers. Retrieved
      from: http://www.chass.ncsu.edu/ccstm/CONNECTIONS/chasm.html

58    Gray, A. (2006).  Retrieved from: http://www.quotationspage.com/quote/34648.html

# CHAPTER 6 — Organizational Behavior

## MEASURABLE LEARNING OBJECTIVES

1. Discuss the Behavioral-based theories of organizational behavior and identify their impact on modern management. Identify the contributions of Thorndike, Skinner and Vroom.

2. Discuss the role of a manager in behavior modification in an organization.

3. Discuss the Need-based theories of organizational behavior and identify their impact on modern management. Identify the contributions of Maslow, Alderfer, McClelland.

4. Identify the impact of ERG theory on a manager's view of an employee.

5. Discuss the Job-based theories of organizational behavior and identify their impact on modern management. Identify the contributions of Herzberg and Hackman and Oldham.

6. Distinguish between functional and dysfunctional conflict and its causes.

7. Identify the different styles of conflict management and the effectiveness of each style.

8. Discuss the role of teamwork within an organization and identify the pros and cons of using teams.

9. Identify the different types of teams and stages of team development.

10. Define groupthink.

11. Distinguish between task and maintenance roles within a group.

12. Distinguish between the characteristics of high and low performance teams.

# Motivation Theories

A leader's job in an organization is to get things done through the employees of that organization. Understanding both how to motivate and what motivates subordinates has been the focus of research ever since the Hawthorne Studies.[1] To make matters more complicated, what motivates employees is constantly changing, but "to be effective, managers need to understand what motivates employees within the context of the roles [those employees] perform."[2]

Motivation is an "inner force that drives individuals to accomplish personal and organizational goals."[3] Understanding what motivates each individual in an organization can lead to better productivity and a more successful organization—perhaps even the survival of the organization is dependent upon motivated employees.[4]

Managers can utilize several approaches to motivate employees. The theories are behavioral-based, need-based, or job-based. Generally speaking, managers will find one theory or method more natural to implement; however, different subordinates will require different methods of motivation.

## *Behavioral Based*

The behavioral based methods for motivating employees involve responding to subordinate behavior with positive reinforcement, negative reinforcement, punishment, or extinction. Positive and negative reinforcement strengthen (reinforce) behaviors and are positive for the subordinate who receives them. Punishment and extinction decrease undesirable behaviors and are negative for the subordinate who receives them.

### *Thorndike's Law of Effect*
Edward Lee Thorndike (1874 - 1949) published five-hundred books and articles on such topics as applied psychology, learning theory, and mental measurement. He studied at Columbia University, where he taught from 1909 to 1940, and served as president of the American Psychological Association. Thorndike's law of effect states that individuals form habitual responses when they produce outcomes that are agreeable.

Thorndike conducted one experiment that involved putting a cat in a cage, latching the door, and placing a piece of salmon outside of the cage. Initially, the cat spent a considerable amount of time trying to reach through the cage or scratching at the door before eventually hitting the latch that opened the door. Each time this experiment was repeated, the cat spent less effort and time on useless activities, unlatching the door sooner.[5] Thorndike concluded that the behavior that produced the desired effect—the cat unlatching the door to reach the salmon—became dominant and occurred more quickly in the successive experiments. This is known as "the law of effect."[6]

Thorndike believed that the positive result reinforced a particular response much more than a negative result would discourage a response. Thorndike's law of effect can be applied to a workplace attendance program: Employees who receive attendance awards would be more likely to maintain perfect attendance; likewise, an employee whose tardiness is logged will try to correct his future behavior—but not with as much enthusiasm as those who received awards for good behavior. Thorndike's law of effect provided the basis for Skinner's operant conditioning analysis of behavior.[7]

### Skinner's Behavior Modification (Reinforcement, Punishment, Extinction)

Behavioral-based motivation was also researched by B.F. Skinner in experiments with rats.[8] Skinner, a Harvard psychologist, played a significant role in research of operant conditioning (that consequences determine future behavior). Skinner argued that creating pleasant consequences for certain forms of behavior would increase the frequency of that behavior. He believed that immediate rewards will bring about desired behaviors from people. Conversely, a behavior is less likely to continue if it is punished or not rewarded.

Skinner utilized a rat held in a special cage that had a pedal against one wall. When the pedal was pressed, a food pellet fell into the cage. One day, the rat accidentally presses the pedal and food appeared in the cage. The rat soon learned that pushing produced food; the connection between the action and the consequence was made. Skinner noted that a behavior that is followed by positive reinforcement is likely to be repeated. Therefore, positive reinforcement in the workplace may get people to do things that they would not normally do by offering rewards for certain behaviors. A positive reinforcer reinforces behaviors when it is offered.[9] Rewards may be monetary or non-monetary and include pay for performance, compliments, letters of commendation, and cash bonuses. Positive reinforcement must be used properly in the workplace. Just as it is a mistake for a father to offer a treat to hush an unruly child, so it is a mistake for a manager to reward negative behavior in the workplace. Negative behavior that is rewarded will continue to the detriment of the organization.

What happens if a rat keeps pushing at the pedal, but does not get any more food pellets? Again, the connection is made that the behavior does not lead to a desired consequence, so the behavior is not repeated. Withdrawal of the positive reinforcement leads to the extinction of the behavior. Examples of extinction in a workplace include not giving pay for extraordinary performance or not providing complements.

Negative reinforcement is not punishment but reinforces behavior when it is withdrawn.[10]  Negative reinforcement increases the probability that the desired behavior will take place by eliminating something that is not liked.  A common use of negative reinforcement is seatbelt alarms—if one fails to buckle up, the alarm begins sounding and does not stop until the seat belt has been fastened.  The annoying alarm reinforces the behavior to buckle up prior to starting the car.

Punishment is the administration of an unfavorable consequence and is often formalized in an organization's policies.  Punishment can include docking pay, leave without pay, shouting at a subordinate, or assignment of an unappealing task.

If managers deal fairly and consistently with unacceptable behavior, employees will generally be respectful of rules and regulations.  A management team that is not consistent or does not deal with destructive behavior will find the workforce constantly testing the boundaries of what they can get away with next.

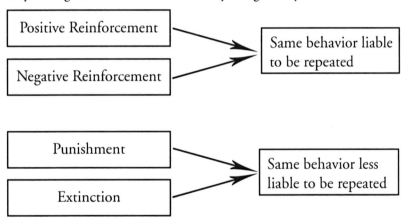

Reinforcement brought about by the consequences of behavior influences future repetition of the behavior.  For example, if the crowd roars with delight as a basketball player hangs on the rim while dunking the ball on a fast break, the chances are the basketball player will hang on the rim given another opportunity. Lack of reinforcement will tend to decrease the likelihood of future repetition of the behavior.  The lack of punishment for undesirable behavior will lead to an increase in the likelihood of repetition.  If the referee ignores the basketball player's violation, the basketball player is more likely to continue hanging on the rim in the future.  Extinction, which is no reinforcement, will decrease the likelihood of future repetition.  If the crowd refrains from cheering a basketball player hanging on the rim, the basketball player will likely get the hint and quit hanging on the rim.

Managers need to be cognizant of the worth that employees place on certain rewards. The manager may believe that a reward is highly valued by subordinates, but the subordinate may not place a high value on the reward. For example, employees in companies that never issue attendance awards may lack positive reinforcement. This lack of positive reinforcement may tempt the employee to call in sick to get a day off. If the punishment is not serious enough, the employee may find the unscheduled day off more satisfying than the negative mark on the attendance sheet. If employees consider the reward valuable, they will opt for the behavior that holds pleasant consequences. According to Skinner, a yearly attendance program does not reward with a high enough frequency to modify behavior.

### Vroom's Expectancy Theory

One of the most widely accepted explanations of motivation is Victor Vroom's expectancy theory, formulated in the 1960s. Vroom proposed that people are motivated by the probability of their actions leading to the successful achievement of specific objectives, which must be desired by the subordinate.[11] A manager must concentrate on three barriers in order for his or her subordinates to succeed:

> First of all, they [managers] need to connect the task to be performed to the likelihood of better results. Secondly, they need to set expectations that there are positive benefits to the employee in achieving those results. Thirdly, they need to ensure that these benefits are of value to the employee.[12]

Expectancy theory argues that one will tend to behave in a particular manner, based on his or her expectation of a favorable outcome. Additionally, the greater the extent to which the individual believes the outcome will be of benefit to them, the greater the likelihood of maintaining that behavior. Therefore, if a subordinate believes that the outcome of an action will be career advancement or an increase in pay, this will motivate him or her to perform the action. Expectancy theory helps to explain why many workers are not motivated on their jobs. Expectancy theory focuses on the three parts of the motivation equation: input, performance, and outcomes. Expectancy theory includes three variables:

1. Expectancy can also be stated as the link between the effort exerted and the performance of the worker. Expectancy is the perceived likelihood that effort will lead to a specific level of performance and is based upon personal experience, self-confidence, and the perceived difficulty of the goal.
2. Instrumentality, or the linkage between the performance and the reward, is measured in the degree to which a subordinate believes that a specific level of performance is in reaching the desired outcome.

3.  Valence is the attractiveness that the reward holds for the subordinate. Each subordinate will place a different weight on potential rewards (outcomes) that are earned, based upon his or her performance.

In order for an employee to be motivated, he must be able to answer "yes" to all of the following questions:

- If I give a maximum effort, will it be recognized in my performance appraisal?
- If I get a good performance appraisal, will it lead to organizational rewards?
- If I'm rewarded, are the rewards ones that I find personally attractive?

The answers to these questions can vary from organization to organization and from person to person; thus, no universal principal exists for explaining motivations. Each individual has a different set of goals and will be motivated only if expectations are appropriately tailored.

The critical issue is how the subordinate perceives the outcomes of job performance: is the reward valued and motivational, or is the reward not personally valued and non-motivating?

A manager must determine what supervision, training, or resources an employee needs and consider what rewards are most important to an individual employee. Examples of extrinsic rewards include benefits, a promotion, free time off, or money. An example of an intrinsic reward is the satisfaction of a job well done. A manager must provide individual motivations to ensure that each subordinate's own values become the motivating factor.

## Need Based

A need is a requirement or necessity for survival and well being. The basic premise of needs theories is that people are motivated to obtain outcomes that will satisfy needs. The needs theories suggest that in order for a manager to motivate his or her employees, he or she must know what needs an employee has and if those needs can be satisfied through the workplace. With this knowledge, a manager will promise to meet an employee's needs when the person performs at a high level.

### Maslow

Abraham Maslow's Hierarchy of Needs theory is based upon the assumption that some needs take precedence over others. The hierarchy's progression, beginning with the most basic needs, is as follows:  physiological, safety, belonging, esteem, and self-actualization. "Maslow's thinking was surprisingly original—most psychology before him had been concerned with the abnormal and the ill."[13]

Maslow referred to the first four levels of needs—physiological, safety, belonging, and esteem—as deficit needs. Maslow believed that if an individual is lacking, he or she will feel the need for more, but if the individual is satisfied, he or she does not miss anything and is not motivated to fill the need further.

In contrast to deficit needs, Maslow described what he calls B-needs—being needs/self actualization. These needs get stronger, even as they are being met. If an individual wants to gain self-actualization, he or she must first have met all of the lower needs. When an individual's lower needs are not met, the person focuses on meeting those needs; therefore, higher-order needs cannot be met nor can potential be reached. As a result, only a small percentage of people are self-actualizing. According to Maslow, self-actualizing people are reality centered.[14] They can tell the difference between lies and truth. They believed that life's difficulties are problems that demand solutions. They feel that the ends will not necessarily justify the means. They believe in values. Maslow believed that society's biggest problem is that very few people are self-actualizers. These people are not really concerned with values because they haven't met their basic needs.[15]

Although Maslow proposed the hierarchy in a fixed order, the hierarchy contains many exceptions. In addition, there is very little statistical evidence that supports the theory.

## ERG Theory

Clayton Aldefer's ERG theory model was developed in reaction to Maslow's theory on the Hierarchy of Needs. Rather than being a sequential order of needs, of which the most basic need must be filled prior to pursuing the next, Alderfer collapsed the five categories of needs into three categories, known as existence, relatedness, and growth—also arranged in a hierarchy.[16]

- Existence needs include physiological and safety needs (Maslow's 1st and 2nd categories).
- Relatedness needs include social and external esteem, which includes involvement with co-workers, employers, friends, and family (Maslow's 3rd and 4th categories).
- Growth needs included internal esteem and self–actualization, which includes the desire to be productive, creative, and meaningful (Maslow's 4th and 5th categories).[17]

Alderfer agreed with Maslow that as the lowest level of unmet need is satisfied, the next level of unmet need becomes the prime motivator. However, unlike Maslow,

Alderfer believed that a person can be motivated by needs at more than one level at a time.

For instance, a college graduate looking for that new job would be in the existence phase. Her primary level of need would be for housing and food. However, as a young executive she knows that to continue with any company, she will need to improve and grow in the position. Five years after graduation, she would have moved past her existence phase and into relatedness or growing. She would nonetheless continue to emphasize existence to some extent, but with a secure job on which she can focus to fulfill her needs at a higher level. Managers must realize that employees have many needs to satisfy at the same time. According to the ERG theory, if a manager focuses on only one need at a time, he or she will not motivate effectively. The key is to get subordinates to pursue growth.

| Alderfer | Maslow |
|---|---|
| Growth | Self Actualization |
| Relatedness Needs | Esteem |
| | Belonging |
| Existence Needs | Safety |
| | Physiological |

## McClelland's Trichotomy of Needs

David McClelland received his Ph.D. from Yale University in experimental psychology in 1941 and is best-known for his research on achievement motivation. He researched the relationship between achievement motivation and economic development and the physiological influences on achievement motivation. David McClelland's research on the needs for achievement, affiliation, and power can be summarized as follows:[18]

- The need for achievement is found in people who desire to perform challenging tasks well and have a strong desire to meet personal standards for excellence. These people tend to set personal goals for themselves and like to receive performance feedback.

- The need for affiliation is found in people who are concerned about establishing and maintaining good interpersonal relations, being liked, and having the people around them to get along with each other.
- The need for power is found in people who desire to control or influence others.

Managerial success is dependent upon how one views these needs. Successful managers at all levels of the organization will have a low need for affiliation and a moderate to high need for power.

## *Job Based*

Job-based motivation is ensuring that a job addresses both extrinsic and intrinsic reinforcers and designing the job in such a way that the individual can experience job rotation, job enlargement, and job enrichment.

Extrinsic reinforcers are rewards given by an organization to individuals who have met high performance standards. These rewards must matter to those whom they are given; they must view the reward as something of value.[19] Intrinsic rewards are those motivations that an individual gains from performing a job itself—the thrill of finding a solution to a problem or the successful implementation of a project.

In an organization that practices job rotation, a worker rotates between jobs instead of spending all his or her time repeating the same task. Job rotation is meant to minimize boredom; however, moving a worker from one boring job to another is not the solution. Individuals should be given an opportunity to rotate into lateral positions to alleviate boredom and frustration, because such rotation may increase retention and keep valuable staff.

Job enlargement is similar to job rotation in that it is meant to decrease boredom; however, an individual whose job has been enlarged will be given additional tasks—at the same level of responsibility—to complete at the same time they are working on their regular tasks. Job enlargement can lead to happier employees. Organizations that enlarged jobs "had the benefits of more employee satisfaction… greater chances of catching errors, and better customer service, but they also had the costs of higher training requirements, higher basic skills, and higher compensable factors."[20]

Job enrichment entails giving an employee additional tasks, but those tasks are of a higher level of responsibility than the employee's current level. Job enrichment is further discussed in Herzberg's two-factor theory and Hackman and Oldham's job design model.

*Herzberg's 2-Factor Theory*

The two-factor theory was formulated by theorist Frederick Herzberg. During the 50s and 60s, Herzberg researched the factors that affect an employee's performance and believed that factors existed that would cause an employee to feel unsatisfied with his or her employment. The first of those factors was called hygiene factors: characteristics of the workplace, such as pay, supervisors, the organization's culture, and the working conditions that can make people dissatisfied, if they are not well managed. If these hygiene factors are well managed, people will no longer be dissatisfied; however, regardless of how well individuals manage these factors, they cannot make people happy or satisfied with their jobs. Hygiene factors are those parts of a job that are extrinsic to the individual.

Herzberg's research led him to define motivators as the key to job satisfaction. Motivators include job responsibilities, feelings of achievement, and an opportunity for personal growth. Herzberg believed that when these factors are present in a job, the job becomes satisfying and motivating. Motivators are those things that are intrinsically rewarding about a job.

Herzberg's theory did not hold up well against later researchers, but it did focus managers on both the intrinsic and extrinsic factors of motivation, as well as lay the groundwork for later motivation theories.

*Hackman and Oldham Job Design Model*

Recent research in job design, such as the job characteristic model proposed by J.R. Hackman and G.R. Oldham, suggests core job dimensions of well designed and enriching jobs:

1. Skill variety: the degree to which the job requires the individual to do different tasks and involves the use of a number of different skills, abilities, and talents.
2. Task identity: the degree to which an individual can successfully complete a job from beginning to end.
3. Task significance: the degree to which the job has a significant impact on others—both inside and outside the organization.
4. Autonomy: the amount of freedom, independence, and discretion the employee has in areas such as scheduling the work, making decisions, and determining how to do the job.
5. Feedback: the degree to which the job provides the employee with clear and direct information about job outcomes and performance.[21]

Job enrichment occurs when all five core job dimensions are present. The five core job dimensions each lead to a critical psychological state and end with personal and work outcomes of high internal motivation, high quality performance, high satisfaction with work, and low absenteeism and turnover.

Adapted from: Hackman, J.R. & Oldham, G.R. (1980). Word redesign. Reading, MA: Addison-Wesley. p90

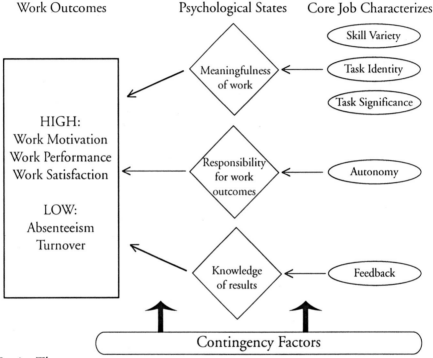

*Equity Theory*

John S. Adams, a behavioral psychologist, proposed the Equity Theory in 1963.[22] Adam's theory recognizes that variable and subtle factors will affect an individual's perception of their workplace and where he or she stands in relationship to his or her work. The Equity theory focuses on how an individual's perception affects motivation and how fairly he or she is being treated. Employees have an idea of what constitutes equity—the appropriate outcomes based upon their inputs.

An individual needs to believe that a balance exists between his inputs and the outcomes (see Figure 6.4). If an individual perceives that the outcomes equal the inputs, this perception will have a positive effect on their job performance and satisfaction. If an individual believes that the inputs are far greater than the outcomes—that the scale is tipped in favor of another individual—the perception will have a negative effect on job performance. The result will be dissatisfaction, and time will be spent in an attempt to restore equity and achieve fairness.

According to Equity theory, individuals compare the ratio of outcomes to their inputs against the same ratio of another.

Inputs: personal sacrifice, commitment, adaptability, skill, enthusiasm, effort, tolerance, loyalty, hard work, trust, ability, support, flexibility, determination.

Outputs: recognition, appreciation, responsibility, sense of achievement, opportunity for advancement and promotion, salary, benefits, perks, pension plans, commissions, bonuses, etc.

Equity is measured against others, both within the organization and in the marketplace.

If the ratios are comparable, then the worker believes that the treatment is fair. If a worker believes that the ratio is lower, the individual will believe that the treatment is inequitable, which will lead to dissatisfaction and an attempt to restore balance. An individual who believes that the treatment is inequitable will normally attempt to restore balance by either reducing inputs, resigning, attempting to increase his or her own outcomes, retaliating against others in the organization, or reducing the outputs of others in the organization.[23]

# Managing Conflict

Conflict is a process that begins when an individual perceives that he or she has been negatively affected by another individual or group.[24] Traditionally, conflict was seen as an unhealthy element in an organization, and managers would seek to avoid it in an attempt to keep the peace. However, the Human Relations view considers conflict to be inevitable, because people are prone to have conflicts and conflict can be constructive within an organization. When conflict arises, the manager deals with the situation appropriately and seeks growth from the incident. On the other hand, the interactionist view welcomes certain types of conflict. The interactionist manager seeks to maintain some level of conflict in order to keep workers within the organization inspired.

## *Functional vs. Dysfunctional Conflict*

A group that does not experience conflict may experience group think. Conflict that hinders group performance is destructive, whereas conflict that supports the goals of the group and improves performance proves functional and constructive. Constructive conflict should take place among group members to ensure creative solutions and full use of group member's knowledge.[25]

Constructive conflict can be promoted in group settings through the use of structured processes, such as devil's advocate or the dialectic approach.[26] The role of devil's advocate is important to ensure that the shortcomings of ideas are exposed and explored. The role is formally assigned to a group member who has the job of highlighting problems. The function of devil's advocacy is to lessen the personal and emotional aspect of conflict.

Dialectic conflict is a structured form of conflict, in which two opposing sides debate opposite courses of action. Each group in the debate advocates an opposing course of action so that the proposal is better understood by all members of the group.

## Causes of Conflict

The causes of conflict in the workplace can be boiled down to three main categories: task, relationship, and process.[27]

### Task Conflict

Task conflict begins when group members have different expectations or vision for the task at hand—concerning facts or the interpretation of evidence. When task conflict is properly channeled, it is associated with effective decisions.

### Relationship Conflict

Relationship conflict occurs when individuals within a group organization fail to communicate effectively. This type of conflict can escalate so that everyone directs attention and energy towards the conflict and little to the organization's goals. Relationship conflict is usually associated with ineffective decisions.

### Process Conflict

Process conflict occurs when the group plans the processes it will utilize to meet a goal. One group member may like to have an entire project planned out, while another prefers only to plan one step ahead; such differences lead to conflict. However, process conflict can lead to improved processes and more effective and efficient groups.

## *Conflict Management Styles*

In order for organizations to succeed, managers must be able to manage conflict in a functional manner. Some researchers believe that managers have aggression to expend and welcome some degree of uncertainty that comes from conflict.[28] Thus, managers should not avoid or discourage conflict but rather strive to manage conflict in the organization. How a manager chooses to deal with conflict will vary depending on the type of conflict. Regardless of whether conflict is functional or dysfunctional, managers deal with conflict in one of the following ways: avoidance, accommodation, competition, compromise, or collaboration.[29]

### *Avoidance*

When managers avoid and ignore conflict, nothing is done to resolve the disagreement. Avoidance is ineffective since the real source has not been addressed. Just ignoring the issue or attempting to stay neutral will not make conflict disappear. Avoidance will draw considerable attention from the work at hand and make the conflict worse.

### *Accommodation*

When accommodation takes place, one individual simply acquiesces to the demands of the other. Accommodation typically takes place to maintain harmony. This method of managing conflict is generally ineffective. If the dominant party continues in this method, the compliant party will not likely cooperate in the future.

### *Competition*

Competition occurs when each individual attempts to maximize his or her own gain, which results in a win/lose situation. Competition escalates easily because competing groups will try to outmaneuver the other. Competition is ineffective because the two sides are generally more concerned about winning than arriving at the best solution. While short term competition may spark new interest and inspiration within the organization, extended competition instills an "us versus them" attitude.

### *Compromise*

When two individuals are concerned not only about their own goals but also about the goals of the organization, compromise may be effective. However, both individuals must be willing to make concessions in order to resolve differences. The result of compromise is that each individual wins a little and loses a little. When each individual fully understands that all are working in the best interest of the organization, compromise is easier to attain.

### Collaboration

Collaboration is a method through which both parties try to satisfy their goals by not making concessions, but by coming up with a satisfactory solution—a win/win situation. Collaboration can occur by emphasizing frequent meetings, listening to each other, and patiently working through differences. Collaborative work management tools help people accomplish or manage group work activities. A summary of major categories of software tools used in enterprise collaborative systems include electronic mail and instant messaging, voice mail, faxing, web publishing, data conferencing, voice conferencing, video-conferencing, discussion formats, chat systems, electronic meeting systems, calendaring and scheduling, task and project management, workflow systems, and knowledge management.[30]

While recent debate has established that some conflict is beneficial to a company, a manager must maintain a healthy work environment. Allowing dysfunctional conflict to go unchecked will weaken any organization. Alternatively, keeping functional conflict at a civil level will help keep a company competitive. One method of precluding dysfunctional conflict is through team building.[31]

# Teams

The use of teams within organizations began in the 1970s, but those teams were usually implemented to accomplish a single project or task and then disbanded or operated separately from the normal work environment. More and more companies are increasing motivation and morale by implementing employee involvement programs.[32] These programs consist of teams who share a common responsibility for specified goals, with the intent of improving productivity and reducing costs. The focus of these teams ranges from a basic safety committee to an advanced process improvement.[33] Studies have shown an increase in job satisfaction for those employees included on teams that also included members of management.[34] The studies reveal that the breaking down of the traditional hierarchical structure of an organization, by including staff from all levels of the organization, can improve overall morale.

## *Pros and Cons of Using Teams*

Teams have become the popular standard in organizations. A team is a small number of people with complementary skills who are committed to a common purpose, performance goals, and approach, for which they hold themselves mutually accountable.[35]

The positive aspects of utilizing a team make it inviting to both the organization and individuals. Individual team members have goals—as well as the team collectively. The team exists for a specific reason. All performance—both the team's and each individual's—is evaluated and based upon the goal of the team.

Some negative aspects have to be dealt with when utilizing a team. When personal conflict arises between individuals on the team, a manager must be aware of how subordinates interact with fellow workers. A manager may also come across individuals who practice social loafing—individuals who become lazy because the responsibility has been dispersed to a number of team members who will pick up the slack. In many cases team members tend to be more risk oriented, because no single person will have to take responsibility for failure.[36]

## *Informal and Formal Teams*

An informal team is a group that has come together with a common goal without any direction or involvement from management. Informal groups are not official and do not serve a stated purpose, but they emerge from impromptu relationships among coworkers. Individuals will naturally find commonalities and form friendship groups or support groups. Informal groups can have a positive impact on the organization by connecting individuals and allowing things to get done in ways that may not be possible within the formal organizational chart.

A formal team is one that management has deliberately created to perform specific tasks to help meet organizational goals. The idea behind a formal team is to disperse the workload among smaller cells of individuals, provide them with the resources needed to complete a project, and delegate authority to the team, so that they can accomplish the goals. Teams have evolved to include many different types—each utilized for a different reason.

## *Primary Types of Teams*

Although they can be referred to by different names in different organizations, there are five primary types of teams: workgroup, committee/taskforce, cross-functional, quality circles and self-managed.

### *Workgroups*

Members of a workgroup have responsibility for a specific process in the organization, such as a department, and work closely together. Authority held by the group can vary greatly from none to full autonomy.[37]

### *Committee/Taskforce*

A committee is a temporary or permanent group of people assembled to act upon some matter. The committee is set to focus on a general issue that needs to be addressed in a continuous manner that may or may not have a conclusion point.

A project improvement team is a temporary team assembled to focus on the development or improvement of a specific business process.[38] A project improvement team has a set beginning and end and a well-defined plan to meet a specific goal.

### *Cross-Functional Teams*

A cross-functional team is a formal team that is comprised of people from different departments that are brought together to achieve a common goal. For example, this type of team can include people from finance, marketing, operations, and human resources departments—and employees from all hierarchical levels within an organization. Members may also come from outside an organization—from suppliers, key customers, or consultants. Cross-functional teams often function as self-directed teams: they respond to broad objectives but not to specific directives. Decision making within a team may depend on consensus, but a manager/coach/ team leader often leads the team.

### *Quality Circles*

A quality circle is a group of workers from the same functional area who meet regularly to uncover and solve work-related problems and seek work improvement opportunities. They are a group composed of workers who meet together to discuss workplace improvement; they also make presentations to management with their ideas. Typical topics are improving safety, improving product design, and improvement in manufacturing process. Quality circles have the advantage of continuity, keeping the circle intact from project to project. Quality circles are also used many times within quality control departments themselves.

### Self-Managed Teams

Members of a self-managed team manage the day-to day operations of a process or department. The team is autonomous and has the authority to make decisions that lie within the scope of their duties. Members also hold the responsibilities traditionally held by single managers—setting goals, allocation of resources, and conflict resolution.[39]

## Benefits of Teams

Teams can be a great asset and benefit to both an organization and individuals.[40] The following reveals some of the most salient benefits:

### To an Organization
- Synergistic process design or problem solving.
- Objective analysis of problems or opportunities.
- Promotion of cross-functional understanding.
- Improved quality and productivity.
- Greater innovation.
- Reduced operating costs.
- Increased commitment to organizational mission.
- More flexible response to change.
- Increased ownership and stewardship.
- Reduced turnover and absenteeism.

### To an Individual
- Enhanced problem-solving skills.
- Increased knowledge of interpersonal dynamics.
- Broader knowledge of business processes.
- New skills for future leadership roles.
- Increased quality of work life.
- Feelings of satisfaction and commitment.
- A sense of being part of something greater than what one could accomplish.

## *Stages of Team Development*

Bruce Tuckman first proposed the Forming–Storming–Norming–Performing–Adjourning model of team development in 1965. He maintained, with the exception of the adjourning stage, that these four phases are both inevitable and necessary in order for a team to grow, to face up to challenges, to tackle problems, to find solutions, to plan work, and to deliver results.[41]

### *Forming*

The first stage of team development is the forming stage. In the forming stage, members join the group because of a work assignment, as in a formal group, or to meet a need—such as belonging or esteem—as in an informal group. During this stage, members identify acceptable behaviors and define the group's purpose, leadership, and structure. A great deal of uncertainty exists during this stage of group development. This stage is concluded when the members begin to think of themselves as a group.

### *Storming*

In the storming stage, conflict and jockeying often arise for positions of power and status among group members, sometimes producing emotional responses. Members deal with conflict during this stage of team development. The group concludes this stage after deciding on both a clear chain of command and a direction.

### *Norming*

The norming stage represents a time of change in which close relationships form an interdependence between members of the group. Members develop a unified sense of identity and are willing and able to express opinions and ideas constructively. The group comes "together" during this stage. The group concludes the norming stage when members have incorporated the standards of group behavior.

### *Performing*

In the performing stage, group members begin to apply their energies to the task at hand and develop solutions. The attention of individual group members shifts from getting to know each other, the group hierarchy, and direction to performance.

### *Adjourning*

Tuckman later added a fifth phase, adjourning. The adjourning stage is the final stage for temporary work groups and is the stage in which group members prepare to disband. The team is dispersed when the task is complete and may feel a bit of loss no longer working together—much like a normal life cycle. The reactions to adjournment may be mixed: some group members enjoy the high of a completed project, while others are disheartened by the loss of the relationships with other group members.

## *Task vs. Maintenance*

Each member plays a role in helping the group reach its goals. Group roles will vary, depending upon the team, its goals, the organization, and even the individual himself. An individual may fill a different role on the different teams of which he or she is a member. Two types of team roles exist: task and maintenance.[42]

A task-oriented role is one in which the holder focuses on getting the job done. Task roles keep the group headed towards their goals and prod members who may be moving along slowly.

A maintenance-oriented role is one in which the holder focuses on relationships of group members. Members who hold this role will encourage various viewpoints and act as mediators.

## *Characteristics of High Performance and Low Performance Teams*

John P. Kotter, in his book, *Leading Change*, states that teams must be built on mutual trust and respect to thrive.[43] Kotter believes that teams can thrive if they possess five characteristics: shared vision and goals, shared leadership and accountability, continuous learning and development, a customer focus, and the capability to gather and utilize data and feedback.

### *Shared Vision and Goals*
The team's vision must be communicated to and shared by all members. A clear vision will direct the actions of the members to focus on the desired outcomes and the direction to take to reach those outcomes.

### *Shared Leadership*
Teams that are successful develop each member's leadership skills so that they can proactively address change. All members are held accountable for team performance and are encouraged to communicate concerns. Members are also cognizant of the talents of all members of the team and utilize and maximize those talents to ensure reaching team goals.

### Continuous Learning and Development

Training and development for team members is an ongoing process. Some high performance teams may spend 30 percent of their time receiving training on technical and interpersonal skills. Training and development may consist of conflict resolution, leadership, team building, and communication.

### Customer Focus

High performance teams must focus on customer requirements, satisfactions, and complaints. By carefully reviewing feedback from both internal and external customers, teams can focus on high performance actions.

### Feedback and Data

High-performance teams consistently review their performance and develop plans for improvement. Using feedback and data allows a team to improve the quality of its product or service and reduce errors. High-performing teams mobilize and reach the performing stage of group development quickly.

> [These teams also incorporate] . . . a number of colleagues into the processes of clarifying the scopes and nature of their projects and of identifying and selecting competent team participants. They held highly participatory launch meetings; [and] as a result, these teams produced high quality outputs during the mobilization and launch phase.[44]

It has been found that low performing teams mobilize relatively slow. The following reveals information about low performing team leaders:

> [Low performing team leaders] . . . utilized limited mobilization strategies that were primarily one-person shows, concentrating on timetables and work plans rather than on the content of their projects, and used political rather than competency criteria to staff their teams. They extended their leader-centered focus into the launch meetings, hoping to spend the time communicating their agendas and focusing on implementing plans. Instead, the meetings denigrated into confusion and futile attempts to clarify project goals and technical content. As a result . . . [the teams] emerged from their launch meetings with very little common understanding of the problems at hand or agreement on how to move forward.[45]

# Conclusion

There are as many ways for motivating employees as there are employees in an organization. Countless books, magazines, websites, and articles tell managers how to motivate their troops. Each manager will find the method or combination of methods that best suits his or her style and personality. However, many fail to acknowledge that for every leadership style, a "follower-ship" style also exists. A good motivator will always remember that he or she is leading a group comprised of individuals; therefore, he or she must find the best method of motivating every individual in the organization. However, a great motivator balances individualized attention and implements various techniques designed to motivate the entire group. If some individuals sense favoritism towards others in the group or a lack of interest in them personally, attempts at motivation can quickly turn to conflict and dissent. Even a rudimentary understanding of what motivates people will prove to be a boon to anyone in leadership. The specific factor that the manager uses to motivate may range from addressing the person's needs, to modifying or reinforcing behavior, to expanding or redefining their job. The same is true with conflict in that there are many ways to diminish morale. Finally, teams will be weakened by less than adequate motivation and too much conflict.

# Impact on the Organization, the Manager, and Employees

Motivation is supplied through addressing the employees' behavior, needs, or job. Not every individual seeks additional responsibility in their job or desires upward mobility. Some merely work because they have to support a family. Others will lose interest in the job if managers do not recognize their contributions. A manager must consider the response of each individual when choosing a particular motivation technique.

A manager needs to pay close attention to how each person in the group is motivated and adapt his or her style and methods to fit the mean of the group. The manager can confidently delegate tasks by identifying those that desire greater responsibility, because those individuals will likely meet or exceed expectations. A manager who bestows additional responsibilities on employees who do not want anything above and beyond their job description will likely induce discontentment in those individuals. Likewise, the manager may alienate those who desire more work.

Managers may find that some individuals take on additional responsibility readily; but the longer the task goes on, the less motivated they become about the job. These people are motivated by the positive reinforcement and accolades of doing the extra work. The manager may have to assume the role of a cheerleader to keep them motivated through task completion. This technique may work out well for the individual completing the task, but the manager may isolate others for not praising their work.

Some managers, especially those in newer positions, may find focusing on and providing the most basic needs of the work force helpful. Ensuring that employees have their basic needs met is more of a passive style than behavioral or job factor motivation. Thus, this method is beneficial to new managers so that they have time to familiarize themselves with the individuals that comprise the group that they lead. Once they know the tendencies of the group, they may take a more proactive stance. According to needs based theories, individuals who find their needs met will seek their own means to the next level. The manager must be cognizant of those who may seek more fulfillment and support that need.

With all the information and guides to motivating an organization, managers must not neglect conflict that arises within the organization. Not only can conflict surface as a result of other factors but also as a result of poor motivational techniques, with respect to the individuals within the group. Conflict, by contrast, can impact the organization faster than a motivator can build it up. If the constant negative feedback on the nightly news is not indication enough, human nature tends to hang on to the negative longer than the positive. Restoring motivation to a team will take much longer than the conflict that took morale down.

Properly balancing motivation techniques and conflict management is foundational to building a strong team. Before the manager can expect to have a great team, he or she must assign the key tasks to the right individuals, reinforce the expected behaviors, and stifle conflict. Once the stage has been set for a strong team, the manager must keep the team focused. Whether the team requires updated or newly designed objectives, the manager can capitalize on momentum gained through completed projects. By keeping the team engaged, the manager will keep motivation high and conflict at a minimum. A team without focus will lose motivation. The lack of purpose and lower morale will leave room for conflict to arise, which spells disaster for the organization.

# Endnotes

1   Terpstra, D. E. (1979). Theories of motivation: borrowing the best. Personnel Journal, 58. 376.

2   Bowen, B. E., & Radhakrishna, R. B. (1991). Job satisfaction of agricultural education faculty: A constant phenomena. Journal of Agricultural Education, 32 (2). 16-22.;Quote is from: Linder, J.R.  (1998). Understanding employee motivation.  Journal of Extension, 36, (3).  Electronic copy retrieved October 25, 2006 from the World Wide Web: http://www.joe.org/joe/1998june/rb3.html

3   Linder, J.R. (1998). Understanding employee motivation.  Journal of Extension, 36, (3). Electronic copy retrieved October 25, 2006 from the World Wide Web: http://www.joe.org/joe/1998june/rb3.html

4   Smith, G. P. (1994). Motivation. In W. Tracey (ed.), Human resources management and development handbook (2nd ed.).

5   Schwartz, B. & Lacey, H. (1982). *Behaviorism, science, and human nature.* New York: Norton, p. 24

6   Ibid, p. 25.

7   Ibid, p. 26.

8   B.F. Skinner Foundation Home Page. Retrieved October 25, 2006, from the World Wide Web: http://www.bfskinner.org/Operant.asp

9   Ibid.

10  Ibid.

11  Vroom, V.H. (1964).  Work and motivation. New York: John Wiley.

12  British Broadcasting Corporation Home Page.  Theories in motivation. Retrieved October 30, 2006 from the World Wide Web: http://www.bbc.co.uk/dna/h2g2/pda/A2860346?s_id=8

13  A Science Odyssey: Abraham Maslow", PBS Home Page. Retrieved October 31, 2006, from the World Wide Web: http://www.pbs.org/wgbh/aso/databank/entries/bhmasl.html

14  Boeree, C.G. (2006, 18 August). *Abraham Maslow.* Retrieved 17 August 2006, from http://www.ship.edu/~cgboeree/maslow.html

15  Hodgetts, R.M., Luthans, F. & Doh, J. P. (2006). *International Management, Culture, Strategy, and Behavior, Sixth Edition,* p. 371. New York: McGraw-Hill Irwin.

16  Alderfer, D. (1972).  Existence, relatedness, and growth: Human needs in organizational settings. Gelncoe, IL: Free Press.

17  Value Based Management. (2006, 1 January). *ERG Theory - Clayton P. Alderfer.* Retrieved 18 August 2006, from http://www.valuebasedmanagement.net/methods_alderfer_erg_theory.html

18   Barbuto, J.E. Jr., Fritz, S.M., & Marx, D. (2002). *A FIELD EXAMINATION OF TWO MEASURES OF WORK MOTIVATION AS PREDICTORS OF LEADERS' INFLUENCE TACTICS: Journal of Social Psychology,* 142 (5), p. 601 – 616 ¶ 21

19  Lawler, III, E.E. & Finegold, D. (2000).  Individualizing the organization: Past,

present, and future.  Organizational Dynamics, (29), 1.  pp. 1-15.

20   Campion, M.A. & McClelland, C.L. (1991).  Interdisciplinary examination of the costs and benefits of enlarged jobs: A job design quasi-experiment.  Journal of Applied Psychology, 76, (2). p. 186.

21   Hackman, R. J., Oldham, G., Janson, R. & Purdy, K. (1975). A new strategy for job enrichment.  California Management Review, 17, (4).  pp. 57 - 71.

22   Adams, J. (1965).  Inequality in Social Exchange.  In Advances in Experimental Social Psychology, Ed. Berkowitz, L.  New York: Academic Press.

23   Skarlicki, D. P., Folger, R. & Tesluk, P. (1999). Personality as a moderator in the relationships between fairness and retaliation.  Academy of Management Journal 42, (1).  pp. 100- 108.

24   DiPaola, M., & W. Hoy. (2001). Formalization, conflict, and change: constructive and destructive consequences in schools, *The International Journal of Educational Management* 15(5), pp. 238-244.

25   Garvin, D.A. & Roberto, M.A. (2001).  What you don't know about making decisions. Harvard Business Review, (79), 8, pp. 108 – 116.

26   Schwenk, C.R. & Cosier, R.A. (1980). Effects of the expert, devil's advocate and dialectical inquiry methods on prediction performance.  Organizational Behavior & Human Performance, 26, (3), pp. 409-424.

27   Jenh, K.A. (1997). A qualitative analysis of conflict types and dimensions in organizational groups. *Administrative Science Quarterly*, 42(3), pp. 530–558.

28   Kelly, J. (1970). Make conflict work for you. *Harvard Business Review* 48 (4), pp. 103-113.

29   Thomas, K.W. (1976). Conflict and conflict management. In M.D. Dunnett (ed.), Handbook of industrial and organizational behavior. Chicago: Rand McNally. pp. 889-935.

30   O'Brien, J.A. (2004). *Management information systems.* New York: McGraw-Hill/Irwin.

31   Garderner, P.D., Simmons, J.E.L. (1998). Conflict in small and medium sized projects. *Journal of Management in Engineering* 14 (1), p. 35.

32   Abbott, J.B., Boyd, N.G., Miles, G. (2006). Does type of team matter: An investigation of the relationships between job characteristics and outcomes within a team-based environment. *Journal of Social Psychology* 146 (4), pp. 485-507.

33   Ibid.

34   Ibid.

35   Katzenbach, J.R. & Smith, D.K. (1993). T*he Wisdom of Teams*, Boston, Harvard Business School Press.

36   Massachusetts Institute of Technology (retrieval date 7/7/06). Strategic Management ocw.mit.edu/.../15-660Strategic-HR-ManagementSpring2003/ F8B8B8FA-9C6E-43FD-8425-0011F2C4A9F9/0/slade.pdf

37   Okes, D. & Westcott, R.T. (2001). editors, Certified Quality Manager Handbook: Second Edition, ASQ Quality Press, pp. 37-41.

38   Ibid.

39   Ibid.

40  Ibid.

41  Tuckman, B. (1965). Developmental sequence in small groups. Psychological bulletin, 63, pp. 384-399.

42  Benne, K.D. & Sheats, P. (1948). Functional roles of group members. Journal of social issues, p. 41-49.

43  Kotter, J.P. (1996). Leading Change. Boston: Harvard Business School Press, 1996.

44  Ericksen, J. & Dyer, L. (n.d.) Uncovering and exploring the mobilization and launch phase of high and low performing project teams, Center for Advanced Human Resource Studies Working Papers. Retrieved November 5, 2006 from the World Wide Web: http://www.ilr.cornell.edu/depts/cahrs/downloads/pdfs/workingpapers/WP02-06.pdf

45  Ibid.

# CHAPTER 7 — Human Resource Management

## MEASURABLE LEARNING OBJECTIVES

1. Discuss the importance of the management of human resources within an organization.

2. Identify the primary US federal laws and regulations with which a manager must be familiar.

3. Discuss the strategic human resource planning process.

4. Distinguish between a job analysis, a job description and a job specification.

5. Identify and discuss the steps in the employment process.

6. Discuss current issues in human resource management.

# Importance of Human Resource Management

Human Resources Management (HRM) is the overarching administration of a Human Resources (HR) department. HR is responsible for determining the following:

- Methods utilized to recruit new employees.
- Administration of the hiring process.
- The types of training and development programs to offer and on whom the programs should focus.
- Oversight of the benefits available, compensation policies, employee records, and personnel policies.

In large organizations, a dedicated department will handle these issues; but in a small organization, one or two staff members handle them.

The HR planning process consists of the activities required for staffing and sustaining an organization. The first activity is the planning process, which consists of aligning the human resource strategic goals with the organization's strategic goals. The planning process will ensure that all activities in which HR engages meet the goals of the overall organization. The planning process includes assessment of jobs within the organization—job analysis, job description, and job specification—and planning for future human resource needs.

When an organization's leaders determine staffing needs, HR will normally attempt to build a pool of good candidates for the position. An organization will have to interview many candidates to find one that has the desired skills, abilities, and fit for the organization. Hiring the best candidate is crucial for the success of an organization, because a poor hiring decision will have repercussions across the entire organization. The employment process involves several areas, such as recruitment, selection, orientation, training, performance management, compensation, and benefits.

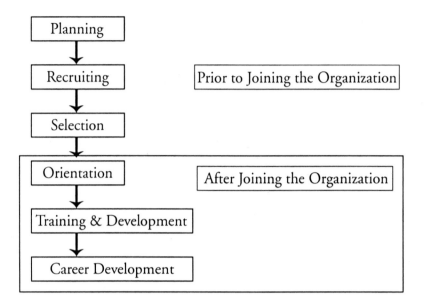

## Recruitment

Recruitment is the first step in the hiring process and is the process of building a pool of qualified job candidates. Recruitment requires the following abilities:[1]

1. Identification of the abilities needed to perform the job successfully. Most likely, a job analysis will be performed to determine the job description and job specifications specific to a position.

2. Determination of how the job will be advertised to ensure that the applicant pool includes those who are candidates for the position.

3. Ensuring that the advertising and applicant pool meets the organization's equal employment opportunity commitment.

HR personnel often focus recruitment efforts on current employees who wish to make lateral or upward moves within the organization, referrals from current employees, print and radio advertisements, and internet advertising.

The skills required for a job and its level within the organization will determine the most appropriate sources to utilize in a search for applicants. According to a survey of 519 small businesses, more than a quarter of respondents stated that one of their top three business worries was to find qualified and motivated employees.[2]

Recruitment can take place internal or external to the organization. Internal recruiting is done by posting an upcoming job opening on bulletin boards, in newsletters, or on electronic message boards. Those who are interested in and qualified for the position, whether it is a lateral or upward move, are invited to apply for the position. Benefits to internal recruiting include the following:

- Allows current employees the opportunity to grow in their careers within the organization.
- The applicant already knows the organization and its policies.
- The applicant is a known entity whose work habits are well documented.
- Internal recruiting is cheaper than external recruiting; the candidate can usually begin in their new position sooner than an external recruit.

Disadvantages to internal recruiting also exist:

- By posting the job first internally, there is the potential that none of the applicants that apply qualify, which opens the potential for a difficult future work environment.
- Employees may expect that promotions or lateral moves are based upon longevity rather than merit.
- Potentially, an internal job posting could be written with a specific individual in mind, blocking out other qualified candidates.

If recruiters determine that none of the internal candidates qualify for the position, the job may then be posted externally. Companies have the ability to reach different target markets, based upon where the job is posted. External recruiting also allows current employees to refer acquaintances. The following reveals the benefits of external recruiting:

- External recruits bring new ideas to the organization.
- Employees hired will have the specialized skills and abilities required for the position.

External recruiting also has its disadvantages:

- May leave current employees feeling neglected and overlooked, encouraging the current employees to begin to look elsewhere for employment, due to real or perceived lack of career growth.
- The applicant's true work ethic is an unknown.
- The recruitment process is more expensive and takes longer.

Whether choosing internal or external recruiting as a means of filling a position, one should understand the advantages and disadvantages of the recruiting plan chosen.

## Selection

Selection is the process of screening applicants to determine the best candidate for a position. Several common screening methods exist.

### Application Forms & Résumés

Application Forms & Résumés provide background information about the applicant's education, work history, and certifications. Unfortunately, studies report that 44 percent of all résumés contain some lies.[3] Therefore, review of the application and résumé is only the first step in the screening process:

In October 1991 [Hatteras Hammocks] . . . abruptly lost its controller. Executive vice-president Jay Branch interviewed several candidates for the position, but one man distinguished himself from the others. Recommended by someone Branch knew, the candidate came with a great resume—B.A. in accounting, M.B.A. from Indiana University, CPA, and several years as controller at a big local corporation. The following March, Branch hired him after a quick call to the previous employer. After a few months it became obvious that the new controller couldn't do the job, and by October Branch had fired him. His replacement quickly saw something wrong with the company's books. The man with the fancy resume had embezzled $60,000. A quick background check turned up no record of either of his degrees or his CPA credentials. The police arrested him and he confessed. . . . Branch, who saw his own name forged on several checks, says, "The whole episode taught me the necessity of checking thoroughly, no matter how good a recommendation is."[4]

Careful scrutiny and confirmation of facts presented on the application and résumé must be completed prior to any job offers.

### Ability Tests

Ability Tests should be based upon a thorough job analysis and measure an applicant's physical, mechanical, mental, or clerical abilities. The tests must accurately reflect job requirements to be considered a valid and reliable screening tool.

### Performance Tests

Performance tests are used to evaluate performance on specific tasks that will be performed on the job. Applicants for a managerial position may be asked to participate in different role-playing scenarios. Those applicants are then assessed according to their actions during the scenario.

*Personality Tests*

Personality tests measure an individual's characteristics, such as degree of extroversion, autonomy, energy, and the need for achievement. Most organizations use personality tests with caution because of the challenge of defending such tests in court.[5]

*The Interview Process*

Although widely debated as to its effectiveness, the interview is universally utilized in the application process.[6] Interview questions should focus on the applicant's job qualifications and abilities. A manager must be aware of the legality of certain interview questions. The following are topics that should not be raised during an interview:[7]

- Children. Whether the interviewee currently has or plans to have children or if the person has arrangements for child care. Such questions single out a particular group and are disallowed by Title VII of the Civil Rights Act of 1964.
- Age. An interviewer cannot ask an applicant's age—even asking a high school graduation date may be shaky. Because The Age Discrimination in Employment Act outlaws discrimination of anyone older than forty, age only becomes relevant when it is a bona fide occupational qualification (BFOQ).
- Disabilities. The Americans with Disabilities Act (ADA) prohibits employers from obtaining information regarding a physical or mental disability that may interfere with a job.
- Citizenship. Although employers can ask applicants if they have a legal right to work in the U.S., applicants do not have to be U.S. citizens. Asking such questions, when not a BFOQ, sets the organization up for a national origin discrimination lawsuit.
- Legal Issues. Employers may not ask if the applicant has ever filed a lawsuit or been arrested.

Limited exceptions do exist for many of these question bans in the form of bona fide occupational qualifications. The following includes a few examples of qualified BFOQs:

- Age sixty as the required retirement age for airline pilots.
- Only female locker room attendants are hired to work in the female locker room.
- Jobs in the federal government may require U.S. citizenship.

For those jobs that do not have BFOQs, the subject of disabilities may be explored only after a conditional job offer is made, based upon satisfactory completion of required physical, medical, or job-related skills tests. If an interviewer discovers any physical or mental condition that may affect job performance, he or she may then ask the candidate direct questions regarding the condition. Even visible evidence of a disability does not automatically disqualify a candidate from either an interview or employment. The organization is required to explore reasonable accommodation to enable the applicant to perform the job's essential functions:[8]

> An employer is impressed with an applicant's resume and contacts the individual to come in for an interview. The applicant, who is deaf, requests a sign language interpreter for the interview. The employer cancels the interview and refuses to consider further this applicant because it believes it would have to hire a full-time interpreter. The employer has violated the ADA. The employer should have proceeded with the interview, using a sign language interpreter (absent undue hardship), and at the interview inquired to what extent the individual would need a sign language interpreter to perform any essential functions requiring communication with other people.[9]

Interviews can be structured or unstructured in their formats. Unstructured interviews are all different in that the interviewer will ask each applicant different questions. In a structured interview, each applicant is asked the same or very similar questions and can be behavioral or situational in focus. All structured interviews will have the following characteristics:

- The questions must be job related and based on a job analysis.
- Each applicant is asked the same questions (different follow-up questions are allowed).
- There is a standard scoring system used to score the applicant's answers to the questions.[10]

A behavioral interview focuses on behaviors exhibited by the interviewee in the past. The questions are structured, open-ended, and focus on abilities needed for the position which the applicant is interviewing. The following questions may be asked during a behavioral interview:

- Tell us about a time in the past year when you had to deal with a difficult team member and describe what you did.
- Give us an example of a time when you used your customer philosophy to deal with a perplexing problem.[11]

A situational interview focuses on hypothetical situations. While the questions are still structured, open ended, and focus on abilities need in the position, a situational question will ask the interviewee how they would handle a certain situation. Questions that may be asked during a situational interview are as follows:

- A customer is angry because the store is out of a product that was advertised for sale. How would you handle the situation?

- You are having difficulties with a co-worker and believe that they are telling your manager untruths about your work. What would you do?

According to Min and Kliner, successful selection depends upon seven steps:[12]

1. Know the exact job specification, including daily interaction, interpersonal skills, and levels of commitment to the organization and experience.
2. Understand what personal characteristics are required.
3. Identify the best recruiting source for the vacant position.
4. Assess qualities, such as technical skills, academic requirements, business knowledge, etc.
5. Check applicant's credentials and employment references.
6. Determine applicant's expertise.
7. Put together information about the top three candidates and decide which one is the best match for the organization.

Hiring good employees who are qualified for the jobs they fill will have a significant positive impact on an organization. When the selection process is completed and an individual is offered and accepts a position, the next step is the orientation process.

## Orientation

"After all, the company isn't just introducing a worker to a new job. It's acclimating him or her to a whole new culture."[13] Well developed orientation programs work to reduce the anxiety associated with beginning a position with a new organization.

Besides the facts concerning pay and benefits, orientation programs help new employees understand the organization's culture and values. The program should be designed to assist a newly-hired employee in adjusting to the work environment.

The new employee should already be familiar with the organization. The company should allow the employee to read employee manuals and policies before orientation. During the orientation, the new employee should become acquainted with the organizational chart and learn how the organization functions. Personal introductions and a tour of the department or working area are important during the orientation to build confidence in the new employee.

Meeting coworkers is an important part of the orientation process, and Persistence Software has a creative way to get the new employee introduced:

. . . [B]agels and bran muffins are the answer. On mornings when someone new joins the 110-person company, a tray of breakfast food is placed strategically near his or her desk. An e-mail invites everyone to come nosh and meet the new colleague. CEO Christopher Keene explains, "If you just send out an E-mail announcing a new hire, it doesn't help the new person meet anybody, and that's really the tough part."—whereas bagels draw coworkers to the new hire's desk. "Everybody troops by," Keene says. "And they're guilted into introducing themselves."[14]

## Training

Employee training is considered an important function of effective human resources management. Training is a process that is intended to equip employees with specific skills and increase the quality of performance in their current jobs. Training is an essential process in improving productivity and providing the best services to the customers. The two types of training organizations commonly utilize are on-the-job training (OJT) and off-the-job training.

On-the-job training is conducted at the employee's worksite and normally monitored by a supervisor or senior employee. This type of training is especially effective in increasing skills unique to a job and may include activities that will develop the skills of employees. On-the-job training includes serving as an assistant to an experienced worker and lateral transfer into a position, which supplements current skills and coaching, where the employee is led by an experienced worker.

Although OJT may sound ideal, some disadvantages do exist. The first of which is the implicit cost of such a training program. The energy and time spent by the trainer could have been used to perform "real" work.[15] However, since this cost occurs in the early training stage, the result of the training should lead to higher productivity and thus pay off in the long run.

Off-the-job training includes classroom training with live instructors, videos, or workbooks. Off-site training provides the advantage of a "distraction free" environment, which promotes creativity and learning.

The disadvantages of off-the-job training are that it keeps the employee away from their job and may involve travel expenses.

## Employee Development

Development is educating employees so that they are prepared for their future within the organization. Certification agencies require that many professions, such as nurses, accountants, and HR professionals, have skills that must be constantly reviewed and upgraded. Most business leaders agree that the success and growth of an organization is closely related to the successful development of employees within the organization.

Efforts should be made to provide the tools and resources necessary to support employees and their career goals. Organizations should institute a variety of courses that develop management and technical skills. Such courses are important especially to those employees who have an interest in upward mobility.

## Performance Management

Performance management is the process of identifying, measuring, and managing human performance in an organization. Performance appraisal and feedback is important in Human Resources Management because it provides managers with important information to make decisions about pay raises, bonuses, promotions, etc. Performance appraisals also help managers to determine which workers are candidates for training. The information provided during a performance appraisal helps an employee understand how he or she is doing in relation to objective standards of performance. The information also helps the supervisor determine what training or development the employee may need. Supervisors counsel employees who are working at levels below acceptable standards. Performance feedback can lead to high levels of employee motivation because it provides employees with detailed information about their strengths, weaknesses, and ways to improve their performance in the future. The following points state a few guidelines for effective performance feedback:

1. An assessment should be written using specific language. The assessment of job performance should be stated clearly and succinctly and supported with facts and examples. One must be sure to focus on behaviors, not on judgments.
2. Performance gaps should be addressed. The difference between the expected level of performance and the actual level of performance One must be sure to include the salient issue—what has occurred and what is expected.[16]
3. Feedback given during a performance appraisal, whether positive or negative, should never be a surprise to the receiving employee. The official feedback should only be confirmation of what the employee has already received through oral or written methods—from his or her supervisor.

## Compensation and Benefits

Employee compensation has three elements: base compensation, pay incentives, and benefits. These three items constitute a remuneration package which the employee obtains for his or her labor. Pay and benefits are the most significant cost in most organizations. In gaining or losing a competitive edge, the effectiveness with which compensation is allocated greatly impacts the organizations and its employees. Compensation affects an individual economically, sociologically, and psychologically.[17] Mishandling compensation issues could have a strong negative impact on employees, and ultimately, on the organization's performance.

Compensation tools are utilized to produce reasonable pay systems that allow the organization to attract, maintain, and motivate employees, while restraining labor costs. Many factors influence the level of compensation and benefits offered by an organization. Those factors are found both internal and external to the organization.[18]

| Factors That Influence Compensation and Benefits | | |
|---|---|---|
| Organizational Factors | External Factors | Employee Factors |
| Management Philosophy<br>Kind of Business<br>Size of Company<br>Profitability of Company<br>Is the organization labor<br>or capital intensive? | Geographical Location<br>Unionization<br>Industry | Kind of Job Performed<br>Employee's Performance<br>and Tenure |

# Legal issues

## *Major United States Federal Laws and Regulations Related to HRM (1963–2005)*

Employers must ensure that the organization itself and all employees in an organization act in accordance with federal laws and regulations. While many important U.S. federal laws and regulations exist, the following delineates a few of them:

| | |
|---|---|
| Equal Pay Act, 1963 | The Equal Pay Act prohibits discrimination based upon gender in the payment of wages and fringe benefits for equal work in jobs requiring equal skill, effort, and responsibility—which are performed under similar working conditions. Pay differences can be based on seniority, merit, or production quota. |
| Civil Rights Act Title VII | The landmark legislation outlawing discrimination based on race, color, creed, or national origin is the Civil Rights Act of 1964. Those activities covered include hiring, promotions, assignments, discipline, performance, appraisal, and all other conditions, benefits, or privileges of employment. |
| Age Discrimination in Employment Act (ADEA) | The Age Discrimination in Employment Act (ADEA) provides protection for persons who are age 40 or over. It does not prohibit; however, all discrimination on the basis of age, such as maximum entry level ages for initial appointment as a law enforcement officer or a bona fide occupational qualification. |
| Occupational Safety & Health Act (OSHA) | Organizations must provide non-hazardous working conditions. |
| Employee Retirement Income Security Act (ERISA) | The Employee Retirement Income Security Act of 1974 (ERISA) is a federal law that sets minimum standards for most voluntarily established pension and health plans in private industry to provide protection for individuals in these plans. |

| | |
|---|---|
| Pregnancy Discrimination Act | The PregnancyDiscrimination Act is an amendment to Title VII of the Civil Rights Act of 1964. Discrimination on the basis of pregnancy, childbirth, or related medical conditions constitutes unlawful sex discrimination under Title VII. Women affected by pregnancy or related conditions must be treated in the same manner as other applicants or employees with similar abilities or limitations. |
| Mandatory Retirement Act | This Act prohibits forced retirement of employees under 70. |
| Consolidated Omnibus Budget Reconciliation Act (COBRA) | The Consolidated Omnubus Budget Reconciliation Act (COBRA) gives workers and their families who lose their health benefits the right to choose to continue group health benefits provided by their group health plan for limited periods of time under certain circumstances such as voluntary or involuntary job loss, reduction in the hours worked, transition between jobs, death, divorce, and other life events. Qualified individuals may be required to pay the entire premium for coverage up to 102 percent of the cost of the plan. |
| Imigration Reform & Control Act | Under IRCA, employers may hire only persons who may legally work in the U.S.—citizens and nationals of the U.S. The employer must verify the identity and employment eligibility of anyone to be hired, which includes completing the Employment Eligibility Verification Form (I-9). Employers must keep each I-9 on file for at least three years, or one year after employment ends, whichever is longer. |
| Worker Adjustment and Retraining Notification Act | WARN offers protection to workers, their families and commuunities by requiring employers to provide notice 60 days in advance of covered plant closings and covered mass layoffs. This notice must be provided to either affected workers or their representatives (e.g., a labor union), to the State dislocated worker unit, and to the appropriate unit of local government. |

| | |
|---|---|
| Americans with Disablities Act (ADA), 1990 | ADA is a federal law that forbids discrimination in the workplace against persons who are disabled. Employers who have 15 or more employees, along with all State and Local Governments are affected. Individuals protected under this act include qualified individuals with a disability, individuals with a history of a disability, and people regarded as having a disability. A qualified individual is defined as an individual who, with or without reasonable accommodation, can perform the essential functions of the employment positions that such individuals hold or desire. |
| Civil Rights Act of 1991 | The purpose of this act was to amend the Civil Rights Act of 1964 to strengthen and improve Federal civil rights laws, to provide for damages in cases of intentional employment discrimination, and to clarify provisions regarding disparate impact actions. |
| Family & Medical Leave Act | Covered employers must grant an eligible employee up to a total of 12 work weeks of unpaid leave during any 12-month period for one or more of the following reasons: (1) for the birth and care of the newborn child of the employee; (2) for placement with the employee of a son or daughter for adoption or foster care; (3) to care for an immediate family member (spouse, child, or parent) with a serious health condition; (4) to take medical leave when the employee is unable to work because of a serious health condition. |
| Sarbanes-Oxley Act | The Act covers a whole range of governance issues—many covering the types of trade that are allowed within a company, with an emphasis upon keeping everything above board. For example, the Act forbids personal loans to officers and directors. Former WorldCom boss Bernie Ebbers had taken considerable loans from his company shortly before it became the center of a corporate scandal. Other measures regulate the responsibilities of audit committees sent in to check the health of companies' compliance. The Act also offers protection to whistleblowers. |

The Equal Employment Opportunity Commission (EEOC) is responsible for enforcing anti-discrimination laws and "provides oversight and coordination of all federal equal employment opportunity regulations, practices and policies."[19]

The EEOC has five commissioners and a General Counsel appointed by the President of the United States and confirmed by the Senate. The five-member Commission makes equal employment opportunity policy and approves most litigation. The General Counsel is responsible for conducting EEOC enforcement litigation under Title VII of the Civil Rights Act of 1964, the Equal Pay Act, the Age Discrimination in Employment Act, and the Americans with Disabilities Act.

## *Best Practices*

Employers can take proactive measures that will reduce the likelihood of violations of EEO policies. Organizations should develop a strong EEO policy that is embraced by top management. The company should train and hold accountable all managers, supervisors, and employees. The organizations should carefully document and explain all employment decisions to those persons affected by these decisions. All hiring and promotions should be done with EEO practices implemented. Businesses should police themselves, ensuring that current employment practices do not violate any individual's right to equal employment. Companies should train and mentor employees to give workers of all backgrounds the opportunity to acquire upper-level jobs. Finally, the business should make known to all employees all promotion criteria and job openings.[20]

# Strategic Human Resource Planning Process

Strategic human resources (HR) planning is the process of establishing programs or procedures to implement HR strategies. Strategic planning for Human Resources must follow the organization's strategic plan. A firm may have a well-composed HR strategy; but if no tactic exists to implement it effectively, the strategy becomes meaningless. In order for HR management to support the future direction of an organization, strategic human resources plans should be developed.[21] All HR programs in an organization are based on human resource planning. This process involves components of a human resource management system, which are designed by managers and ensure that these components are consistent with organizational architecture, strategy, and goal.

The objective of human resource planning is to ensure that an organization has the necessary resources to produce certain amount of products or services. In order to obtain the necessary resources, HR should conduct several activities prior to the employment process—creating detail job analysis, job description, and job specification.

## Five Aspects of Implementing Strategy

Human resources from a strategic perspective include assessment of human capital and an accountability framework.[22] The five aspects of implementing strategy in HR are strategic alignment, leadership and knowledge management, results-oriented performance culture, talent management, and accountability.

### Strategic Alignment

Strategic alignment is the planning stage and aligns the strategies of the human resources function with the mission, goals, and objectives of the organization. This alignment is accomplished through analysis and measurement of HR programs.

### Leadership and Knowledge Management

Leadership and knowledge management is the first step in the implementation stage and ensures continuity of leadership. A business establishes continuity of leadership through the identification of potential gaps in leadership and addressing those gaps. The organization then implements programs that capture organizational knowledge and promote learning.

### Results-Oriented Performance Culture

The second part of the implementation stage is the promotion of a results-oriented performance culture. During this stage, an organization's HR managers implement and maintain effective performance management systems and award programs to promote a diverse, high-performing workforce.

### Talent Management

The third step in the implementation stage is managing the organization's human resource talent. In this step, human resource managers must address all gaps in competency that employees may have and implement and maintain programs to attract, acquire, develop, promote, and retain quality individuals.

*Accountability*

The final stage, evaluating results, contributes to the organization's performance by ensuring accountability of Human Resource leaders. In this stage, the organization monitors and evaluates policies, programs, and activities. The company must also analyze compliance with merit systems and identify and monitor improvements during this stage.

# Job Analysis

Job analysis is the process of pinpointing duties of a position and explaining the significance of how those duties relate to a particular job.[23] While observations are made of a person performing a job, the analysis is of the specifications and description of the job, not the person. Job analysis identifies the competencies of knowledge, skills, and abilities directly related to the performance of a specific job.

> It is a systematic procedure for gathering, documenting and analyzing information about the content, context, and requirements of a job. . . . A competency is a measurable pattern of knowledge, skills, abilities, behaviors and other characteristics that an individual needs in order to perform work roles or occupational function successfully.[24]

Although a job analysis does not have to be completed each time a manager seeks to fill a job, constant organizational changes require that a job analysis should be conducted periodically on jobs within the organization.

# Job Description

Although management guru Tom Peters believes that job descriptions should be abolished, a job description is simply a general list of responsibilities and tasks of a specific position. It contains information about the knowledge, training, education, and skills necessary for a particular job—a summary of information collected in the job analysis phase. Well-crafted, carefully-worded job descriptions prevent unnecessary misunderstandings by ensuring that job candidates and hiring managers understand the requirements for a job. Job descriptions also provide a basis from which to determine whether a disabled applicant is otherwise qualified for the job, and if so, to assist in determining what accommodation the applicant would require to be able to perform the essential functions of the position.

## *Job Specification*

A job specification describes the minimum characteristics and qualifications necessary to effectively perform a job. Therefore, an applicant must possess these qualifications to be considered for a job. Job specifications include critical expertise and proper education.

Job specifications should be specified as exact as possible to benefit managers during the interview process, thus avoiding hiring over- or under-qualified candidates.[25]

# Current issues

## *Managing Workforce Diversity*

Characteristics, visible or not, that distinguish one individual from another is referred to as diversity. These differences include age, gender, race, ethnicity, religion, sexual orientation, and disabilities. Diversity is one of the most important issues facing organizations today. Managers must ensure an inclusive workplace, utilizing the skills of all employees and treating all employees with respect and professionalism.

Workplace diversity is about people—employees who bring differences to an organization. Diversity is about making differences work to the benefit of all. Managers recognize that diversity is a resource that enhances performance within an organization.[26]

Biases based upon race, sex, age, national origin, disability, or religious beliefs can create disharmony in the workplace and serious legal issues. Managers and supervisors should recognize that developing awareness through diversity training will create a respectful workplace. Understanding discrimination laws and the importance of embracing diversity will not only lower the risk of lawsuits but also, more importantly, create a healthy work environment for all.[27]

Valuing diversity in the business world today means creating a workplace that respects differences, recognizes individual contributions, and creates a work environment that maximizes the potential of all employees. Teams made up of culturally diverse individuals yield more creative, synergistic, and effective outcomes.[28]

Workplace diversity focuses on inclusion and how a diverse workforce can impact an organization's profits and losses. Leveraging workplace diversity is a vital strategic resource for competitive advantage. Organizations that link workplace diversity to strategic goals and objectives are holding managers accountable for results.[29]

## *Sexual Harassment*

Sexual harassment is a form of sex discrimination that violates Title VII of the Civil Rights Act of 1964. Unwelcome sexual advances, requests for sexual favors, and other verbal or physical conduct of a sexual nature constitute sexual harassment. The following examples clarify sexual harassment:[30]

- Submission to such conduct is made either explicitly or implicitly a term or condition of an individual's employment, also known as Quid Pro Quo.
- Submission to or rejection of such conduct by an individual is used as the basis for employment decisions affecting such an individual.
- Such conduct has the purpose or effect of unreasonably interfering with an individual's work performance or creating an intimidating, hostile, or offensive working environment.

Harassment can be subjective, where the victim perceives an abusive environment or objective, where a reasonable person in similar circumstances would perceive an abusive environment.

Sexual harassment can occur even if the victim is not of the opposite sex. The victim, as well as the harasser, may be male or female. Victims can include anyone affected by the offensive conduct.[31]

Sexual harassment in the workplace presents a large liability for organizations. Defense against legal action proves difficult. When the harasser is a supervisor or manager, the organization is liable for tangible employment action—unless the employer used reasonable care to prevent and correct harassment or the victim unreasonably failed to make a complaint under the employer's prevention policy.[32]

When the harasser is a co-worker, an employer must take immediate corrective action upon becoming aware of the harassment. If the harasser is not an employee, liability will still be an issue if the employer knew or should have known of the conduct and failed to take corrective action.

The greatest thing an organization can do to prevent sexual harassment liability is to develop a policy prohibiting sexual harassment. The policy must define and explain zero tolerance for this type of conduct. All organizations should have a complaint procedure in place, and all employees should acknowledge receipt and understanding of this policy.[33]

## *Hostile Work Environment*

Unwelcome comments or conduct based on legally protected characteristics that interfere with an employee's work performance can constitute a hostile work environment. The interference must be unreasonable and create an intimidating or offensive work environment. This type of harassment can be committed by a supervisor, co-worker, or even a non-employee. The victim of a hostile work environment complaint does not necessarily have to be the individual toward which the offender directs his or her conduct. Whomever the harasser affects with negative conduct can be a victim.[34]

While no laws mandate that an employer be courteous, certain laws do protect employees from abuse and a hostile work environment. Like sexual harassment, employers must establish a workplace that is free of hostile conduct.

A hostile work environment is a violation of civil rights, based on gender, sexual orientation, race, nationality, ancestry, ethnic origin, mental or physical handicaps, etc. A hostile work environment exists when an employee experiences workplace harassment that includes an offensive, intimidating, or oppressive atmosphere, created by an individual in the workplace.

Many actions tend to create a hostile work environment, such as staring or leering in a sexually suggestive manner. While not all inclusive, the following are examples that may create a sexually hostile environment:[35]

- Offensive remarks about body parts, clothes, looks etc.
- Touching, patting, pinching, or intentional brushing.
- Sexual jokes or sexual gestures.
- Sexual emails, letters, notes, or images.

One should not assume that only actions of a sexual nature can create a hostile work environment. Many non-sexual actions arise that may also result in hostile environment harassment. These include the following:[36]

- Racially derogatory words, phrases or epithets.
- Gestures, pictures, or drawings that depict a particular racial or ethnic group in an offensive manner.
- Comments about skin color or other ethnic characteristics.
- Offensive religious comments.
- Negative stereotype expressions.
- Negative age comments.

If an employer fails to take appropriate corrective action, or if it can be proven that an employer knew or should have known about an incident of harassment, then the employer is liable. Title VII prohibits retaliation against an employee who makes a complaint of harassment or supports the claim of another employee. Retaliation can include dismissal, transfer, demotion, or negative evaluation.[37]

# Career Management

In the early stages of a career, an individual should place himself or herself near or in situations with colleagues and supervisors whom he or she wants to emulate. For example, one place to gain experience and network is volunteering on company projects, such as the newsletter or volunteer activities external to the organization. Volunteering brings one in contact with individuals from all levels and departments within the organization and provides exposure throughout the organization.

Other areas of career management that tend to get overlooked include dress code and punctuality. Employees need to dress appropriate to the part and rank towards which they aspire. If an employee works on the manufacturing line but wishes to one day be the line manager, then he or she must learn the policies and procedures inside and out. Also, the employee needs to set themselves apart from the others in the group: show up for work a few minutes ahead of schedule and report back early after lunch. An employee might consider volunteering to stay late to meet the project deadline or offer to learn skills which are needed by the organization.

In an office environment, the principles are the same as those on the manufacturing line, but there are more deadlines to manage. Two deadlines that are carelessly overlooked include responding to emails and voicemails. One should respond to emails and voicemails promptly, because lack of response sends a negative message regarding work ethic.

Mentors are a key to career management. Whether one has been in the workforce for two days or twenty years, he or she should have a mentor. Mentors are individuals that provide career guidance and advice and help with obstacles along the way. Mentors are individuals that can explain office culture and politics or give insight into how to make a presentation to the Manager of Accounting. Mentors have been in the same shoes and know the ropes about the business and the company; their knowledge is another's power. Good mentors will provide sound career advice, serve as a sounding board, and can also offer feedback.

## *Career Paths*

When an employee transfers from one position to another within the company, three different types of career paths are available: linear, spiral, and steady-state.[38]

### *Linear*

In a linear career path, the employee progresses up though an organization's hierarchy, generally in one functional area, such as marketing or finance. One who follows a linear career path will move up within the organization by taking on more responsibility and expanding his or her skills in a series of jobs. The employee on this track may do so at one organization or change companies during the career climb.

### *Spiral*

In a spiral career path, upwardly mobile employees will often start in one position, such as an electrical engineer, become an engineering manager, transition to director of Human Resources planning, and wind up in recruiting. Each of the different jobs held by one in a spiral career path will build on the previous jobs and provide a broad base of experience.

### *Steady-State*

When an individual chooses a career as a lifetime profession, he or she follows the steady-state career path. This type of career is common, with individuals practicing professions such as a physician or minister.

## *Job Hunting*

Whether one is competing for a promotion within an organization or looking for a job in the marketplace, optimal self presentation is critical for success. Job applicants are removed from consideration throughout all of the stages of the recruitment/ interview process. Sarah Needleman has gathered input from various recruiters and developed a list of things that every job hunter should know:[39]

1. Be concise when answering interview questions. A candidate can talk himself or herself out of a job by giving long-winded answers to interview questions. A candidate should practice answering common interview questions. It is a balancing act to provide the interviewer with enough information to make a decision, but not so much that they can find something wrong with the answers.

2.  Résumés should be free of all factual discrepancies. Any falsifications—such as academic record or awards—will immediately disqualify a candidate. Even noting that a Bachelor of Arts was earned instead of the actual degree of a Bachelor of Science may have recruiters questioning a résumé.

3.  Candidates must exhibit strong communication skills during an interview. A candidate shows strong communication skills by making eye contact, speaking with confidence, and using complete sentences and thoughts, without excessive slang or verbal crutches.

4.  If communicating with a recruiter via email, use plain fonts, no background wallpaper and check spelling, punctuation, and grammar prior to sending. Be sure that a personalized email account is appropriate—sleezgirl@ might not get the wanted response. If using a cell phone as a contact number, be sure the voicemail message is appropriate and professional.[40]

5.  Present an air of professionalism and remember that a candidate may be assessed from the time they enter the parking lot. How a candidate treats the organization's receptionist may be considered just as important as credentials or responses to questions during the interview. Candidates should get rid of gum and be aware of habits—such as foot tapping or hair twirling—and listen to mom's advice and stand up straight.

6.  Recruiters do not want candidates who act nonchalantly during an interview. Genuine enthusiasm, energy, and passion, regarding both previous accomplishments and the opportunity available in the position for which the candidate is interviewing, should be displayed during the interview process.

7.  A candidate must have a professional appearance—in both dress and demeanor. Clothing should not be outdated and special attention should be given to the entire outfit. Polish shoes, iron the wrinkles, and wear a minimum amount of jewelry.

8.  Finally, be cautious about personal information that is available on blogs or other places on the web. Recruiters regularly use Google and other search engines to check on candidates. According to a 2005 survey of 102 executive recruiters by ExecuNet, an executive job-search and networking organization, 75 percent of recruiters use search engines to uncover information about candidates, and 26 percent of recruiters have eliminated candidates because of information found online.[41]

The entire hiring process from résumé to interview is carefully scrutinized by recruiters, and job candidates must ensure that they navigate the entire process with enthusiasm, care, and professionalism.

# Conclusion

Human Resource Management is vital to every organization, regardless of its size. Polices need to be established that will guide both the organization and its employees through the steps needed to build a world class workforce. These policies not only protect the company but also the employee. Human Resource Management impacts all aspects of the company and their employees.

Laws that pertain to personnel were established to protect both the organization and employees. These laws need to be integrated into the organization through policies and procedures. Established policies will guide managers through the processes of hiring, retaining, and termination.

# Impact on the Organization, the Manager, and Employees

Without solid foundations and guidelines on how to handle typical employee issues, organizations may be vulnerable to legal recourse. Managers need to understand how the hiring/termination process works to ensure that they are acquiring and maintaining the right personnel for the job. Employees have the responsibility of knowing polices under which they work and how these will impact their career and advancement.

# Endnotes

1   UC Berkley. (2006). *Guide to Managing Human Resources*. Retrieved on July 19, 2006 from http://hrweb.berkeley.edu/guide/employment.htm#recruit
2   Kelin, E. (1993). *Heroes for Hire*. D&B Reports, pp. 26–28.
3   Kluger, J. (2002).  Pumping up your past. Time 159, (23), p. 45.
4   Cronin, M.P. (1993).  This is a test. Inc., 15, (8). P 64, 5p.
5   Adler, S. (1994). Personality tests for sales force selection: Worth a fresh look.  Review of Business, 16, (1). P. 27, 5p.
6   Harris, M.M. (1989). Reconsidering the employment interview: A review of recent literature and suggestions for future research. Personnel Psychology, 42, (4).  pp. 691-726.
7   Pauliot, J.S. (1992). Topics to avoid with applicants. Nation's Business, 80, (7).  pp. 57-58.
8   Ibid.
9   Equal Employment Opportunity Commission Web Site.  Enforcement guidance: reasonable accommodation and undue hardship under the Americans with disabilities act.  Retrieved from: http://www.eeoc.gov/policy/docs/accommodation.html#reasonable
10  Aamodt, M. (2001). Technical affairs. International Public Management Association Assessment Council. Retrieved: http://www.ipmaac.org/acn/feb01/techaff.html
11  Vogt, P. (2006). Acing behavioral interviews. Wall Street Journal, Retrieved October 1, 2006 from: http://www.careerjournal.com/jobhunting/interviewing/19980129-vogt.html
12  Min, J.C. & Kleiner, B.H. (2001). *How to hire employees effectively,* Management Research News, 24, (12) p. 31–38.
13  Hoffman, M. (1999). Do I know you?  Inc. 21, (15). P211, 2p.
14  Ibid.
15  Van der Klink, M.R. & Streumer, J.N. (2002). Effectiveness of on-the-job training. Journal of European Industrial Training, 26, (2/3/4). pp. 196–199.
16  Washington State Department of Personnel Home Page. Performance feedback. Retrieved November 1, 2006 from the World Wide Web:  http://hr.dop.wa.gov/PDPGuide/performance/PDPGuide-Part5PerfFeedback10.htm
17  Melcher, R.A., Cohn, L., & Symonds, W.C. (1999). *You may come home again–with a raise.* Business Week 3638. p. 44-45.
18  Henderson, R.I. (1994). Compensation management. (6th ed). Upper Saddle River, NJ: Prentice Hall.
19  EEOC Home Page. (2006). Equal Employment Opportunity Commission. Retrieved July 8, 2006, from Equal Employment Opportunity Commission Web site: http://www.eeoc.gov/
20  EEOC. (2006). Equal Employment Opportunity Commission. Retrieved July 8, 2006, from Equal Employment Opportunity Commission Web site: http://www.eeoc.gov/abouteeoc/task_reports/best_practice.html
21  HRVS. (2002). Human Resources Planning. Retrieved on July 8, 2006, from http://www.hrcouncil.ca/hr_overview/pg003_e.cfm#1a
22  Office of Personnel Management. Retrieved October 23, 2006 from: http://www.opm.gov/hcaaf_resource_center/2-2.asp

23 HR-Guide. (1998). *Job Analysis: Overview.* Retrieved on July 8, 2006 from http://www.hr-guide.com/data/G000.htm

24 Office of Personnel Management Handbook. Retreieved October 2, 2006 from: http://www.opm.gov/deu/Handbook_2003/DEOH-Section-7.asp

25 Min, J. C. and Kleiner, B. H. (2001). *How to hire employees effectively,* Management Research News, 24, (12) p. 31 – 38.

26 Workplace Diversity. Retrieved July 18, 2006, from Cornell University ILR School Web site: http://www.ilr.cornell.edu/library/subjectGuides/workplaceDiversity.html?refresh=true&cat_id=773

27 Preventing Workplace Diversity. Retrieve July 18, 2006 from AHI's Workplace Compliance Training Center Web site: http://www.ahipubs.com/training/diversity.shtml

28 Workplace Diversity. Retrieved July 18, 2006, from Foothill-De Anza Community College Web site: http://hr.fhda.edu/diversity/

29 Lockwood, N. (2005). Workplace diversity: leveraging the power of difference for competitive advantage. *HR Magazine, 50, (6).*

30 (Rev. 2002). *Code of Federal Regulations Title 29, Volume 4* (29CFR1604.11).

31 EEOC. (2006). Equal Employment Opportunity Commission. Retrieved July 8, 2006, from Equal Employment Opportunity Commission Web site: http://www.eeoc.gov/facts/fs-sex.html

32 (September 2004) LW356A, Title VII *Sexual Harassment,* FBI National Academy, Quantico, VA.

33 Ibid.

34 The Office of Workplace Diversity. Retrieved August 16, 2006, from Federal Communication Commission Web site: http://www.fcc.gov/owd/understanding-harassment.html

35 Ibid.

36 Ibid.

37 Legal Aspects, *Legal Definitions of Sexual Harassment*, Retrieved August 16, 2006, from http://www.de2.psu.edu/harassment/legal/

38 Driver, M.J. (1988). Careers: A review of personnel and organizational research. In C.L. Cooper and I. Robertson (eds.). International review of industrial and organizational psychology. New York: Wiley.

39 Needleman, S.E. (2006). A job hunters guide to recruiter's code words. Wall street journal. Retrieved from: http://www.careerjournal.com/jobhunting/interviewing/20060509-needleman.html

40 Flesher, J. (2005). What to do (and not do) when emailing recruiters. Wall street journal. Retrieved October 4, 2006 from: http://www.careerjournal.com/jobhunting/resumes/20051025-flesher.html

41 Flesher, J. (2006). How to clean up your digital dirt before it trashes your job search. Wall street journal. Retrieved October 4, 2006 from: http://www.careerjournal.com/jobhunting/usingnet/20060112-flesher.html

## MEASURABLE LEARNING OBJECTIVES

1. Discuss the motivations to accept an expatriate assignment.

2. Identify expatriate selection procedures and success indicators.

3. Discuss compensation and taxation issues for expatriates.

4. Examine personal security issues in the Age of Terrorism.

5. Identify and discuss the following overseas travel issues: planning an itinerary, proper documentation, assistance from U.S. consulates, medical concerns, safety procedures, travel insurance, currency conversion, planning for cross-cultural communication and meetings, and transportation modalities.

# Introduction

Organizations are deploying increasing attention and resources, such as energy, capital, and time to develop managers for overseas business assignments. The rationale behind deploying these resources is to create the managerial global perspective essential for success in global markets. This global perspective empowers managers with business knowledge, basic skills, and a keen sensitivity of the cultures of other countries in which they may be assigned. Thus, managers must be equipped with a global mindset and skills needed to thrive in cultures completely different from their own.

This chapter is divided into two inter-related sections. The first section deals with working overseas as an expatriate, including (1) motivations to accept an expatriate assignment, (2) expatriate selection procedures and success indicators, (3) adjusting to cultural change, (4) compensation and taxation issues for expatriates, and (5) personal security in the Age of Terrorism.

# Working Overseas

Those who work overseas are sometimes referred to as expatriates—or ex-pat for short. The term expatriate, derived from the Latin *ex*, meaning out of, and the Greek *patria*, meaning country, is used to describe a people temporarily or permanently residing in a nation other than their own or where they hold citizenship. Most would not consider managers who travel overseas for business meetings and negotiations expatriates.

## *Motivations to Accept an Expatriate Assignment*

Motivations for accepting an expatriate assignment can be examined from the perspective of the employer and the employee. Organizations investigate every possible advantage, including expatriation, when it comes to establishing and operating businesses in a foreign environment. Successful organizations invest the necessary resources in the professional development of managers who agree to live abroad in cultures that may be very different than their own. The two most prevalent motivations are control over global operations and career development. Control over global operations is the organizational motivation for expatriate assignment development. Expatriatism promotes consistency in operations across the company, as the expatriate manager maintains close professional relationships with the home office. Employees are more comfortable when they know that predictable decisions and management practices are in place. Career development provides motivation for providing key employees with an expatriate assignment. Career development motivations can be quite diverse, as the following proves:

- Expatriate assignments offer the opportunity to manage an overseas operation in order to gain experience in management autonomy and self sufficiency.
- Employees may accept the expatriate assignment to enhance personal growth, expanding their value to the organization by seeking a challenging role with greater responsibility and decision-making authority.
- Many hold the common belief that an international assignment will enhance one's future career. The employee might be motivated to gain exposure to managers or executives at higher levels in the company, which can enhance career progression within the organization.
- Employees may seek expatriate assignments to gain higher levels of compensation. Many organizations will offer premium compensation packages in order to make these types of assignments more appealing— particularly in the less desirable countries.
- The promise of exciting adventures also prompts individuals to seek the excitement and challenge of foreign assignments. The thrill of international adventure, seeking to discover all of the various cultural treasures, which are normally only envisioned or imagined by many, inspires some individuals to seek expatriate status.

Other reasons for accepting an expatriate assignment include opportunity to travel, interest in a different culture and work, and getting back to one's roots.[1]

## Selection Procedures and Success Indicators

The screening and selection of candidates for expatriate assignments is one of the more critical decisions for the organization. The recruiting and selection of a successful candidate can first be attributed to headquarter leadership practices. For example, leadership may decide that only employees who have completed at least one foreign assignment will be considered in the management succession planning process.[2] Leadership must consider local culture and labor practices in determining candidates for expatriation assignments. Candidates who are intimately familiar with the local culture and labor practices of the host country are less likely to be surprised or intimidated by communication barriers, local customs, or any other environmental factors. Hence, the adjustment for the expatriate is relatively seamless and positive, and results occur much more quickly and efficiently. Expatriates who have a host country background have a tendency to be more successful than those who do not. "Expatriates with an in-depth knowledge of host environments, including shared mental models with locals, are better placed to make wise selection decisions."[3]

Companies may consider the cross-cultural capabilities of potential expatriate candidates in addition to technical proficiency and managerial experiences. Decision makers may review the potential expatriate's relational abilities with a diverse workforce. Some firms develop more formalized criteria for selection, including an emphasis on cultural sensitivity, a selection board composed of expatriates, previous international experience, hiring foreign born employees who can serve as expatriates at a future date, and screening candidate's spouses and families.[4] Organizations consider expatriate involvement in the selection process appropriate, even encouraging it. The expatriate should fully understand the assignment outcomes and expectations. In this manner, a company clearly and concisely gives an overview of the company requirements and expectations to the expatriate in order to prevent any misunderstandings. If a company has a clear picture of what the expatriate expects career-wise, then it will be easier to meet those expectations or tell the expatriate beforehand that it will not be possible.[5] Regardless of the process, senior management must be involved in the overall expatriate candidate selection decision—just as their involvement, commitment, and direction are key to the successful implementation of any meaningful expatriation process.[6]

Five key steps play a significant role in expatriate success: conducting an expatriate audit, conducting a cultural diversity audit, refining expatriation selection, providing cross-cultural training, and providing repatriation assistance:[7]

1.  An expatriate audit requires decision-makers to review current expatriate practices in order to identify expatriate failure rates and address the causes of costly expatriate failure. Auditors also evaluate success stories to determine the causes of success as well. Therefore, organizations can improve upon the success rates of future expatriate assignments.

2.  A cultural diversity audit identifies the organization's diversity capabilities for managing in culturally complex environments. Companies can utilize this information for assistance in selecting expatriates.

3.  The expatriate is selected.

4.  The expatriate becomes engaged in cross-cultural training, designed to reduce expatriate and foreign venture failure. Cross-cultural training is not a fail-safe solution, but it does help the expatriate adjust to the foreign environment.

5.  The final step includes repatriation assistance, whereby the organization allows the repatriate to reap the rewards of the completed foreign assignment. Some organizations fall short in this area by failing to utilize or reward the valuable cross-cultural skills and knowledge that an expatriate brings home. Some companies fail to reward repatriates with assignments at home that

enhance career aspirations. In other cases, repatriates have discovered that companies assign them to positions inferior to the one previously vacated, causing the individual to seek employment elsewhere.

## Adjusting to Cultural Change

Successful expatriate placement depends upon how well these individuals react to the new culture. Culture and norms of host countries are often much different than the expatriate's home country—this can be a source of great stress on an expatriate and family. Expatriates may experience a stress-induced reaction known as "culture shock" when confronted with the reality of their new work and home environment. Key factors that can affect expatriate culture shock include the following:

- The training the expatriate receives.
- The demographic characteristics of the expatriate.
- The dispositional and personality characteristics of the expatriate.
- The level of organizational support provided to the expatriate.
- The level of technical competence of the expatriate.[8]

Managers tend to be very upbeat and excited at the beginning of their overseas assignment, but this can change gradually as they begin to encounter frustration and stress from communication barriers and other cultural differences with the local population. Undoubtedly, there will be many stressful experiences in store for the expatriate as a result of cultural differences, but many problems arise among fellow expatriates. Although not widely recognized by management back home, subcultures exist within overseas expatriate circles. Sometimes these differences can cause more stress than the difficulties arising from dealing with locals on a daily basis.

## Communication Barriers and Training

Although expatriates use the English language extensively, companies highly value expatriates who are fluent in multiple languages. Foreign language skills training is very important for the expatriate manager; paradoxically, many of today's multinational corporations consider training in this area a weakness. Business etiquette training is another important aspect of doing business overseas. Knowledge of the practices of a particular region can prove invaluable when negotiating business arrangements. For example, some cultures frown upon beginning a business conversation by talking about business. Business managers in such cultures desire to first establish a social relationship prior to developing a business relationship. Trust is a very important relational characteristic in foreign cultures, so Westerners should be prepared to invest a considerable amount of time into forging a foundation of trust before trying to force negotiations prematurely.[9] Often, the social aspects of a business relationship are just as important to foreigners as the business aspects.

## Cultural Norms

Cultures and norms vary widely across the globe. One's attitude towards time is very important and significantly affects international business. A U.S. expatriate relocating overseas will undoubtedly have to adapt to the host country's attitude toward time. In the U.S., most consider making someone wait for a business appointment for more than half an hour past the scheduled meeting time insulting behavior. In other cultures, such as Latin America or the Middle East, waiting could mean just the opposite. Latin American or Middle Eastern executives may be taking care of the minor details of business so that they can attend to their important visitor without interruption. Whether U.S. expatriates should follow the local or U.S. custom depends. In Spain, a general rule is to never be punctual, as Spaniards consider punctuality being early. Middle Easterners know the punctuality tendencies of U.S. firms well; if an American is late, they consider him or her rude. However, the Middle Easterner can be late and not be looked upon as impolite because he or she is following the local custom.

## Non-verbal Communication

Non-verbal communication is another type of "language" that varies greatly from culture to culture—and its use may be conscious or unconscious. Knowledge of non-verbal communication common to a particular country or culture is helpful in establishing relationships and one's own credibility as a person who respects and appreciates the foreign culture. The main classes of non-verbal communication that are of interest to the expatriate are chronemics, kinesics, paralinguistics, proxemics, and haptics, which often occur together, with or without verbal expression.

*Chronemics.* Chronemics is the use of time to convey a message, including punctuality, the amount of time spent with another person, and the amount of time a person is kept waiting. Two classifications of chronemic culture include monochronic and polychronic. In a monochronic culture, individuals promptly keep appointments, meetings start on time, people do not tolerate interruptions easily, and business relationships focus strictly on the task at hand. In polychronic cultures, it is acceptable to keep someone waiting past an appointed meeting time as a normal part of doing business, and business relationships are closer and more personal.

*Kinesics.* Kinesics describes the physical messages communicated by gestures, such as facial expressions, body movement, posture, and gait. While some of these messages are universal in nature, such as sad or angry facial expressions, culturally significant kinesics can be an important way of communicating respect for another person and his or her culture. For example, bowing in Japanese culture conveys respect—even for enemies—when greeting, thanking, or saying goodbye to others. Knowledge of appropriate times and situations to bow to a Japanese person can convey the expatriate's willingness to learn and appreciate Japanese culture. In Arab countries, the gesture of placing one's hand over one's heart when conveying a greeting is a gesture of respect for people of that culture. When a foreigner offers such a gesture in addition to a verbal greeting, the Arabs appreciate the gesture even more.

*Paralinguistics.* Paralinguistics, or the vocal cues other than words, include volume, rate of speech, pitch, and pauses and silences used in speaking. These vocal cues require some knowledge of the local language, which requires additional training in a foreign language. Though English is a second language in many countries of the world, knowledge of the local language carries advantages that cannot be gained through the use of English alone, especially in countries where English is not widely spoken. Since citizens of the expatriate's host country conduct their own business, often in their own language, knowledge of paralinguistics unique to the local culture can be useful in everyday business transactions, especially negotiations in which some or all of the talking may be done in the local language.

*Proxemics and Haptics.* Proxemics consists of the spatial cues, such as interpersonal distance, territoriality, and other spatial relationships. Haptics refers to contact cues, such as the frequency, intensity, and type of touch. In Arab nations, men commonly step in close to each other to conduct normal personal or business conversations, and men will hold hands with other men with whom they are close friends. Arabs consider being physically close to or touching women disrespectful and offensive, if done by men outside the immediate or extended family. This type of behavior should be avoided, including shaking a woman's hand—even if done by a non-Arab. Knowledge of these types of cultural conventions is important to maintaining proper decorum in a foreign country so as not to offend or insult one's hosts.

## *Expatriate Compensation*

Companies typically compensate U.S. expatriates well, because all overseas benefits usually are based on the U.S. salaries. U.S. expatriates can expect to receive a "foreign service" or mobility premium of about 10 to 15 percent of their regular pay. Additionally, expatriates receive a 20 to 40 percent premium for serving in a location that may be dangerous, lacks U.S. amenities, or has many hardships.[10] Other parts of a typical expatriate compensation package include a cost-of-living adjustment, free housing or housing allowance, a car or car allowance, tax assistance, educational allowances for children, and other benefits. Typical expatriate compensation packages include allowances, such as tax assistance, housing and utilities, assistance with goods and services, educational allowances, car allowance, home travel provisions, paid emergency leave and vacation, completion bonus, relocation bonus, health care benefits, home sale assistance, and expenses for spouse and dependents.

## *Tax Considerations*

U.S. citizens working overseas have an obligation to pay their U.S. taxes. American expatriates may experience lower tax bills as the first eighty thousand dollars in income is tax exempt, but any remainder is taxable. The exemption also includes the first eighty thousand dollars of a spouse's income. Expatriate citizens must file an income tax return each year of overseas duty. In addition to salary, other items are taxable, including stipends for housing and education expenses for accompanying children. Compensation for housing is exempt from taxation, if paid by the employer. An expatriate may also be obligated to pay taxes to the foreign government. An expatriate should become thoroughly familiar with any tax rules that might apply to his or her individual situation to ensure that applicable taxes due to either country are paid on time. These details should be thoroughly covered with one's employer before taking an assignment overseas.

## *Personal Security and Terrorism*

Personal security is often a reflection of the socio-political situation in each country. Countries that are less stable socially or politically are often less secure for foreigners—who make good targets for kidnappers and other criminals. Expatriates should carefully consider the risks of criminal exposure and personal safety in the country to which they will be assigned. These considerations should include where in the country to live and whether or not to take family along for the duration of the assignment. If required, some companies provide security for their employees, and this should be clearly identified prior to moving to the new location. For example, in Iraq and other politically unstable nations, companies hire their own security personnel or private security firms to provide bodyguards for employees and security for its facilities. Even in more stable countries, companies provide bodyguards to protect their more important or senior employees.

In recent years, Westerners (U.S. citizens in particular) have been the target of international terrorists and their organizations, consisting of multiple, independent cells in various countries around the world. Unfortunately, in this environment, an organization cannot guarantee the personal security of expatriate citizens because their status as American citizens makes them a target. While the statistical risk of an individual American citizen being directly affected by a terrorist attack abroad is very low, the possibility still exists and responsible consideration of this possibility is important before making any decision to go overseas.

Information is available from the United States Department of State regarding terrorism, in the form of travel warnings, issued periodically as the situation warrants by conditions in various countries and distributed to citizens overseas by the embassy in each country. These general steps help decrease vulnerability:

- Keep a low profile. Your dress, conduct, and mannerisms should not attract attention. Make an effort to blend into the local environment. Avoid publicity and don't go out in large groups. Stay away from civil disturbances and demonstrations.

- Be unpredictable. Vary your route to and from work and the time you leave and return home. Don't exercise at the same time and place each day, never alone, on deserted streets, or on country roads. Let people close to you know where you are going, what you will be doing, and when you should be back.

- Be Alert. Watch for anything suspicious or out of place. Don't give personal information over the telephone. If you think you are being followed, go to a pre-selected secure area. Immediately report the incident to your company security officer and local law enforcement agencies. In overseas areas without such above agencies, report the incident to the US Embassy.[11]

The expatriate must know the environment in which he or she will be living and working and know what appropriate actions to take in advance in response to a possible threat. Any actions taken should be planned in advance with company security personnel, including escape routes, emergency contact numbers, and any other appropriate security information.

# Business Travel Abroad

Business travel abroad is becoming a vital part of international trade and business. Before business transactions occur in a foreign country, leaders recommended that company officials visit the countries to study their markets first. The United States prefers business transactions in person rather than conducting business over some other form of communication. Traveling abroad to cultivate new relationships with other companies in other countries will prove to be an important aspect of international business dealings. Companies must consider certain pre-travel requirements and other affects that come with international travel prior to conducting business in person overseas.

## *Planning an Itinerary*

Preparation is the key to effective business travel abroad. A travel itinerary is created in order to aide in the preparation of a business trip. The itinerary enables the traveler to make the best use of their time, while staying organized. Oftentimes, the use of a travel agent expedites the planning process. Travel agents are able to find the best travel rates for air, hotel, and vehicle rental. Their knowledge can be very helpful regarding proper documentation for travel to specific countries. The itinerary, if properly organized, can allow the traveler to be effective yet not overworked. Since international travel is expensive, careful planning is crucial. A well-organized trip will allow up to three appointments evenly spaced throughout the day to ensure the business traveler is adequately rested and not overly stressed. Companies must confirm appointments before departure. The following travel tips should be kept in mind while planning a trip:
- Travel plans should reflect goals and priorities.
- Obtaining names of possible contacts, arranging appointments, and checking transportation schedules should be accomplished before the trip begins.
- Confirm the normal workdays and business hours in the countries being visited.
- The U.S. businessperson should be aware that travel from one country to another might be restricted.

## *Proper Documentation*

An essential aspect of traveling abroad is obtaining the proper documentation. While foreign countries may individually vary on their documentation requirements, a traveler must have certain basic documents. Passports, visas, and ATA carnets are documents that are needed for overseas traveling.

### *Passports*

The first and most basic form of travel documentation is a passport. A passport is an internationally recognized travel document that verifies the identity and nationality of the bearer. Passports may be obtained from any passport acceptance facility. Only the U.S. Department of State has the authority to grant, issue, or verify United States passports. Applicants must present the agency with proof of U.S. citizenship, a valid form of photo identification–such as a driver's license or military identification tag–and two identical passport photographs. Photography shops and drug stores are common places were applicants can have their passport photographs taken. Additionally, some post offices and U.S. district courts will accept passport applications as well. The passport applicant may apply by mail or in person, although certain requirements pertain to each. In most cases, a passport will be issued within six weeks of the agency receiving the application. If an emergency arises where a passport must be expedited within fourteen days of travel, the applicant can schedule an appointment at one of the thirteen regional passport agencies. There is an additional charge to expedite the process, and sometimes the agency will require customers to show proof of departure for urgent travel needs.[12]

### *Visas*

A visa is an official authorization appended to a passport, permitting entry into and travel within a particular country or region. The visa is a formal document that is issued by a country giving permission to an individual requesting entrance to the country during a certain period of time to fulfill a specific purpose. Most countries require a valid visa for those traveling to a foreign country. In order to obtain a visa, one must go to the foreign country's embassy or consulate located in the United States. One should notify the consulate that the travel is for business, because some countries require visas for business travel but not tourist travel.

Many foreigners who desire to do business in the United States might encounter some difficulty in obtaining a visa. The U.S. offers over twenty types of non-immigrant, temporary stay visas to foreigners seeking entrance into the country. Noncitizens who wish to do business in the U.S. need to obtain a B-1 visitor visa. This visa allows international business people to come into the U.S. and consult with business associates, attend a scientific, educational, professional or business convention, settle an estate, negotiate a contract, and participate in a short-term training.

Concerning U.S. citizens who desire to travel overseas, the Bureau of Consular Affairs offers these steps to remember in applying for a visa:

1. Review visa status and find out if a U.S. visa or a renewal is needed.
2. Review the visa wait times information for interview appointments and visa processing at each embassy and consular section worldwide. Visit the embassy or consular section website to apply for visa and find out how to schedule an interview appointment, pay fees, and other instructions.
3. Plan on an interview at the embassy or consulate. Usually, a fingerprint scan is required.[13]

## ATA Carnets

ATA (Admission Temporaire) Carnet is a standardized international customs document used to obtain duty-free temporary admission of certain goods into the countries that are signatories to the ATA Convention. Basically, a company wanting to take certain goods into a country, such as product samples, would need to obtain a carnet. A carnet is usually valid for up to a year. The U.S. Council for International Business issues a carnet for the entrance of commercial samples, tools of the trade, advertising material, cinematographic, medical, and/or other professional equipment. The ATA Convention approves these carnets. A fee is incurred by the company, based on the value of the goods being imported. If the imported goods are not re-exported, then the company is charged the cost of the duties and taxes. Before embarking on travel, the carnet holder must issue a bond or bank guaranty of 40 percent of the good's value to ensure that everything is done properly and that the fees will be covered.[14]

## Extra Copies of Documents

Traveling can be unpredictable and oftentimes things can be lost or stolen along the way. Travelers should have two copies of their passport identification page. In case the passport is stolen or lost, the extra copies will be helpful. The traveler should carry one of the copies and give the second copy to someone back home, such as a family member or friend. While an individual should not publicize all of his or her travel plans, the traveler should leave at least a copy of the traveler's itinerary with a family member or friend, in case of emergency.

*Current Documentation*

Over the course of time, passports, visas, and other documents might become outdated. As mentioned earlier, travelers can renew passports by mail if they fall under certain criteria. The passport may be renewed by mail if the most recent passport has not been damaged and is able to be submitted, if the passport was received within the past fifteen years, if the passport holder was over the age of sixteen when it was issued, and if the legal name is still the same, Sometimes a visa may be mistakenly called an "expired visa" when actually the visa's status has changed. One should know when the visa status changes so that the traveler can plan well in advance to get it updated.

## Assistance from U.S. Embassies and Consulates

U.S. embassies and consulates are a key element to successful overseas business travel. The embassies and consulates serve several different purposes, including issuing visas to foreigners and providing assistance to U.S. citizens abroad. Over 160 U.S. embassies are located in capital cities of the world. Of those 160 U.S. embassies, 60 are U.S. consulates general—regional offices of embassies. They seek to provide as much help as possible to traveling U.S. citizens. Oftentimes, consular officers have to assist in emergency situations. If a passport is lost while in another country, the consul can issue a replacement, usually within twenty-four hours. They also aid in needed medical assistance, loss of financial resources, death of a U.S citizen abroad, and disaster/evacuation.[15]

A consular can help in many situations but is not able to act in a role other than its own. If another country arrests a consular's citizen, the consular officer cannot protect them against the laws of that country. Legally, that U.S. citizen is under the control of that country's authority. Before embarking on a trip, business travelers should contact the local Export Assistance Center[16] to discuss their needs and any services that they might be able to receive from an embassy. Travelers should contact the U.S. embassy in the foreign country two weeks prior to leaving to inform them of their business travel plans.

## Medical Concerns

Whenever traveling to a foreign country, diseases, allergies, and water contamination become valid concerns. Many other countries do not have the same health standards as the United States. Business travelers must remember to keep all required and recommended vaccinations up-to-date, and to be knowledgeable of any known allergies and diseases that tend to be prevalent in that particular country. A person must do research before going to a country to find all possible contamination's that have been reported for the area to which he or she is traveling. Major medical concerns include vaccinations, food allergies, and water contamination.

## Vaccinations

Different vaccinations are needed for travel to different countries. Most physicians will know the different vaccinations that an individual may need for individual countries or sections of the world. However, anyone traveling should to take the initiative to learn what precautions to take when entering a particular foreign country. Due to the fact that most vaccinations take time to become effective and require more than one dose over many days or weeks, an individual should see their local doctor four to six weeks prior to leaving the country.[17]

## Food Allergies

Food allergies and contaminated foods are also specific concerns for anyone traveling abroad. Many countries in the world partake in food that is rarely or never eaten in the United States. For example, Latin or Caribbean nations use many different spices, unique to those regions, in the preparation of the food. Furthermore, some countries may prepare foods such as certain domesticated animals or iguana. Many people in the United States believe they do not have food allergies and therefore eat what they want when they travel, but can become very sick if the proper precautions are not taken. The best way to prevent an adverse reaction is to know what is being served, and if at all possible, eat only foods that are common and known to be non-allergenic. When this becomes impossible, one should do research before entering a country and try to find a doctor who can do a test for food allergies.

## Water Contamination

Probably the largest concern for anyone traveling abroad is the safety of the drinking water. No human being can live for very long without water, so an individual must have access to purified drinking water, if the country's tap water is unhealthy. Water is not necessarily the healthiest liquid to drink in foreign countries. One reason for this is that some nations do not use sanitary waste disposal methods and will allow sewage to drain into the same pipes as water. In cases where purified water or bottled water is not available, be prepared to conduct water purification procedures, such as boiling the contaminated water, bringing portable water purifiers, or adding chemicals, such as iodine to disinfect the water.

*Disease and Disaster*

The final two medical concerns when traveling are the possibilities of disease and disaster. Reports of outbreaks of diseases have been cited for years across many nations, both under-developed and developed. The same can be said for natural disasters. Once overseas business travel has begun, preparation for dealing with an outbreak or disaster is very difficult. Business travelers should develop contingency plans, based on the research conducted prior to traveling. For example, consider the case of SARS (Severe Acute Respiratory Syndrome), which occurred during 2002-2004 across the nations of China, Singapore, Taiwan, and Canada. Although most travelers were at low risk for contracting SARS, people were advised not to travel to countries where SARS was prevalent.

## Safety Procedures

Since the terrorist attacks on the United States on September 11, 2001, the U.S. government has attempted to increase security in airports, subways, and train stations. Although the government has established many precautions in order to protect Americans while traveling, U.S. citizens must be aware of continuing threats to security before traveling overseas. The events of September 11 have not only effected the way Americans feel about traveling but has also brought an awareness of the growing tensions between the U.S. and other countries. Thus, business travelers must be aware of the possible dangers they could face while in other countries.

Although terrorist attacks can take place in any nation, U.S. nationals should take extra precautions to remain safe in certain areas of the world. Before leaving for a business trip, one should obtain a Consular Information Sheet, issued by the Department of State, to learn valuable information about the country to be visited. The information sheets are available for every country in the world and give important information such as entry requirements, currency regulations, unusual health conditions, the crime and security situation, political disturbances, areas of instability, and special information about driving and road conditions. The sheets also provide the telephone numbers and addresses for U.S. embassies and consulates. One should take into consideration all of the information given on the Consular Information Sheet before making the decision to make a business trip overseas.[18] Additionally, Public Announcements are regularly published regarding possible international security issues. These announcements are made when the U.S. perceives a threat, even if it does not involve U.S. citizens as a particular target-group. Announcements have been issued in the past dealing with pre-election disturbances, violence by terrorists, as well as anniversary dates of specific terrorist events.

Business travelers can take specific actions to reduce the risk of being a victim while overseas. When planning for a trip, one should carefully consider what is to be packed in luggage. A businessperson needs to be aware of the culture that he or she will be entering and pack accordingly. U.S. culture can be quite different from that of the foreign nation. An American can easily be spotted by the clothes worn, so one key to not being a target overseas is to dressing conservatively. Do not dress in a way that draws attention to oneself, especially with expensive jewelry and clothes. Blending in with the culture is better than looking like a tourist. One should pack as light as possible and leave all valuable things behind.

## Safety on the Street

In the end, remaining safe in a foreign nation requires, in most cases, the use of common sense. Always be aware of the local surroundings and do not get into situations that pose a potential risk. If safety might be jeopardized, one would wisely postpone overseas business travel until the risk of being harmed is not an issue. Travelers should use the same common sense overseas that would normally be used in the United States. One should avoid crowded places–such as subways, train stations, and elevators–because of the increased risk of being a victim of pickpockets. Foreigners should not travel alone at night. If necessary, one should avoid short cuts and poorly-lighted streets. The key to not being a victim is to act like a native, not a tourist. Travelers should walk around with confidence, not confusion. If a situation arises where police or help is needed, a few phrases should be learned in the foreign language so help can be sent.[19]

## Safety in the Hotel

As a rule of thumb, hotel doors should remain locked and meetings with business associates should take place in the lobby instead of the room. Due to the possibility of items in a hotel room being stolen, valuables or money should never be visible in the room. A hotel business card may be useful in the event of an emergency or if one gets lost. As with safety on the street, the best form of self defense is to use common sense.[20]

## Safety on Public Transportation

Public transportation in other nations can be dangerous for the uninitiated business traveler. Criminal activity may be systematic and well organized on or near public transportation. Some tips for safe use of public transportation include the following:

- Never sit or stand too close to strangers.
- Do not accept food or drink from strangers. Criminals have been known to drug food and drinks in order to rob.
- Hide valuables in a safe place, if possible, and never expose large amounts of cash in a public place.
- One should not to fall asleep in places that are unfamiliar since criminal gangs are common overseas.
- Be careful to drive and walk in safe, well lit areas.
- If traveling by way of taxi, be sure the taxi is clearly identified with official markings.
- Always trust common instincts and avoid buses and city trains, if possible.[21]

## Travel and Medical Insurance

Travel protection consists of insurance coverage and assistance services that will safeguard a traveler before, during, and after the trip. Numerous benefits accrue to those obtaining travel insurance prior to overseas travel, such as protection of cost incurred due to a cancelled trip, twenty-four hour emergency medical referral and assistance during travel, reimbursement of unexpected travel expenses incurred during an emergency, and coverage during a medical emergency. Additionally, the astute traveler ensures that his or her health care insurance covers emergencies abroad. Some medical insurance policies do not cover medical emergencies outside of the United States. In cases where medical coverage is valid, a policy may not cover personal evacuation from a remote area or part of the country where medical facilities are inadequate. One should consider purchasing a short-term health and emergency policy that is designed specifically for travelers, especially the option that covers personal evacuation in the event of a serious illness or emergency.

## Currency Guidelines

International currency exchange has been a major issue for business travelers. This problem has been effectively solved in Europe, with the development of a common currency—the Euro—among European Union members. However, when traveling to other areas of the world, currency exchange can be problematic. Currencies in the regions of Asia, Africa, or South America are not unified and can cause problems with exchange. Many airports have exchange locations in them, but the more remote the location the fewer exchange stands will be available.

While some U.S. international travelers may understand that different currencies hold different values, they may not be able to mentally convert the value from the U.S. dollar. Therefore, Americans end up paying too much for something, as foreign vendors often take advantage of the situation. Normally this is seen with tourists, but it can happen very easily with a businessperson. Another problem is the ability to freely convert one currency from another. This can be problematic in nations where the currency is not very valuable and the exchange rate is unfavorable.

The astute business traveler carries minimal cash, as credit and debit cards have become increasingly popular across borders. The issuing companies will convert the purchases at the most favorable rate available on the day of transaction. One can purchase traveler's checks locally and then cash them at virtually any bank in the world. This is a common way of avoiding the currency problems that exist. However, many people do not want to take the time or do not have the time before leaving the United States to visit a bank to obtain traveler's checks. Therefore, they are forced to rely on the exchange of currency in the country where they are going. Currency exchange can be a problem for the traveler who does not take the time to become educated on exchange rates. The business traveler must research exchange conversion rates prior to embarking on business travel overseas.

## Check List for Business Meetings and Travel Abroad

One should ensure—prior to departure—that trip essentials are handled, such as travel itinerary to medical information, as well as being educated on the country where the meetings will take place. The traveler should consider an additional list for the business meeting, which is the purpose for the whole trip in the first place. The wise traveler develops a list of important things to remember before leaving for a business trip:

- A successful business meeting starts before leaving the country. The meeting needs to be set up before leaving the United States, and the business needs to determine whether or not an interpreter will be needed before arriving in the country for the meeting. Those in the meeting should convey the correct message, because poor communication can have a devastating effect on the outcome of the meeting.

- Business cards are always something a businessperson makes sure they have on them; but when traveling overseas for a business trip, one should have business cards not only in English but also the language of the country in which the meeting will be held. Individuals also must familiarize themselves with the culture in which they will be entering. One needs to learn the basic cultural traits, such as hand signals, road signs, and common courtesy traits such as tipping.

- If a person uses electrical appliances during the presentation, he or she should make sure to bring a transformer and/or plug adapter. Many outlets used in other countries are different than those used in the United States.[22]

## Cross-Cultural Communications

The ability to communicate successfully with other cultures is imperative when conducting a business meeting oversees. "The advent of the global economy is changing the fundamental nature of our governments, businesses, organizations and populations. No longer are people constrained by state boundaries but have all become part of an interdependent international network."[23] If one intends on conducting business in an international territory, communication is a part of life. Cross-cultural communication is a crucially important matter that should not be overlooked. Parents fail to communicate with their children; bosses often do not communicate well with their staff; men and women often have trouble communicating to one another. Communication failure tends to be a universal problem that people experience within their own culture and language. The lack of communication often leads to unnecessary problems. Therefore, communication is obviously an important aspect of business in the United States, as well as when conducting business travel abroad. When one chooses to engage in business internationally, he or she must consider many aspects of cross-cultural communication. Language barriers, foreign holidays, the time-zone changes, the usage of global telephones, and global internet access can sometimes be overlooked when preparing for a business trip. Furthermore, knowledge of acceptable forms of body language and gestures will be a great asset when communicating properly in different cultures. The astute business traveler can prepare for proper communication techniques via formal and informal training programs aimed at helping improve cross cultural communication. Typical cross-cultural communication areas for consideration include language barriers, foreign holidays, time-zone changes, acceptable forms of business communications, and gestures.

### Language Barriers

"It is now recognized that linguistic and cultural knowledge are the two most vital areas of knowledge that organizations must come to acquire if they are to integrate, progress and succeed in the marketplace."[24] Inexperienced U.S. business travelers incorrectly assume that all of their international colleagues speak and understand the English language.  English is frequently the language used in global business, even though it is not the language spoken by the majority of people in the world.  English is taught in many other schools overseas, where it is a second language in many other countries.  However, the method of instruction emphasizes reading and grammar to the point that foreigners often can read English fluently but are unable to understand it.  The following suggestions are offered to English speaking travelers when dealing with non-English speaking persons:

- Slow down and be patient.  Avoid the attempt to raise your voice louder.
- Remember others are trying something new and different to them; speak clearly.
- Keep sentences short.
- Avoid asking "either/or" questions and negative questions and contractions.
- Avoid idioms, colloquialisms, slang, and jargon
- Use visuals if ever possible, such as graphs, charts, or models.[25]

Finally, the business traveler should not go to the other extreme and assume business associates are not fluent in English, as this could lead to embarrassing or negative situations.

## Foreign Holidays

Travelers must consider foreign holidays before making international business travel arrangements.  Foreign nations may not recognize the holidays that Americans typically observe. For example, German culture celebrates Vincent's Day, Assumption Day, and Reformation Day.  Germany does not observe U.S. holidays, such as Good Friday, Easter, and Labor Day.  Some cultures may have more religious holidays than others. Other nations may celebrate the birthdays of ancient emperors, as well as the dates of events not recognized in the United States.  Holidays may be observed in a combined week, so one should not attempt to conduct a business trip during a holiday week.  Therefore, a businessperson should be aware of the holiday schedule before scheduling the trip abroad and scheduling meetings with customers or associates.

## Time-Zone Changes

Just as in considering the holiday schedule before traveling, one should also be aware of the different time zones.  This is an easy but important consideration when making travel arrangements, as the date may change depending on the direction of global travel. For example, two calendar days are lost, depending on the time of departure, when traveling from the eastern U.S. to China. Conversely, one only loses a couple of hours–despite all day travel–when returning from Europe to the U.S. The traveler should also realize that many other countries do not observe daylight savings time.

### Acceptable Forms of Business Communications

When traveling abroad, one needs to consider how to maintain communication between foreign associates, the home base office, family, and friends. The use of international prepaid phone cards is acceptable across the globe. Prepaid international phone cards are available for purchase at most retail stores. If using a reusable card, one should make sure that it has enough minutes "loaded" for all communication needs. However, some of these cards are only useful calling internationally from the United States. One should make sure that the phone card works from inside another country. Additionally, cell phone companies have added international service as an option to global travelers. Individuals should pay bills on time and have a prepaid phone card as a back up. International travelers often have no way to recharge their cell phone batteries, because other countries sometimes have different electrical outlets and voltage settings that do not fit the standard battery chargers for U.S. cell phones.

Travelers should observe the same precautions whenever accessing the Internet and checking email. With prepaid phone cards, global roaming Internet access service is available. The technology provides worldwide access from anywhere to anywhere through a local number. Prior to departure, one must be sure that the account is paid in advance to assure access for the length of the entire trip. Global phone access and global internet access are two important items that business travelers need when traveling abroad. These items should be taken care of before departing on the trip.

### Acceptable Forms of Body Gestures

Body language is an important form of communication across cultures and sometimes differs greatly from the body gestures that are used in the United States. For example, a "thumbs up" in America is a positive gesture; however, it is an offensive gesture in certain other cultures. A "wink" to someone in America is also a positive gesture, but it often carries a different meaning in other cultures. This is an area in which one should be educated when traveling to a foreign country for business. To the inexperienced traveler, gestures that seem harmless and acceptable in American culture can be quite offensive to those in the foreign culture. Therefore, one should observe appropriate gestures while doing business in a foreign country.

## *Other Cultural Factors*

Culture is a set of behavior patterns that are learned and shared through common experience. Culture is learned—it impacts everyone and serves as the means of processing and interpreting information. Every land has its own culture, and every culture is different from one to another. Cultural factors are important areas that business travelers need to study prior to traveling abroad. "The single greatest barrier to business success is the one created by culture."[26] Other important areas that could become potential barriers include religious factors, history, local laws, and the relationship between customs and foreign goods.

### *Religious Factors*

Religious factors are a very serious situation in certain regions of the world. In the United States, people often take for granted the freedom to observe religious practices in any manner. A religious ruling class controls some nations where freedom of religion does not exist. Bibles and other religious paraphernalia can be very offensive to foreign cultures. Possession of such may involve negative legal repercussions. The religious beliefs of some cultures strongly affect all aspects of personal and business life.

### *History*

Just as respecting the religious beliefs of other nations is important, one also needs to respect the history of the culture. Business associates in other cultures may be sensitive to attitudes concerning their nation's history and culture. An example would be the Chinese civilization, which has flourished for over 3500 years. When visiting historical sites, care should be taken to show respect for the historical significance of that location. Such respect communicates to foreign associates a heightened level of appreciation for the culture, which may lead to more favorable business relationships.[27]

### *Local Laws*

The experienced business traveler understands and observes the laws of "the land" when traveling overseas. If one violates the rules and regulations of another nation, the United States Embassy can do little besides provide a list of local attorneys. If one violates a local law while in a foreign nation, the offender should ask the arresting authority to notify a consular officer at the nearest Embassy. Individuals should inquire about the local laws before arriving in a new culture and obey them while in that nation.

*Customs and Foreign Goods*

Custom regulations obviously vary from country to country and are constantly under revision. Concerning the import and export of goods across borders, the experienced business traveler is aware of contraband items. Many fruits and specific food products are banned from transport across borders. One tip is to not attempt to convey contraband through the customs process of the foreign nation. Similar limitations may be placed on items upon return to the U.S. Current U.S. Customs law allows only four hundred dollars worth of merchandise to be brought in the country before levying a tax against it. One should keep receipts of all purchases. A foreigner should never carry a package for someone else when entering a new country.

## Transportation Modalities

As in travel across the U.S., airlines, rails and ferries, taxis, and buses provide public transportation services overseas. Traveling by rail is a more popular method of transportation in other countries, especially in tourist areas. The experienced business traveler researches the various modes of transportation available in the foreign nation and is aware of the procedures for securing such services. Trains and buses may require exact change, so one needs to be aware of the cost and plan appropriately. One should always possess a passport and valid photo ID–in addition to possessing a planned itinerary of the trip.

If choosing air travel, businesses have two options: commercial or charter flights. Charter flights, more convenient than commercial travel, are typically reserved for larger corporate use. If the business decides to travel by charter, one should secure the service from a reputable company. Smaller "fly-by-night" airlines have been known to "go out of business" in the middle of the travel dates, abandoning business travelers.

Rails and ferries are available for cross-border travel. Train travel may be more cost effective than air travel. For example, Europe and Asia boast rail systems that travel at high speeds and can be as quick as air travel. International rail systems are rated high in safety performance and passenger safety. Ferries are also a common way to travel in certain areas, as they provide safe and reliable service as well. Many consider rail and ferry travel a safe and reliable method of travel overseas.

Car rentals offer another option for business travel. One should do business with a known company or one that has well identified markings. To avoid being a target, foreigners should not rent luxurious or flashy cars Since most U.S. auto insurance's do not cover overseas rentals, the traveler should purchase the insurance offered by the rental company. Some companies only have cars with the steering wheel on the opposite side of the car. Many accidents have resulted due to the unfamiliarity of the vehicle. If at all possible, one should not rent a car while overseas—to save much stress and money.

If one must rent a car while oversees, the embassy or consulate of the country teaches about specific vehicle operator requirements. Many countries do not recognize a U.S. driver's license. However, most countries accept an international driver's license. An international driver's license can be obtained prior to departure at the local American Automobile Association. Certain nations require a permit instead of tolls on certain roads. The absence of this permit may result in a severe financial fine. The traveler is responsible to observe all laws and road signs, even if they are not in English. Be aware of odd traffic patterns and the fact that many countries, compared to what Americans are used to, drive on the opposite sides of the road.

# Endnotes

1     Haldemann, P. (1999). *Building the Bridge for a Successful Expatriation Process.* Retrieved November 15, 2005, from http://www.relojournal.com/sept2000/business_report.htm

2     Swaak, R. (2002). *Managing the Expatriation Process Is One of the Thorniest Issues for Global Managers.* Retrieved November 15, 2005, from http://www.frankallen.com/Executive_Reports/ HR_and_The_Global_Marketplace/Repatriation/repatriation.html_

3     Australian Centre for International Business. (2001). *Expatriate Management: A Business Model for Diversity Management.* Retrieved November 13, 2005, from http://www.diversityaustralia. gov.au/_inc/doc_pdf/exp_manage_model.pdf

4     Treven, S. (2001). *Human Resource Management in International Organizations.* Retrieved November 13, 2005, from http://www.efst.hr/management/Vol6No1-2-2001/11-Treven.doc

5     Elenius, J., Garvik, L., & Nilsson, F. (2003). *An Evaluation of the Repatriation Process at Company X.* Retrieved November 14, 2005, from http://www.handels.gu.se/epc/ Archive/00003646/01/inlaga%5F2003%5F16.pdf

6     Swaak, R. (2002). *Managing the Expatriation Process Is One of the Thorniest Issues for Global Managers.* Retrieved November 15, 2005, from http://www.frankallen.com/Executive_Reports/ HR_and_The_Global_Marketplace/Repatriation/repatriation.html_

7     Australian Centre for International Business. (2001). *Expatriate Management: ABusiness Model for Diversity Management.* Retrieved November 13, 2005, from http://www.diversityaustralia. gov.au/_inc/doc_pdf/exp_manage_model.pdf

8     Sims, R. & Schraeder, M. (2005). A*n Examination of Salient Factors Affecting Expatriate Culture Shock* The Journal of Business and Management, Vol. 10 Issue No. 1. pp. 73-88.

9     Salacuse J. (2005). Ivey Business Journal. Negotiating: *The Top Ten Ways that Culture Can Affect Your Negotiation.* Retrieved November 18, 2005 from http://www.iveybusinessjopurnal. com/ibjmarchapril/2005.htm

10    Capell, P. (2004). *Employers Seek to Trim Pay for U.S. Expatriates.* Retrieved November 16, 2005 from http://www.careerjournal.com/myc/workabroad/20040412-capell-expat.html

11    Government Printing Office. (July, 1996). *Service member's personal protection guide: A self-help handbook to combating terrorism.* Retrieved 10 November, 2005, from http://www.dtic.mil/ doctrine/jel/cjcsd/cjcsi/gude5260.pdf

12    United States Department of State. Passports. (2006). Retrieved October 15, 2006 from http:// travel.state.gov/passport/passport_1738.html

13    United States Department of State. Visas. (2006). Retrieved October 15, 2006 from http:// travel.state.gov/visa/visa_1750.html

14    United States Council for International Business. ATA Cartnet Export Service (2006). Retrieved November 1, 2006 from http://www.uscib.org/index.asp?documentID=718

15    United States Department of State. U.S. Embassies, Consulates, and Diplomatic Missions (2006). Retrieved October 15, 2006 from http://usembassy.state.gov/

16    United States Department of Commerce International Trade Administration. Export Assistance Center (2006). Retrieved November 1, 2006 from http://www.export.gov/eac/index.asp

17    United States Department of State. Medical Information for Americans Traveling Abroad. Retrieved November 1, 2006 from http://travel.state.gov/travel/tips/health/health_1185.html

18    United States Department of State. Consular Information Sheets. Retrieved November 1, 2006
      from http://travel.state.gov/travel/cis_pa_tw/cis/cis_1765.html

19    A Safe Trip Abroad. (2006). Retrieved November 1, 2006 from http://www.friendlytravels.com/
      asafetripabroad.htm

20    Ibid.

21    Ibid.

22    Small Business Notes. (2006). Retrieved November 5, 2006 from http://www.
      smallbusinessnotes.com/international/exporting/businesstravel.html

23    Ibid.

24    Proozm. Voice Between Network Announces New Foreign Language Translation Website.
      (2006). Retrieved November 15, 2006 from http://www.przoom.com/news/1359/, ¶ 3.

25    Ibid, ¶ 4.

26    Cultural Savvy. (2006). Retrieved November 15, 2006 from http://www.culturalsavvy.com/

27    Martin, B. & Larsen, G. (1999). Taming the tiger: key success factors for trade with China.
      Marketing Intelligence & Planning.  Volume 17 Number 4 1999 pp. 202-208.

# Index

**A**

Achievement-oriented leadership, 110
Adams, John S., 158
Administrative management theory, 35–38
Aldefer, Clayton, 154
Argyris, Chris, 38, 55
ATA
   admission temporaire, 211
Autocratic leader, 103, 118
Autocratic manager, 4

**B**

balanced scorecard (BSC, 18
Barnard, Chester, 39
Barriers
   to communication, 125–128
Basic planning process, 64–69
Behavioral-based motivation theories
   Skinner's Behavior Modification, 150–152
   Thorndike's Law of Effect, 149–150
   Vroom's Expectancy Theory, 152–153
Behavioral management theory, 38–45, 154
Behavior modification
   extinction, 150
   in management, 152
   negative reinforcement, 151
   operant conditioning, 150
   positive reinforcement, 150
   punishment, 151
Behavior theories
   of leadership,, 105–106
Benchmarking, 70–71
Bennis, Warren, 6, 7, 99. *See* Bennis and
      Nanus
Bennis and Nanus, 5
Body gestures
   acceptable forms of, 220
Bona fide occupational qualification
      (BFOQ), 179
Bonaparte, Napoleon, 16
Breakeven analysis toolkit, 81
Brockman and Morgan, 17
Burns, J.M., 4

Business communications
   acceptable forms of, 220–221
Business travel abroad
   and foreign currency guidelines, 216–217
   check lists, 217
   cross-cultural communications, 218–220
   documentation, 210–212
   medical concerns, 212–214
   planning an itinerary, 209
   safety procedures, 214–216
   travel and medical insurance, 216
   U.S. embassies and Consulates, 212

**C**

Career management
   and the importance of mentors, 194
   career paths, 195
   dress code and punctuality, 194
   job hunting, 195
Career paths
   linear, 195
   spiral, 195
   steady-state, 195
Change leadership, 116–117
Charismatic leadership, 37, 55
*Cheaper by the Dozen* (Gilbreth), 34
Chief Executive Officer, 3, 10
Chief Operating Officer, 3
Chronemics
   monochronic, 205
   polychronic, 205
Coercive power, 101
Collins, Jim, 113
Communication barriers
   for expatriates, 204–206
Communication process, 124–126
Compensation and benefits
   three elements of, 183
Concentration strategies, 71
Concentric diversification, 71
Conflict
   definition of, 159

functional vs. dysfunctional, 159
management styles, 161–163
types of, 159–160
Conflict management styles
    accommodation, 161
    avoidance, 161
    collaboration, 162
    competition, 161
    compromise, 161
Conglomerate diversification, 71
Consulates
    functions of, 212
Contemporary structures
    network structure, 88–89
Contingency models of leadership
    Fiedler contingency model, 105–106
    Hersey-Blanchard situational theory,
        107–108
    House path-goal theory, 110–111
    Vroom-Jago decision-making model,
        110–111
Control systems and tools, 79
Corporate governance, 90
Covey, Stephen, 115
*Creative Experience* (Follet), 39
Cross-cultural communications, 218–220
Cultural factors
    customs regulations, 221
    history, 221
    local laws, 221
    religious, 221
Cultural norms, 205–206
Culture
    definition of, 221

**D**

Delegation, 91–92
Democratic leader, 104, 118
Democratic manager, 4
Dining etiquette, 135–136
Directive leadership, 110
Disease and disaster
    when travelling abroad, 214–215
District managers, 4
Divisional structure, 16
Documentation

ATA carnets, 211
    current, 212–213
    extra copies of, 211
    passports, 210
    visas, 210
Dress codes, 140–141
Drucker, Peter, 39, 57, 79

**E**

EEOC, 188
Email etiquette
    general guidelines, 134–135
Emotional intelligence, 5
Employee discipline systems, 80–81
Empowerment, 92
Equal employment opportunity commission
        (EEOC), 188. *See* EEOC
Equity theory, 158
Ergonomics, 142
ERG theory
    example of, 155
    three categories of, 154–155
Ethics
    definition of,, 102
Executive managers, 12. *See* Top managers
Expatriates
    and barriers to communication, 205–207
    and compensation, 207–208
    and cultural change, 204–205
    and tax considerations, 207
    definition of, 201
    five keys to success, 203
    motivators for, 201–202
    security and terrorism threats, 207–208
    selection procedures, 202
Expert power, 8

**F**

Fayol, Henry, 33, 35, 54, 90
Federal HRM laws, 185–187. *See* Human
        resources management laws
Fiedler's contingency model, 106, 119
Fiedler, Fred E., 48, 106
*Fifth Discipline* (Senge), 52
Filtering, 126
Finance managers, 11

First line managers, 4. *See* Operational
    managers
Five aspects of implementing strategy, 189
    accountability, 190
    leadership and knowledge management,
        189
    results-oriented performance culture, 189
    strategic alignment, 189
    talent management, 189–190
Follet, Mary Parker, 38, 39, 55
Followership, 6–8
Food allergies
    when travelling abroad, 213
*Force for Change* (Kotter), 4
Foreign holidays
    to consider when travelling, 219
Fourteen principles of management, 36–37,
    54–55
French and Raven, 8, 101
Functional manager, 10
Functional structure, 16, 84, 85
*Functions of the Executive* (Barnard), 40, 47

**G**

General manager, 10
Gilbreth, Frank and Lillian, 54, 58. *See
    also* Therbligs
*Good To Great* (Collins), 113
Good to great concept
    building the organization's vision, 114
    confront the brutal facts, 114
    first who, then what, 114
    hedgehog concept, 114
    level 5 leadership, 114
Gray, General Alfred
    famous quote, 144
Greenleaf, Robert, 115
Groupthink
    eight ways it occurs, 139–140

**H**

Hackman, J.R., 157
Hackman and Oldham job design model
    five core dimensions, 157–158
Haptics, 206

Herzberg's 2-factor theory
    hygiene factors, 157
    motivators, 157
Herzberg, Frederick, 157
Hierarchy of needs, 42, 55. *See* Maslow,
        Abraham
Hostile work environment
    examples of, 193–194
House, Robert, 109
*Human Problems of an Industrial Society*
        (Mayo), 41
Human resource managers, 12
Human resources management
    employee compensation, 183
    employee selection process, 178–181
    importance of, 175
    performance management, 183–184
    planning process, 175
    recruitment, 176–178
    training and developing, 182–183
Human resources management laws,
        185–187
*Human Side of Enterprise* (McGregor), 43,
        59

**I**

Ideal bureaucracy, 38, 55
Industrial Revolution, 32, 54
Information and financial controls
    ratio analysis, 81
Internal controls
    communication monitoring, 78
    control activities, 78
    control environment, 78
    information monitoring, 78
    risk assessment, 78
Interview process, 179–182
    bona fide occupational qualification
        (BFOQ), 179
    seven steps to successful selection, 181
    structured or unstructured, 180
    topics to avoid during, 179
Inventory modeling, 45, 56
Itinerary
    purpose of, 209
    tips for planning, 209–210

**J**

Janis, Irvin, 139
Job-based motivation theories
    Equity theory, 158
    Hackman and Oldham job design model,
        157–158
    Herzberg's 2-factor theory, 157
Job hunting
    things one should know, 195
Jobs, Steve, 130
Juran, Joseph M.
    (father of quality), 51

**K**

Kaplan and Norton, 18
Katz, Robert, 12
Kinesics, 206–207
Kotter, John P., 4, 117, 167
Kouzes and Posner, 7, 100

**L**

Laissez-faire leader, 104, 118
Laissez-faire manager, 4
Language barriers
    for English speakers, 218–219
Leader-member relations, 48, 106
Leadership
    definition of, 100
    transactional, 4
    transformational, 4
*Leadership Challenge* (Kouzes and Posner), 7
Leadership styles
    autocratic, 103–104
    democratic, 104
    laissez-faire, 104
Leading, 3, 106
Least preferred coworker scale, 48, 106
Legitimate power, 8, 101
Lewin, Kurt, 117
Likert, Rensis, 105
Linear programming, 45

**M**

Machine bureaucracy, 15
Major federal HRM laws, 185–187

    *See* Federal HRM laws
Management
    definition of, 3
Managerial decision styles
    autocratic, 4, 43, 99, 103, 108, 118, 143
    democratic, 4, 99, 103, 118
    laissez-faire, 4, 99, 103, 104
Managerial roles
    Decisional, 9
    Informational, 9
    Interpersonal, 9
Managerial skills
    Conceptual skills, 13
    Human skills, 13
    technical skills, 13, 14
Managing conflict, 159–168
*Managing People is like Herding Cats* (Bennis), 99
Maslow's hierarchy of needs theory, 153
Maslow, Abraham, 40
Mathematical forecasting, 45, 56
Matrix organization, 16, 86
Mayo, Elton, 40
McClelland, David
    achievement motivation, 155
McGregor, Douglas, 38, 43, 55
Medical concerns
    when travelling abroad, 213–214
Meetings
    guidelines for strong meeting leadership,
        133–134
    six keys to success, 132–133
Meilinger, Colonel P., U.S.A.F., 6
Middle managers, 3. *See* Project managers
Min and Kliner, 181
Mintzberg, Henry, 9, 14. *See also* Managerial
    roles
Mission statement, 3, 8, 12, 17, 18, 70
Mixed messages, 128
Motivation theories
    behavioral based, 149–153
    job based, 156–159
    need based, 153–156
Munsterberg, Hugo, 38, 39, 55

**N**

Narrow span of control, 17, 91
Need-based motivation theories
   ERG theory, 154–155
   Maslow's Hierarchy of Needs theory, 153
Needleman, Sarah
   on job hunting, 195–196
Network structure, 88–89
Noise, 125
Non-verbal communication
   cultural variations, 205–206
   definition of, 127
   in the communication process, 124
Norms, 138–139
Nutt, Paul, 68

**O**

Office etiquette, 136
Office layout
   features to consider, 141–142
Office politics
   dress codes, 140–141
   groupthink, 139–140
   norms, 138–139
   office layout, 141–142
   utilizing in an ethical way, 137–138
Ohio State leadership model, 105
Oldham, G.R., 157
One-way communication, 125
Operational managers, 19
Operations management, 11, 81
Operations manager, 11
Operations research, 44
Oral communication, 124
Organizational environments, 19–20
Organizational stakeholders, 21
Organizing, 3, 83
Owen, Robert, 38, 58

**P**

Paralinguistics, 206
Participative leadership, 110
Passports, 210
Perception, 126

Performance management
   guidelines for, 183
Pericles, 128
*Personality and Organization* (Argyris).
      *See* Argyris, Chris
Peters and Townsend, 17. *See also* Narrow
      span of control
Phone etiquette, 135
Planning, 3, 63–64, 74, 93
Position power, 107
Power, 8–9, 39, 39–40, 101
President, 3, 114, 188
Principle-centered leadership, 115–117
*Principles of Scientific Management* (Taylor),
      33
Professional bureaucracy, 15
Professional presentations, 128
   strategy, 129
   structure, 129
   style, 129
   substance, 129
   supplement, 130
   support, 130
Project management, 74–76
Project managers, 4, 74
Proxemics
   suggestions for use, 142–143
Proxemics and haptics, 206

**Q**

Quality Control Handbook, 51. *See* Juran,
      Joseph M.
Quantitative theory. *See* Management sci-
      ence theory
Queuing theory, 46
Quid pro quo, 192

**R**

Recruitment
   internal and external, 177
   process of, 176–178
Referent power, 8, 101
Relationship-motivated behaviors, 106. *See
      also* Fiedler's contingency model
Relationship behavior, 108
Reward power, 8, 101

**S**

Safety
  in the hotel, 215
  on public transportation, 215–216
  on the street, 215
  procedures, 214
Scenario planning, 75–76
Schon, Donald, 44
Scientific management, 32
Selection process
  ability, performance, and personality tests,
    178–179
  applications & résumés, 178
  interview process, 179–181
Senge, Peter, 52
Servant leadership, 115
Sexual harassment
  and Civil Rights Act of 1964, 192
  examples of, 192
  prevention of, 192
*Shortcut to Persuasive Presentations* (Pericles),
    128
Simple structure, 15
Simulations, 56
Single- and double-loop learning, 44, 55
Situational analysis, 64, 65, 66
Skinner, B. F., 150
Smith, Adam, 31
Span of control, 91
Stogdill, Ralph, 105
Strategic human resource planning process
  definition of, 188
  implementing strategy, 189–190
  job analysis, 190
  job description, 190–191
  job specification, 191
  objective of, 188
Strategic management, 17, 28
Strategic managers, 3, 12
Strategic planning, 69–72, 188
Strategy formulation, 71–72
Structured interviews
  characteristics of, 180
Supportive leadership, 110
SWOT analysis, 12, 18, 65–68, 93
Systems-thinking, 52–53

Systems approach to management, 21, 47
Systems theory, 47

**T**

Tactical managers, 3
Tactical planning, 18
Task-motivated behaviors, 106. *See
    also* Fiedler's contingency model
Task behavior, 108
Task structure, 106
Taylor, Frederick Winslow, 33–34
Team development
  stages of, 166–167
Teams
  benefits of, 165–166
  high and low performance, 167
  informal and formal, 163
  maintenance-oriented role within, 167
  pros and cons of using, 162–163
  stages of development, 166–167
  task-oriented role within, 167
  types of, 164–165
*Ten Rules of Good Followership* (Meilinger).
    *See* Meilinger, P., Colonel
*Theory of Social and Economic Organizations*
    (Weber), 37
Theory X and Y management (McGregor),
    43, 55
Therbligs, 35, 54
Thorndike's Law of Effect, 149–150
Thorndike, Edward Lee, 149
Tichy and Devanna, 5
Time-zone changes
  when travelling, 219
Top managers, 3, 12. *See* Chief Execu-
    tive Officer (CEO); *See* President;
    *See* Strategic managers
Total responsibility management (TRM), 22
Traditional structures
  functional structure, 85–86
Training
  off-the-job, 182
  on-the-job, 182
Trait theories, 104–105
Transactional leadership, 4, 112, 113
Transformational leadership, 5, 112

Transportation modalities
  when travelling abroad, 222–223
Tuckman, Bruce, 166
Two way communication, 125

**U**

U. S. Embassies
  functions of, 212
University of Michigan Leadership Model,
    105
Unstructured interviews, 180

**V**

Vaccinations
  when travelling abroad, 213
Vertical integration, 71
Visas
  steps in applying for, 210–211
Vision, 100–101
Vision statement, 12, 18, 70
Vroom's expectancy theory
  three parts of, 152–153
Vroom, Victor, 152
Vroom-Jago decision-making model,
    110–111

**W**

Walton, Sam, 112
Water contamination
  when travelling abroad, 213
Weber, Max, 33, 35, 37, 40, 55
Welch, Jack, 10, 20
*Why Decisions Fail: Avoiding the Blunders
    and Traps that Lead to Debacles*
    (Nutt), 68
Workplace diversity, 191–192